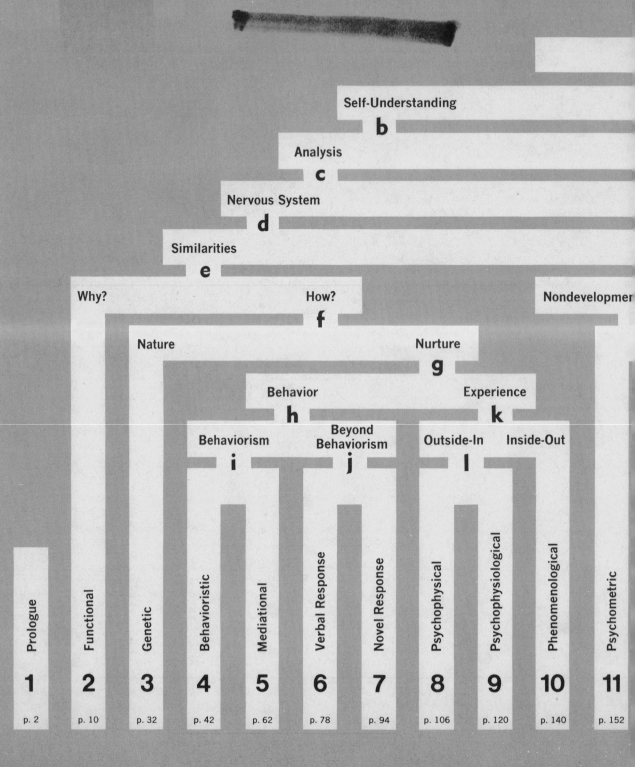

Self-Understanding **b**

Analysis **c**

Nervous System **d**

Similarities **e**

Why?   How? **f**   Nondevelopmer

Nature   Nurture **g**

Behavior **h**   Experience **k**

Behaviorism **i**   Beyond Behaviorism **j**   Outside-In   Inside-Out **l**

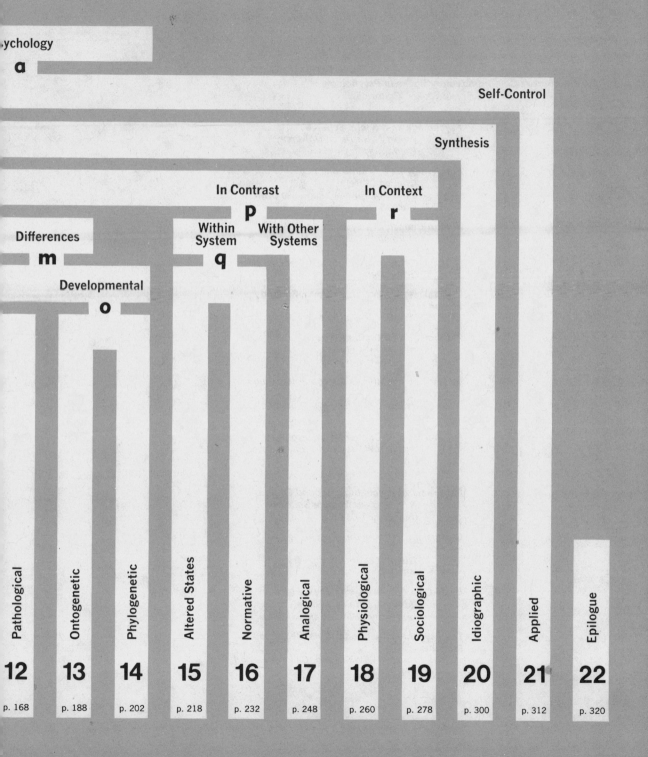

ychology

a

Self-Control

Synthesis

Differences

m

In Contrast

p

In Context

r

Within System

q

With Other Systems

Developmental

o

Psychology:

A Story of a Search

Second Edition

W. Lambert Gardiner

Brooks/Cole Publishing Company
Monterey, California

A Division of Wadsworth Publishing Company, Inc.

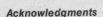

Acknowledgments

Figure 2-4. Adapted from H. Schlosberg, The description of facial expressions in terms of two dimensions. Journal of Experimental Psychology, 1952, **44**, 229–237. Copyright 1952 by the American Psychological Association. Reprinted by permission.

Figure 9–2. From Julian E. Hochberg, Perception. © 1964 by Prentice-Hall, Inc., pp. 4, 59. Reprinted by permission.

Figure 11–5. From J. P. Guilford, The Nature of Human Intelligence. © 1967 by McGraw-Hill Book Company. Reprinted by permission.

Poem, page 269. From The Dinosaur, Bert Laston Taylor (1866–1921), "A line-o'-type or two," Chicago Tribune. Reprinted by permission.

Quotation, pages 286–287. From E. H. Schein, The Chinese indoctrination program for prisoners of war: A study of attempted "brainwashing." Psychiatry, 1956, **19**, 162–164. Reprinted by permission.

Quotation, page 287. From An Anatomy for Conformity, by E. L. Walker and R. W. Heyns. Copyright © 1967 by Wadsworth Publishing Company, Inc. Reprinted by permission of the publisher, Brooks/Cole Publishing Company, Monterey, California.

Quotation, pages 161–165. From Primary Mental Abilities, by L. L. Thurstone. Copyright © 1938 by University of Chicago Press. Reprinted by permission.

39068

ISBN: 0-8185-0118-9
L.C. Catalog Card No.: 73-89595
Printed in the United States of America

1 2 3 4 5 6 7 8 9 10—78 77 76 75 74

Production Editor: Micky Lawler
Interior & Cover Design: Linda Marcetti
Cartoons: Tony Hall
Typesetting: Holmes Composition Service, San Jose, California
Printing & Binding: Kingsport Press, Kingsport, Tennessee

Preface to the Second Edition

The traditional introductory text organizes psychology around processes (remembering, learning, thinking, problem solving, and so on). An alternative organization, which I glimpsed when writing the first edition of this text, is becoming clearer. This second edition is organized around approaches. Each chapter in the body of the text focuses on one approach to the understanding of the function of the nervous system. Thus, for example, Chapter 12 focuses on the pathological approach, in which the function of the nervous system is studied through observation of its malfunction, and Chapter 18 focuses on the physiological approach, in which the function of the nervous system is studied through observation of its structure.

Typically, in each chapter I present the logic of the approach, provide an illustration of the approach in action, and discuss issues in the use of the approach. Do not be alarmed by the untraditional chapter headings; the traditional topics lurk underneath. "Emotion" and "Motivation" simmer below "Functional Approach," and "Creativity" is alive and well and living under "Approach through Novel Response." It is the same psychological pie I am serving, but it is cut at right angles across approaches rather than across processes.

The slight disadvantage of the unfamiliar headings is more than offset by the many advantages. This organization emphasizes the process of science, whereas the traditional organization emphasizes the product of science. The disorderly product, in the early stages of a science such as psychology, makes sense only in terms of the orderly process that generates this product. This organization around approaches keeps the focus on the phenomena we are trying to understand, whereas the traditional organization around processes tends to focus on the accumulated body of information, which represents the residues of the attempts to understand those phenomena. The need to focus on the phenomena rather than on the literature was pointed out to me by my 13-year-old niece, Dorothy. She dropped into my office while I was trying to tease a paragraph on Freud out of a dozen or so books I had accumulated by and about him.

> How do you write books, Uncle Lambert?
> I read all those books, and then I write a paragraph.
> Oh, you copy?
> No, no. When I take my paragraph from one book, I'm copying. When I take it from several books, I'm doing research.
> I don't see the difference.
> Beat it, kid.

Now that it has been brought to my attention, I'm not sure that I can see the difference myself. I am sure, however, that I should keep my focus on the phenomena and use the literature only to sharpen that focus.

A second advantage of organization around approaches is that this method does not distort the subsequent content that is accumulated. It provides a copious basket into which the facts can be gathered rather than (as does the traditional organization around processes) a ward of Procrustean* beds into which the facts are forced.

A third advantage is that the approaches conform more closely than the processes to the major criteria of a good classification. That is, they are more mutually exclusive and exhaustive.

The traditional categories are, by no means, mutually exclusive. Remembering is involved in learning, which is involved in thinking, which is involved in problem solving in a complex of overlapping and interacting processes. The approaches, on the other hand, are mutually exclusive, since only one approach can be applied at any one time. This does not imply that every psychologist can be pigeon-holed as an exponent of one particular approach or that every research article can be classified as an illustration of one particular approach. Though psychologists are not obliged to apply any one approach consistently throughout their careers or even throughout a single article, they would benefit by being aware of the logic of the approaches they are applying.

The particular approaches presented in this text may not be exhaustive, but approaches are potentially exhaustive. Any failure to meet this criterion is due to

*Procrustes was a notorious outlaw who laid his victims on a bed and chopped down those who were too long and stretched those who were too short.

limitations in me rather than to any intrinsic limitations in the classification. Further developments in psychology and in this psychologist will reveal approaches not considered here. During the evolution of this text, tentative chapters entitled "Humanistic Approach," "Ecological Approach," "Structural Approach," and so on appeared and disappeared. In subsequent editions they may reappear. Many specialists will find this generalist's view limited because their specialty is inadequately or inaccurately represented. I am indeed short-sighted and even astigmatic and can only plead that books, like boxes, have a limited capacity and thus cannot be both broad and deep.

The most glaring omission is a chapter entitled "Humanistic Approach." However, the term "humanistic" is both too narrow and too broad to describe an approach. The entire book could reasonably be called "Psychology: A Humanistic Approach," because its means—it is written person-to-person rather than station-to-station—and its ends—self-understanding and self-control—are humanistic. But the term is too narrow; it has come to be identified with a third force, and I want to represent the first force and the second force and many other forces too. This third force has been a refreshing reaction to the excesses of the first and second forces of behaviorism and psychoanalysis. It has righted many balances in going beyond Skinner and Freud. This reaction is recorded throughout the book, and these balances are, hopefully, maintained. It is ironic that, because of historical accident, the behaviorists who emphasize reacting in theory are acting in practice and the humanists who emphasize acting in theory are reacting in practice. That we are being reminded that we are human is a reflection not of a great conceptual breakthrough in psychology but of the sad state of our science before this humanistic howl of protest. Although "humanistic" is too broad a term to describe any one of them, four major concerns of humanistic psychologists are represented in this book. The concern for the subjective world of the subject as well as the "objective" world is reflected in "Phenomenological Approach," the concern for states of consciousness other than "normal" is reflected in "Approach through Altered States," the concern for potential man as well as "actual" man is reflected in "Normative Approach," and the concern for the specific individual as well as the "average" individual is reflected in "Idiographic Approach."

Were I not so modest, I would recommend that introductory courses in psychology survey approaches (as does this text), that advanced courses focus in more detail on each of the approaches, and that very advanced courses survey the approaches again but at greater depth and with more emphasis on the interrelationships among them. Thus the entire curriculum would reflect the "tell-them-what-I'm-going-to-tell-them, tell-them, tell-them-what-I-told-them" organization of this text.

Since writing the first edition, I have written an advanced text entitled *An Invitation to Cognitive Psychology.* Some of that book has been incorporated into this second edition. The advanced text reflects changes in me between the first and the second editions of this introductory text, and a revision should record changes in the author as well as in his field. If this second edition is of more value than the first edition in helping you understand psychology, it is because I understand psychology better now than I did then.

Frankly, I was not looking forward to revising. I saw it as a grim, teeth-gritting chore after the creative work of writing the original. It turned out, however, to be as enjoyable a process. Surveying one's chosen field and trying to reflect changes in it and in yourself are exhilarating enterprises. I look forward now to revising again, from time to time, in the exciting years that lie ahead in psychology. The impressive changes over the last few years have resulted not so much in dramatic breakthroughs as in shifts of emphasis and attitude. For instance, psychology seems to be less timid and tentative than it was a few years ago. Our science is perhaps growing out of its adolescent apprehensions. You may not agree, as I argue in the Prologue, that psychology is the central discipline, but you will probably agree that it is becoming less of a grab bag of bits and pieces pirated from other disciplines. The sections of the first edition on research methodology and statistics have therefore been graciously relinquished to their disciplines and appear in this second edition only when they help us to understand a particular approach to the function of the nervous system, which is presented here as the true focus of psychology.

I have corrected errors kindly pointed out by students and professors who used the first edition. However, although I have not consciously left any errors, I secretly hope that I have not entirely spoiled the sport of finding them. A student is not at all harmed by finding his professor and his textbook writer in disagreement. It breeds a healthy suspicion that one or the other (and probably both) is fallible and the wholesome attitude that he as a student must ultimately evaluate the evidence himself and reach his own conclusions.

I am encouraged to find that my text tends to be used by good teachers who want to do their own teaching and do not need the security blanket of an encyclopedic text. I have not toned down overstatements, because those good teachers can right the balance by reacting against them. I have retained controversial experiments (McConnell, Spitz, Hess, and so on), because those good teachers can introduce the recent evidence that challenges their conclusions. The student will, in this way, get a better feel for the haphazard process by which science progresses. Typically, the professor and the textbook writer present a solid authoritarian front that overwhelms the humble opinions of the student, and they present science as a series of success stories that discourage the student when his or her first few fumbling efforts fail.

I'd like to thank my publisher, Brooks/Cole, for providing me with the space and the time to write undisturbed by mundane maintenance matters. I also received competent and congenial help from cartoonist Tony Hall, copy editor Micky Lawler, permissions editor Joyce Quinn, proofreader Cece Munson, and designer Linda Marcetti. I shared an office (and practically a skin) with another author-in-residence, Guy Lefrancois, while he was writing *his* introductory psychology textbook, *Of Humans*. Guy was a most stimulating environment to which much of this second edition is a response and will no doubt continue to be when we two elderly scholars work side by side on our fourteenth and fifteenth revisions.

I also extend my thanks to those who adopted the first edition of my book and thus vindicated the faith of myself and my publisher that the academic world is ready for less formal and more friendly texts. My further thanks go to those who not only adopted my baby but wrote to tell me how it is getting along.

Norbert Yager of Henry Ford Community College, Jerome Brown of the State University of New York, College at Geneseo, George Martin of Mount San Antonio College, William H. Tedford, Jr., of Southern Methodist University, Alice Van Krevelen of Berea College, N.H. Pronko of Wichita State University, David W. Martin of New Mexico State University, Andrew Neher of Cabrillo College, Christopher J.S. Tuppen of the University of British Columbia, R. J. Senter and Richard E. Butcher, both of the University of Cincinnati, and Larry Swenson of West Valley College provided an incredibly valuable set of suggestions for transforming the first edition into this second edition. Ed Walker, my consulting editor, who continued to lend me his scholarly and his fatherly hands, assured me that this was the best set of reviews he had ever seen. It is more important to be understood than to be appreciated. Those reviewers understood. Indeed, some of them, through working with my book in a number of classes, seemed to know it better than I did. Forcing down twinges of jealousy, I thank them for taking the trouble. Larry Swenson, who not only reviewed the book in writing but elaborated on his review in a long conversation in his home, left me with the following advice: "You should deal with advice for changing your text as my wife and I deal with advice for raising our baby. We listen respectfully and consider carefully, but we proceed on the basis of the gut gestalt." I took his good advice, so no reviewer need feel any more responsible for inadequacies in this text than Larry's friends feel for inadequacies in his baby.

W. Lambert Gardiner

Preface to the First Edition

First, a Word to the Teacher

This text (if it is a text and sometimes I wonder) is unlike any other introductory text in psychology. I state this at the outset not as an apology but as an admonition—not as an excuse for adding yet another product to an overflooded market but as a warning that, if you are seeking a conventional text, you will waste precious time by reading any further. For certain mundane reasons, usually attributed to my Scottish blood, I would like this book to become recognized as a text. It certainly can be used as such, for it hits every major topic in psychology, although some admittedly only a glancing blow. For more noble reasons, I would be delighted to overhear that a more standard source was assigned for the body of findings and that this book was prescribed (as a complement rather than a supplement) for the spirit of the search that uncovered those findings. I will use it as a text myself, although it makes me obsolete, for it constitutes the content of my lectures. Not to assign it, however, would be hypocritical, because it contains what I strongly believe the introductory student should be exposed to.

Some of the symptoms of the textbook writer's syndrome are listed below. The rationale (or rationalization?) whereby *this* textbook writer avoids them is indicated to illustrate, in somewhat whimsical fashion, the manner in which this text differs from more conventional texts.

The Compulsion to Be Comprehensive

As the body of significant findings has increased, the texts have grown thicker. The writer feels obligated to cram as many of them as possible into a book that can be bought, carried, and read by a student of average wealth, strength, and stamina. Since there is not yet, in these early days of our science, a coherent, theoretical framework within which those findings can be housed, the text degenerates into a catalog. A text organized around empirical findings is thus artificially difficult—since there is no structure to contain old findings—and immediately obsolete—since the daily output of new findings not only must be included but determines the subset of old findings that should be preserved. Today's physicist would probably find the content of a physics text written at the same stage in the development of *his* science difficult to learn and mostly not worth learning. The texts that aim to systematize the findings represent brave but futile attempts to make cosmos out of chaos. Indeed, an orderly presentation of disorderly findings could perhaps, tongue-in-cheekily, be criticized as a distorted picture of our science. This text is organized around the search that unearths the findings rather than the findings themselves. Thus a particular finding appears because it illustrates a point rather than merely because it exists. There is no need to scale the mountain of literature merely because it is there. The story of the search is told logically rather than chronologically, so that the emphasis may be on currents rather than on eddies. Various logical approaches used by man to understand himself are illustrated in turn. Such a presentation is incomplete but not obsolete, since the search continues although the story must end.

The Compulsion to Be Correct

Textbook statements are invariably dressed impeccably in precise terminology and shrouded discreetly in careful qualifications. Such scientific precision and reticence are commendable in journal articles and advanced texts but may perhaps not be appropriate in introductory texts. They tend to leave the student with some bland impression that, on every theoretical issue, there is much to be said on both sides, and, in every content area, further research is necessary. This text favors "fat rats" over "hypothalamic hyperphagics with lesions in the ventramedial nuclei" and the danger of overstatement over the security of understatement. The emphatic statement in nontechnical language will be better remembered by students. It will do them no harm to have it qualified in advanced courses or —better still—to qualify it themselves by reacting against it. One of the attitudes to be learned by students, too long conditioned by authoritarian teaching, is that science deals not with absolute truth but only with successive approximations to the truth. Half a truth is better than no truth at all.

Textbooks favor the third over the first person and the passive over the active voice. The psychologist-as-researcher must be objective, but not necessarily the psychologist-as-teacher. Personal reference may be of heuristic value. "You are a student of Gardiner, who was a student of Ryan, who was a student of Bentley, who was a student of Titchener, who was a student of Wundt, who founded the first psychological laboratory" conveys a sense of the shortness of the history of our science and the place of the student in that history more effectively than "The first psychological laboratory was founded at Leipzig in 1879 by Wilhelm Wundt." Reference to the personal lives of the major characters in the history of our science also serves a heuristic function. Pavlov's relationship to his wife is not relevant to his findings but is relevant to the capacity of the student to digest those findings.

Then, a Word to the Student

This text is designed to be studied rather than simply to be read. Some heuristic devices have been incorporated to encourage you to go beyond that left-to-right, top-to-bottom, page-x-to-page-x + 1 scanning that usually passes for studying. In addition to the traditional table of contents, the hierarchical structure of the book is provided following the front cover, and, in place of the traditional glossary, a classification of the technical terms (which appear in boldface in the text) is provided preceding the back cover. The former shows how the book is organized from top to bottom, and the latter shows how the book is organized from bottom to top. The former chart is described in more detail in the prologue, and the latter chart is described in more detail in the epilogue. The prologue contains a statement of the basis for each distinction within the hierarchy. This section is dull and difficult. Skim it (or perhaps even skip it) on the first reading. It is simply a bird's-eye view of the book that will make more sense after the worm's-eye view that follows. It is recommended, however, that, at the end of each chapter, you review the previous distinctions to see where you are, where you have been, and where you are going. The epilogue contains the before-the-fact rationale (or after-the-fact rationalization, if you prefer) for the set of categories into which the technical terms are organized. The resultant chart bears the same relationship to a thesaurus as a glossary does to a dictionary. Thus it proceeds in the more meaningful direction from idea to word rather than from word to idea.

An outline is provided to clarify the structure of each chapter. This, too, is probably more useful during the reading of the chapter, to see where you are, and after the reading of the chapter, to test whether you can return alone to where you have just been. Each chapter is designed to be short enough to be devoured in a single sitting and coherent enough to be digested as a whole. This organization should save the time usually spent counting the number of pages to the end of the chapter and should keep each chapter within the capacity of your behind as well as of your mind. Psychologists have demonstrated that black on yellow is the most readable combination. We should practice what we teach. Therefore the book is printed on yellow paper. I always add comments to my books and am often frustrated by cramped books that do not grant reasonable space to talk back to them. We should teach what we practice. Therefore the book has wide margins so that you can create your own unique copy by recording your reactions as you read. The chaff-to-wheat ratio is higher than in most texts. This book is essentially my introductory lectures in psychology written down. Those lectures are delivered to 700 rambunctious youths late in the afternoon and 700 tired adults late in the evening. It is necessary to swoop to oratory and stoop to pun to keep the former group attentive and the latter group awake. Those hammy elements are preserved, since it is probably no less necessary to keep a reader awake by chaff so that he may benefit from wheat. I hope you enjoy my jokes but are not distracted by them from the point they are designed to make. May you have as much fun reading this book as I had writing it.

And, Finally, a Word to All My Teachers and Students

Any book is inevitably, in some sense, the product of every lecture and seminar, book and journal article, bull session and tête-à-tête in the experience of the author. After the information from those various sources has been mulled through his mind, it is difficult to disentangle it again into its elements, label each with a source, and give credit for them. This book is dedicated, then, to every teacher and student, formal and informal, with whom I have come in contact. They will all, I hope, recognize their contribution, take their subjective credit for what they like, and absolve themselves of the blame for what they don't like. One person must, however, be singled out. Henry Gleitman swept through the Cornell campus for one brief but eventful year. I had the good fortune to be one of his assistants. He taught me that a lecture can be a work of art and inspired me to strive to become an artist on my own small canvas. I assimilated his course so thoroughly that it is difficult to know where Gleitman ends and Gardiner begins. In striving to write my best of all possible books, I have found myself using his illustrations embarrassingly often. His name crops up throughout the book, whenever a particular illustration is recognized as his, but his spirit pervades the entire book.

So much for the sources of ideas in my head. It is still, however, a long way from the information in my head to the book in your hand. The good people of Brooks/Cole Publishing Company—Bonnie Fitzwater, Charles T. Hendrix, Konrad Kerst, and Jack N. Thornton (it's a small, friendly company for a small, friendly book)—granted me the luxury of two summers as author-in-residence in their delightful offices in the California hills with nothing to do but read and think and write. During those two pleasant and productive summers, Sue Ramsay Arnold, Kristine Lundquist, Linda Honeysett, and Lois Gift took turns mothering me so that I was protected from the harsh realities of life and could work undisturbed. Frank Costin at the University of Illinois, James A. Dyal at the University of Waterloo, Robert W. Eichinger at the University of Minnesota, P. James Geiwitz at Stanford University, Garvin McCain at the University of Texas at Arlington, Clifford T. Morgan at the University of Texas, and Edward L. Walker at the University of Michigan all provided valuable reviews. Ed Walker went far beyond the call of a consulting editor's duty by lending one fatherly hand to the author as he applied one scholarly hand to his manuscript. The reviews were encouragingly extreme. The reviewers loved the book or hated the book or loved some features and hated others but never offered the insult of indifference. The negative comments improved the quality of the manuscript, and the positive comments improved the morale of the author. The one feature that divided the reviewers most is those somewhat casual asides that one cannot resist in lectures but that are typically purged in the transition from hot air to cold print. Some were delighted by them and said leave them in; some were appalled by them (I shudder sympathetically myself sometimes) and said throw them out. I compromised by pushing them to the bottom of the page as footnotes but not right off the page as recommended. Thus, those who want to read the expurgated version can just read the text and ignore the footnotes, and those who want to read the "un" of the unexpurgated version can just read the footnotes and ignore the text. I am very grateful to the reviewers for making this a better book and absolve them of blame for my stopping so far short of a perfect book. Flaws remain because sometimes I wrote things beyond redemption and sometimes I pigheadedly ignored their advice. Carol Ann Hege picked up the typing where Kali Coull of Sir George Williams University left off. Micky Stay copyedited the manuscript, kindly eliminating many inelegant aberrations but permitting my pet deviations from English. Lon Driggers and John Odam designed a handsome book, and John enlisted the aid of his friend Tony Hall, back home in London, to garnish it with creative cartoons. So, with me writing and Carol typing and Micky copy-editing and Lon and John designing and Tony drawing and everyone else yelling encouragement from the sidelines, together we built a book. Here it is.

W. Lambert Gardiner

Contents

Know then, thyself, presume not God to scan
The proper study of mankind is man.

Alexander Pope
An Essay on Man

The purpose of psychology is to give us a completely different idea of
the things we know best.

Paul Valéry
Tel Quel

Oh wad some power the giftie gie us
To see oursels as others see us!
It wad frae monie a blunder free us
An' foolish notion.

Robert Burns
To a Louse

I wished, by treating Psychology *like* a natural science, to help her
become one.

William James
Collected Essays and Reviews

It is not enough that you should understand about applied science in
order that your work may increase man's blessings. Concern for man
himself and his fate must always form the chief interest of all technical endeavors, concern for the great unsolved problems of the organization of labor and the distribution of goods—in order that the
creation of our mind shall be a blessing and not a curse to mankind.
Never forget this in the midst of your diagrams and equations.

Albert Einstein
Address, California Institute of Technology

1

Prologue

This is the story of man's attempt to know himself through the scientific study of himself—that is, through careful observation and clear thinking. We are all familiar with the application of scientific method to the understanding of the world around us or, at least, with the fruits of this understanding. Some of these fruits are sweet, like the techniques of mass communication that bring us closer together; some of these fruits are sour, like the weapons of mass destruction that threaten to spread us apart. Despite mixed feelings about the products of science, we cannot quibble about the effectiveness of the process of science. Man has, by this means, gained a profound understanding of the world in which he lives. Can this way of thinking be applied to an understanding of himself? It can. It has been done in the past, it is being done at present, and it will continue to be done in the future. This is the story unfolded in this book.

The two major frontiers of man are the very far and the very near. The exploration of outer space is discussed daily in our newspapers and on our television sets; the exploration of inner space, not so well documented by the media, is discussed here. The conquest-of-outer-space story is becoming a bit boring—not only because moonshots tend to go so clockworky well from blastoff to splashdown but because we cannot participate except as spectators. Each of us can, however, participate in the conquest of inner space. You are your own unique laboratory. You are the world's foremost authority on yourself.

It is only fair to state now that the story told here is a to-be-continued story. Indeed, it is only the beginning of a story. I can report only the first few bumbling steps of an infant science. Psychology as a science is younger than Canada as a nation. Great progress has been made in this first century of the scientific study of man, but our understanding of ourselves still lags far—perhaps dangerously far—behind our understanding of the world in which we live. This lag stems from the fact that psychology is not only a young science but a difficult science as well. Let's glance at some of the factors that make psychology perhaps the most difficult of all sciences.

Science is the study of systems. Physics is the study of the system called the atom, astronomy is the study of the system called the universe, and psychology is the study of the system called the nervous system.* Since the nervous system is the system that studies all the other systems, psychology is the central science.

*Some psychologists consider the organism or the organism-and-environment as their system, but it is more productive, perhaps, to focus on the nervous system and consider the internal environment (other subsystems of the organism) and the external environment only insofar as they provide input to the nervous system. Focusing on the nervous system does not mean that this entire book will be about neurons, cerebelli, hypothalami, and other gucky things. One approach to the understanding of the function of the nervous system is to examine its structure. The physiological approach will be considered in Chapter 18, but it is only one of 20 approaches that will be considered.

Psychologists pay a price for this central role. The fact that the subject and the object are the same in our discipline (that is, one nervous system is studying another nervous system) leads to much conceptual confusion. Indeed, some philosophers of science argue that our story will *always* be a to-be-continued one because it is impossible for a system to fully understand itself. Further confusion arises when the process being studied is the same as the process by which it is being studied (that is, one nervous system is thinking about another nervous

system thinking). The issue is even further muddled by the fact that each nervous system can study itself (that is, I can not only think about you thinking but I can think about me thinking). This situation can lead to an infinite regress, as I think about myself thinking about thinking about thinking, and so on. Or, it can lead to an eternal badminton game, in which I think about you thinking about me thinking about you thinking, and so on.

The system studied by psychologists, the nervous system, is the most complex of all systems. The human brain (variously described as the great raveled knot, the cerebral jungle, a can of spaghetti, or a bowl of porridge) contains more than 10 billion cells, which may be combined in an uncountable number of ways. Such a system is much more complex than the atom, which has challenged our greatest minds for centuries and still retains much of its mystery.

A further difficulty in studying psychology is the ethical problem. Physicists smash atoms and no one complains; psychologists cannot smash people without a roar of anguish from them and a roar of protest from others. When a physicist wishes to find the function of an element in his system, he can remove it and observe the effects. When a psychologist wishes to find the function of the cerebellum, he cannot indiscriminately remove it from another person and observe the effects. Of course, such restrictions on the extent to which man can

tamper with man are commendable and necessary. I am not advocating that they be reduced but merely pointing to yet another difficulty confronting the scientist who is foolhardy enough to choose man as his subject.

A final difficulty is prejudice. The study of man by man is often opposed by man. Many persons who accept the application of scientific method to the study of the world around them refuse to accept the application of scientific method to themselves. Perhaps this attitude is a residue of the same violent reaction to the ideas of Copernicus, Darwin, and Freud, whose theories offended—or seemed to offend—the dignity of man. Copernicus plucked man from the center of the universe, where the geocentric theory had him, and placed him on a broken-off fragment of one of a myriad of stars. Darwin plucked man from an exclusive niche, where the theory of special creation had him, and placed him where he belonged, with the other animals. Freud dealt a further blow by suggesting that man is not even a rational animal but is driven by instinctive forces of which he is not even aware. The reaction has become progressively less vicious. Things are getting better all the time. Copernicus' contemporaries tried to burn his body; Darwin's contemporaries burned his book; Freud's contemporaries simply burned. There is still a whiff of burning in the air.

My personal prejudice is that it is not at all offensive to the dignity of man to be studied. The rainbow's beauty is not marred by putting it through a spectroscope. Indeed, it is yet more awesome when understood. It is refreshing that man at last has the courage to look himself straight in the eye and accept the truth about himself rather than believe what he wants to believe. I agree with Hans Selye, a brilliant medical researcher at the University of Montreal, that "the ugliest truth is more beautiful than the loveliest pretense." Whether man should or should not study himself is, however, a purely academic question. He has been turning the searchlight of science on himself for some time, he is doing it now, and he will do it more and more in the future. His curiosity will not be curbed by force or by fiat. I can only report what man is doing and leave to you the question of what man should do. An informed public is the best insurance that the study of man by man will benefit man.

The story is told in 20 chapters (Chapters 2-21), bracketed by a prologue (Chapter 1) and an epilogue (Chapter 22),* and is presented sequentially—that is, as one chapter after another and, within each chapter, as one word after another. This is one of the unfortunate limitations of verbal communication. Sequential presentation tends to mask hierarchical organization.† The hierarchical structure of each chapter is provided in an outline at the beginning of the chapter, and the hierarchical structure of the book, within which those chapters are organized, is provided following the front cover, from which the book may be digested in what the eminent art critic Ross Parmenter would call one "eye gulp." Each chapter in the body of the text focuses on one approach to the understanding of the nervous system. The chapters are generated by a series of distinctions represented by a letter at each branch in the hierarchical structure. The distinctions can be described as follows.

a. The aim of pure science is understanding; the aim of applied science is control. The aim of pure psychology is self-understanding; the aim of applied psychology is self-control. Since I am pure, the emphasis in this book is on self-understanding. However, the applied approach (Chapter 21) will focus on self-control.

b. Like all sciences, psychology emphasizes analysis, in which a system is broken into its elements. However, the idiographic approach (Chapter 20) will focus on synthesis, in which the person is studied as a whole.

c. Some approaches focus on the nervous system per se and some on the nervous system in contrast with other systems or in the context of other systems.

*This organization was inspired by a remark made by Professor Allan C. Goldstein while I was at Cornell. When asked for the secret of his beautifully organized lectures, he said: "I tell them what I'm going to tell them; I tell them; I tell them what I told them." In the prologue I tell you what I'm going to tell you, in the body I tell you, and in the epilogue I tell you what I told you.

†This theme is evident in the writings of Marshall McLuhan, the Toronto prophet who would lead us out of the wilderness of "linear literacy" into the promised land of "all-at-onceness." Perhaps the presentation of the hierarchical structure can circumvent the limitations of the—to marshal a McLuhanism—"alphabet strung like beads on a line" and still remain within the familiar verbal framework.

d. Any two nervous systems are similar in some ways and different in other ways. Some approaches focus on similarities and some on differences.

e. Some approaches focus on the function of the nervous system (why does the nervous system do what it does?) and some on the mechanisms underlying the function (how does the nervous system do what it does?). The functional approach (Chapter 2) focuses on the function of the nervous system.

f. Some approaches emphasize genetic factors (nature) and some environmental factors (nurture). The genetic approach (Chapter 3) examines the function of the nervous system as determined by genetic factors.

g. The nervous system is the only system that can be viewed from the inside as well as from the outside. The functioning of the nervous system as viewed from the outside is behavior, and that viewed from the inside is experience.

h. Some approaches focus on the functioning of the nervous system as viewed from the outside (behavior). Behaviorism is the attempt to explain behavior purely in terms of the environment. However, some psychologists argue that it is necessary to go beyond behaviorism.

i. The behavioristic approach (Chapter 4) attempts to explain behavior (output of the nervous system) purely in terms of environment (input of the nervous system). The mediational approach (Chapter 5) explains the output of the nervous system in terms of its input plus "something" that mediates between input and output.

j. Certain classes of behavior are difficult to explain purely in terms of environment. Approach through verbal response (Chapter 6) and approach through novel response (Chapter 7) focus on two of these classes.

k. Some approaches focus on the functioning of the nervous system as viewed from the inside (experience). Some view experience from the outside in, and some view experience from the inside out. The phenomenological approach (Chapter 10) focuses on experience from the inside out.

l. The psychophysical approach (Chapter 8) explains experience purely in terms of physical energy. The psychophysiological approach (Chapter 9) explains experience in terms of physical energy plus the physiological processes that mediate between physical energy and experience.

m. Some of the approaches that focus on the differences between two nervous systems consider differences that are results of development, and some consider differences that are not results of development.

n. The psychometric approach (Chapter 11) focuses on differences among "normal" people, and the pathological approach (Chapter 12) focuses on differences along the "normal-abnormal" dimension.

o. The ontogenetic approach (Chapter 13) focuses on development from child to adult, and the phylogenetic approach (Chapter 14) focuses on development from animal to human.

p. Some approaches focus on contrasts within the nervous system and some on contrasts between the nervous system and other systems. The analogical approach (Chapter 17) focuses on the comparison of the nervous system with other systems.

q. The approach through altered states (Chapter 15) contrasts the nervous system in one state with the same nervous system in another state. The normative approach (Chapter 16) contrasts how a nervous system does work with how it ought to work.

r. The nervous system is an element within a hierarchy of systems. The physiological approach (Chapter 19) focuses on subsystems of the nervous system, and the sociological approach (Chapter 20) focuses on the system of which the nervous system is a subsystem.

There warn't anybody at the church, except maybe a hog or two, for there warn't any lock on the door, and hogs like a puncheon floor in summertime because it's cool. If you notice, most folks don't go to church only when they've got to; but a hog is different.

Mark Twain
Adventures of Huckleberry Finn

Intellect is to emotion as our clothes are to our bodies: we could not very well have civilized life without clothes, but we would be in a poor way if we had only clothes without bodies.

Alfred North Whitehead
Dialogues of Alfred North Whitehead

2 Functional Approach

2.1 The Theory of Evolution

2.11 Charles Darwin

The curtain rises on a quiet country home in an English village. The first character in our cast is seen puttering about in his greenhouse and muttering about in his study. It was in this place and in this manner—apart from a famous voyage around the world—that Charles Darwin spent most of his life. Yet this uneventful life of this unassuming man in this unspectacular setting probably had a greater impact on our world than did the lives of some of the more flamboyant figures—the Caesars, the Napoleons, the Hitlers—who have stomped around our globe. Darwin created a revolution. Not that shoddy shift in political personnel that typically passes for a revolution, but a *real* revolution—a change in man's view of himself. After carefully collecting and collating evidence for 17 years, Darwin gently but firmly told man that he was not a special creation of God with an exclusive soul but an animal on the same scale as his dogs and his cows. After the inevitable violent reaction—*Scopes v. State of Tennessee, Professor Huxley v. Bishop Wilberforce*—man swallowed this bitter pill. Indeed, he now finds it not only palatable but sweet. Most of us feel better as raised apes than as fallen angels.

2.12 The Theory

Everyone is familiar with the basic principles of the **theory of evolution**, but I will present them briefly anyway. There are individual differences among the members of any species. Because of certain environmental conditions, the members at one end of a particular scale have some advantage. Because of this advantage, they are more likely to survive. Because they are more likely to survive, they are more likely to reproduce. Because traits are inherited, the next generation of this species will be, on the average, farther along toward the desirable end of the scale. This generation in turn breeds another generation even farther along, and so on.

Let's take a concrete example. Giraffes differ in the length of their necks. The longer-necked giraffes are better able to feed off the leaves in high trees and are thus more likely to survive and reproduce. Since long-necked giraffes tend to have long-necked babies, the next generation will have, on the average, longer necks. They in turn will breed an even longer-necked generation, and so on. Note that no giraffe has ever grown a longer neck during its lifetime by stretching it to reach leaves and then passed its longer neck on to its progeny. This idea is Lamarck's erroneous concept of the inheritance of acquired characteristics.*

*Lysenko made this theory the basis of Soviet biology. Since Communism (and capitalism, too, come to think of it) is a conspiracy to keep people working, it is convenient to make believe that the fruits of a hard-working life can be passed on to one's children. They can, indeed, be passed on culturally, but they cannot be passed on genetically. The theory is wrong, and no amount of political pressure can make it right. Scientific laws cannot be passed or repealed in courts of law.

2.13   As Basic Theory in Psychology

We tend to think of the theory of evolution as a biological rather than a psychological theory—as concerned with the development of structure rather than of function. Perhaps the emphasis has been on structure because, with the death of an organism, structure survives and function fades. Much evidence for evolution is therefore based on structure (skeletons) or the imprint of structure (fossils). However, modern evolutionary theory is beginning to swing to an emphasis on function. The giraffe survives not only because it has a long neck but also because it can use it. The structure-function relationship involves the chicken-egg problem. We do not know whether an egg is one hen's way of producing another hen or whether, as Samuel Butler suggested, a hen is one egg's way of producing another egg. We do not know whether birds have wings because they fly or fly because they have wings.

The theory of evolution is not only a psychological theory but is *the* basic psychological theory. The broad question in psychology is "What is the function of the nervous system?" and the broad answer provided by the theory of evolution is "to enable the organism to survive." The need-reduction theory (Section 2.2) and the activation theory (Section 2.3) represent attempts by psychologists to fit psychology within this basic framework of the theory of evolution (Section 2.1). How does the organism survive? It moves toward things that are good for it (for example, things that it eats) and away from things that are bad for it (for example, things that eat it). The need-reduction theory describes how the organism approaches things that are good for it, and the activation theory describes how it avoids things that are bad for it.* Both theories describe the nervous system as a mediator between the organism's internal environment and its external environment. According to the **need-reduction theory,** the function of the nervous system is to mediate between a state of deprivation in the internal environment (a need) and a thing in the external environment that will satisfy that need (a goal), so that the organism will approach that thing. According to the **activation theory,** the function of the nervous system is to mediate between a thing in the external envi-

*In the first edition I described need reduction as a theory of motivation and activation as a theory of emotion. This traditional distinction between motivation and emotion is not very useful. There is both a motivational and an emotional component to all functioning of the nervous system. We tend to talk of motivation when observing the functioning from outside (behavior) and of emotion when observing the functioning from inside (experience). In this second edition I describe need reduction as a theory of positive drives and activation as a theory of negative drives, reflecting the current tendency within psychology. This distinction is more useful but is still unsatisfactory. In the third edition I hope that I can report a comprehensive new theory, incorporating elements from both old theories, that will describe both positive and negative drives.

ronment and the internal environment, so as to activate the organism to avoid that thing.

2.2   The Need-Reduction Theory

2.21   Homeostasis

You are alive. You are in a precarious state. Life is a narrow tightrope with death on either side. To stay alive, you must maintain yourself within a narrow range of temperature, blood-sugar concentration, metabolic rate, and so on and so on. Let us focus on temperature. You have been set by the great temperature-setter at 98.6°. You are allowed to vary a little bit above or below this optimal temperature, but a little too much or a little too little and you die. You have certain physiological mechanisms for maintaining your temperature at the optimal level, despite variation in the temperature of your environment. If the temperature goes too low, you shiver; if the temperature goes too high, you sweat. Alligators neither shiver nor sweat. Why are all alligators not boiled alligators or frozen alligators? A group of alligatorologists made an expedition to Africa to find out. A few thousand miles and several thousand dollars later, they discovered that, when an alligator gets too warm, it slides into the cool

water; when it gets too cold, it climbs onto a hot rock. Thus the alligator maintains its optimal temperature by adjusting the environment to itself, rather than by adjusting itself to the environment. It behaves. The process whereby an organism maintains itself in an optimal state is called **homeostasis.** When it deviates from this state, it may return to it by adjusting itself to the environment or by adjusting the environment to itself. Man, of course, uses both mechanisms. He shivers and sweats and builds air conditioners and central heaters. The former mechanism is the province of physiology; the latter is the province of psychology (see Figure 2-1, inner circle).

2.22   Need, Drive, and Goal

Let's take a closer look at the psychological mechanism involved in homeostasis (see Figure 2-1, middle circle). Imagine a hypothetical contented organism, which has just been wined, dined, and loved. It is in its optimal state. However, it cannot remain thus for long. The mere passage of time conspires against a continuation of its bliss. It gets thirsty. It gets hungry. This physiological state of deprivation is called a **need.** The need can be satisfied by appropriate behavior with respect to some appropriate object in the environment—by drinking water in the case of thirst or by eating food in the case of hunger. This object that will satisfy the need is called the **goal.** Since the nervous system is the only system within the organism that "knows" the environment, the need must be transformed into its psychological counterpart, which orients the organism to the appropriate goal. This psychological counterpart is called the **drive.** By making the appropriate response with respect to the goal, the drive is removed, the need is satisfied, and the optimal state is regained.

There tends to be a drive for every need and a need for every drive. Cases exist, however, of needs without corresponding drives and of drives without corresponding needs. Pilots have died because their need for oxygen at very high altitudes was not transformed into a corresponding drive. Since man is not supposed to be flying around at such altitudes, nature has not equipped him with a mechanism for recognizing that the same relative amount of oxygen in the air is absolutely not enough. The much-documented sex drive has no corresponding need. An organism would survive without sex—an unhappy organism but a live organism. The sex drive is designed for the preservation of the species rather than for the preservation of the individual.*

2.23   Hunger, by Way of Example

Let's take an even closer look at the psychological mechanism involved in homeostasis (see Figure 2-1, outer circle) by reviewing the story of the search for the physiological basis of the need and the drive in the case of hunger.

*This statement raises three points, none of which are important. First, sex is the basic altruistic drive. "It's not for me, Dear; it's for the species." Second, sex is here to stay. Since nature is more concerned with the preservation of the species than with that of the individual, we are loaded with a powerful drive that will not be legislated, rationalized, or explained away. Third, "I don't need you, Dear, but I want you" is not only psychologically healthy but scientifically sound.

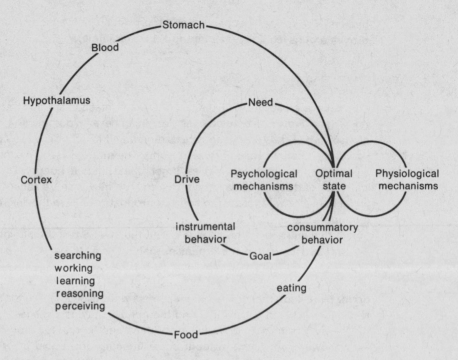

Figure 2-1. Homeostasis. The process of homeostasis is diagramed here and described in the text at three progressively more detailed levels. The inner circle represents simply the psychological means of regaining the optimal state, as opposed to the physiological means on the right. The middle circle represents the general model of the stages in the process of homeostasis. The outer circle represents the specific structures and processes involved in the case of hunger.

2.231   Stomach

The most obvious first place to look is the stomach. Cannon had subjects swallow tubes with balloons at the end.[14]* The balloons were inflated and deflated at irregular intervals, and the subjects were asked to press a key every time they felt hunger pangs. It was found that the pattern of key pressing mirrored that of balloon inflating. Since inflating the balloon produced the same effect as contracting the stomach—that is, pressure against the stomach walls—it was concluded that stomach contractions are the basis of hunger.

*The superscript numbers refer to the References at the end of this book.

2.232 Bloodstream

For the need to be transformed into the drive, it is necessary that there be some mediator between the stomach and the brain. Since the brain and the stomach are connected by the vagus nerve, this was a first possibility. However, rats with cut vagus nerves continued to eat. Since the stomach and the brain are bathed in a common bloodstream, blood was a second possibility. A number of experiments suggest that blood is indeed the mediator. When blood from a hungry dog was interchanged with blood from a satiated dog, the hungry dog became satiated and the satiated dog became hungry. Cafeteria studies in which an organism is permitted to choose from a variety of foods suggest that we have not one but many hungers, each associated with a particular chemical in the blood. The body appears to "know" what it needs; even an infant will choose a balanced diet and will favor food rich in a chemical in which it is deficient.*

2.233 Hypothalamus

For the bloodstream to act on the nervous system, there must be some point of contact. Certain observations have directed attention to a small structure in the brainstem called the **hypothalamus.** Satiated animals resumed drinking when salt was injected near the hypothalamus. Human patients with tumors near the hypothalamus became obese. Following these clues, Teitelbaum began the famous case of the fat rats.[99] He destroyed a part of the hypothalamus in rats and observed that they got fat. They got fat, he noticed, by overeating. They overate by eating more at each meal rather than by eating more meals. They overate until they reached a particular body weight and then ate only enough to maintain it. Moreover, they were more finicky about their food than ordinary rats; that is, they began to refuse food with a lower concentration of impurity. Teitelbaum could not explain this strange set of facts as long as he asked the obvious question "Why did the fat rats continue to eat?" He suddenly realized that the fruitful question was "Why did the fat rats stop eating?" His answer began to emerge. Both normal and fat rats stop eating. The only difference is that fat rats stop later. Could it be, then, that some chemical in the bloodstream, whose concentration is correlated with body weight, acts on the part of the hypothalamus responsible for switching off eating behavior? The smaller the area, the greater the concentration required to turn it off and the greater

*A number of tragic errors have been made because of ignorance of this fact. A child is taken to a hospital because he insists on eating the plaster off the walls. In the antiseptic, plasterless world of the hospital, he dies. He dies of rickets. That is, he dies because his body is deficient in calcium. He had been curing himself by eating plaster.

the body weight. Teitelbaum followed this line of thought by varying the amount of hypothalamus removed. He found that, indeed, the more he removed, the greater the body weight before the rat stopped eating. The apparently incongruous fact that fat rats are finicky eaters now makes sense. The greater the concentration of this chemical in the bloodstream, the greater also the concentration of any impurity and the greater the awareness of it. The only missing link is the exact nature of the chemical. I don't know what it is; Teitelbaum doesn't know what it is; nobody knows what it is. Perhaps you can find out.

2.234 Cortex

For the drive to trigger appropriate behavior with respect to the goal, there must be some link between the hypothalamus and the cortex (the upper crust of the brain where the information from the environment is received and organized). Only the cortex "knows" that steaks are appropriate to satisfy the hunger drive and sticks are not. The exact nature of this link is not known, but we do know it must be two-way. Not only does the hypothalamus act on the cortex, but the cortex acts on the hypothalamus. We all know that the sight of a juicy steak or the sound of a dinner gong can arouse the hunger drive. This principle is applied in steak houses with steaks sizzling on a grill by the window. Schachter, while confirming that the facts about fat rats also apply to fat people, discovered that such arousing stimuli in the external environment control the eating behavior of obese people more than that of nonobese people.[86] Obese people, therefore, lose weight when put on a bland liquid diet in a hospital but regain it when they return to the tempting everyday world.

2.24 Beyond Need-Reduction Theory

2.241 Yerkes-Dodson Law

It would seem reasonable to assume that, the greater the need, the stronger the drive and the more efficient the surmounting of the barriers to the goal. This is true only up to a point. When a need increases beyond a certain level, the organism weakens, its drive lessens, and its efficiency decreases.* Birch has demonstrated a more subtle limitation to our common-sense assumption.[8] He varied the hunger drive in chimpanzees by depriving them of food for vary-

---

*A corpse could be considered, whimsically, as a case of maximum need and minimum drive and efficiency.

ing amounts of time and then observed the effects on the efficiency of solving problems to get bananas. As expected, the chimps performed progressively better as they got hungrier; but they reached a peak, after which they got steadily worse. Overhungry chimps get no bananas. This curvilinear relationship between motivation and performance is called the **Yerkes-Dodson law** (see Figure 2-2). It is reflected in the comment by actors that it is good to be a little nervous, but not too nervous, before a performance.

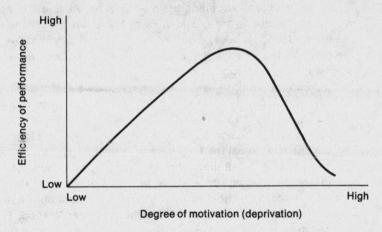

Figure 2-2. Yerkes-Dodson Law

There is a corollary to this corollary . A psychologist asked two groups of students to solve a series of problems. Members of the first group (low drive) were asked simply for their anonymous contribution in establishing norms for the test. Members of the second group (high drive) were told that it was a test of intelligence, innate decency, sense of humor, and sexual potency; that they must write their name on it; and that, incidentally, the university was a little overcrowded. The first group did better on the difficult tasks; the second group did better on the easy tasks. A clue to the explanation of this finding is found through a qualitative analysis of Birch's study. The chimps did worse at low and high levels of drive than at medium levels. They did worse for different reasons: at low levels, because they just fooled around and were easily distracted; at high levels, because they continued with an inappropriate strategy and did not try alternative strategies. That is, at high levels of motivation they fell victim to **set,** the tendency to persist with a particular approach to a problem. Perhaps a difficult task is one in which the obvious thing to do is the wrong thing and an easy task is one in which the obvious thing to do is the correct thing. Thus highly motivated students, who tend to persist with the obvious solution, will do well on easy tasks and poorly on difficult tasks. When you take an examination, sweat if it is easy, but relax if it is difficult.

2.242 Functional Autonomy

Consider the newborn baby cast from the cozy womb into the cruel world. Previously his optimal state was maintained by physiological mechanisms; now he must utilize psychological mechanisms. At first the appropriate goals to satisfy his needs are provided by obliging adults. The nipple is seldom more than a few cries away from the mouth. Gradually, however, barriers build up between the drive and the goal. That is, problems develop. The child must learn to get the food from his plate to his mouth, to go to the corner store to pick up the food, to earn the money to pay the storekeeper, to get the job to earn the money, to go to school to get the job. A need-reduction theorist would perhaps explain your motivation for reading this book as follows: you read the book to pass the course to get the degree to get the job to earn the money to buy the food to eat the food to reduce the hunger need to return to the optimal state to survive. All the complex psychological processes would be viewed as means of attaining goals. However, some of these means can become ends in themselves by a process that Allport calls **functional autonomy.**[2] At first we shop in order to eat, but later we shop in order to shop. Thus current motives can grow out of previous motives but be independent of them, just as the adult grows out of the child and the oak out of the acorn.

2.243 Needs of the Nervous System

The need-reduction theory explains everything we do in terms of reducing needs to return to an optimal state to survive. This model of motivation implies that an organism without needs would not behave.* The nervous system is simply a device to mediate between needs and goals to reduce those needs.

The model is tantalizing, because it reduces the vast complexity of human motivation to a simple framework that fits neatly within the well-established evolutionary theory. Yet, intuitively, we recognize that it is inadequate. It would perhaps explain the behavior of our dogs or our early ancestors or ourselves if we were marooned on a deserted island. Yet even our dogs fetch sticks and slippers, our remote ancestors took time off from the struggle for survival to draw pictures on cave walls, and we would devise games to pass the time on

---

*The nervous system, then, is seen as a physical object that will remain at rest or continue with uniform motion in a straight line unless acted on by some external force. The psychologist, in his eagerness to be scientific, has perhaps too slavishly followed in the footsteps of the physicist. He cuts the umbilical cord from philosophy and, right away, grafts it onto physics.

our deserted island. Such activities appear to be engaged in for their own sake. They do not contribute to survival; they are not means to an end but ends in themselves. Recent studies of such just-for-the-sheer-hell-of-it activities suggest that the nervous system is not merely a static servant waiting to be prodded into the service of the rest of the organism. The nervous system has needs of its own.

It sounded like a good deal: $20 a day for lying in a comfortable bed doing nothing, with visors over the eyes, pillows around the ears, and cuffs around the hands so stimulation could not spoil the leisure. Yet the McGill undergraduates who were presented with this paradise for students were soon clamoring to get out of it.[44] **Sensory deprivation** turned out to be a very disturbing experience. Their thought processes deteriorated, their emotional responses became childish, and they had fearful hallucinations. It appears that, just as the belly needs food, the brain needs a certain amount of stimulation to function normally. Moreover, the organism seeks stimulation for the brain, just as it seeks food for the belly. Monkeys will work hard to unfasten latches to open a window to see what is going on in the laboratory outside.* More dramatically, monkeys will work hard to unfasten latches—for nothing. They enjoy the manipulation of the latches for its own sake; the activity is its own reward. Even the lowly rat is curious about the world in which it lives. It will often take the long, scenic route to the goal box in the maze rather than the short, dull route; it will spend more time around a novel stimulus introduced into its cage than around a familiar stimulus. The activities of exploration and manipulation provide the nervous system with the stimulation it needs, just as the activities of eating and drinking provide the rest of the organism with the nourishment it needs.

In his famous studies on love, Harlow demonstrated that we need not only stimulation per se but a special sort of stimulation. Most psychologists have been reluctant to investigate that mysterious emotion we call love, not only because it is positive but partly because it is complex and partly because it is sacred. The limited consideration of the topic has tended to focus on food as the basis for love. The infant who suckles at the mother's breast comes to love the breast, then the owner of the breast, then the owners of other breasts. Harlow was intrigued by the close attachment of infant monkeys to pieces of cloth provided for bedding.[39] They carried them around as Linus carries his blanket, and they sulked when the cloths were taken away to be washed. He reasoned that perhaps such **contact comfort** is important in the development of love. He

*Monkeys are as curious about man as man is about monkeys. An experimenter once tried to observe the behavior of a monkey by locking him in a room and watching him through a keyhole. All he saw was one large, brown, baleful eye.

tested the relative importance of food and contact comfort by giving infant monkeys two mothers, one a wire mother from which they received milk and the other a cloth mother from which they received contact comfort. The monkeys spent considerably more time on the cloth mother than on the wire mother. Indeed, they behaved with respect to the cloth mother very much as they would have to the real mother. When frightened, they ran to her; when in a strange place, they used her as a base from which to explore; when permitted a glimpse of her, they worked to obtain such a glimpse. Contact comfort would appear, then, to be an important element in the development of love. Harlow raised some monkeys with wire mothers only. They grew up to be neurotic, spending most of their time huddled in a corner of the cage. Monkeys raised with both wire and cloth mothers appeared to be normal. However, they turned out to be poor lovers. The males were impotent, and the females were frigid. The few females who conceived were poor mothers. Real mothers cannot yet be replaced.

This fact is true for monkeys, but what about us? Spitz investigated the high mortality rate in foundling homes. [97] He found that the children were dying from a lack of tender loving care. Those who survived were physically weaker, less emotionally secure, and intellectually duller than children raised in normal homes. We need fondling during the first few months of life. If we don't get it, we will be permanently emotionally stunted.*

A group of psychologists arranged to have some observers infiltrate an organization that believed the world would end at a particular time on a particular date.[23] They were curious to find out what would happen to the members' belief when that time passed and the world remained. The psychologists found that those persons who were only peripherally involved with the group ceased to believe, but those who were strongly committed to the group (that is, who had stated their belief in interviews with the press, who had sold their belongings, and so on) continued to believe. These true believers argued that the destruction of the world had been postponed, that it had been canceled because of their vigilance, that there had been a mistake in the date, and so on and so on. This result suggested to Festinger the concept of **cognitive dissonance.** When two items of information do not fit together, there is a tendency for one of them to be changed. For instance, the two items of information "I smoke" and "smoking causes cancer" are dissonant. Festinger finds that significantly fewer smokers than nonsmokers believe the latter statement. Persons who have those two items within their cognitive world tend either to stop smoking or to stop believing. Research on cognitive dissonance has led to a number of antigrandmotherish findings. Not only do we own a car because we read ads for it, but we read ads for a car because we own it; not only do we say what we believe, but we

*We can't make up for it later, although it's fun trying.

come to believe what we say; not only do we own the things we like, but we come to like the things we own; not only do we know what we like, but we come to like what we know. Thus the nervous system has a need to know what it needs to know.

2.3 The Activation Theory

The activation theory has been inspired by the discovery of a structure in the brain called the reticular activating system. Let's look at the traditional view of emotions before that structure was discovered (Section 2.31: Emotions as Negative Drives), at the structure itself (Section 2.32: The Reticular Activating System), and then at the modern view of emotions that it inspired (Section 2.33: Emotions as Activation plus Perception).

2.31 Emotions as Negative Drives

Let's turn now from the positive to the negative drives—from the tendency toward things we want to the tendency away from things we don't want, from the tendency toward things we eat to the tendency away from things that eat us. "Away from" is not to be interpreted too literally in spatial terms, but in the experiential terms of removing something we do not like from our psychological field. There are two ways in which this can be done: one can remove the thing, or one can remove oneself. The first technique is accomplished by fight; the second is accomplished by flight. The emotion underlying the first is rage; the emotion underlying the second is fear. These primitive emotions must have played a dominant role in the life of early man. Consider one of your remote ancestors confronted by a saber-toothed tiger. He has a tiger in his psychological field. He can remove it or remove himself. He can kill it or run away. The only good tiger is a dead tiger or a distant tiger.

There is some evidence that rage and fear involve the secretion, respectively, of two different hormones, **noradrenalin** and **adrenalin.** Tigers have a high proportion of noradrenalin, and rabbits have a high proportion of adrenalin. Tigers are equipped for fight, and rabbits are equipped for flight. Funkenstein made some Harvard undergraduates angry by presenting them with awkward problems, criticizing their performance, and ridiculing their solutions.[25] In an interview afterward, he asked them to describe their feelings during the experiment. He found that they directed their anger either out at the situation or in at themselves. The anger-out reaction was correlated with the secretion of noradrenalin and the anger-in reaction with the secretion of adrenalin.

We all recognize three broad effects of an emotion-arousing stimulus —experiential (we feel angry or afraid), physiological (there are certain changes in our bodies), and behavioral (we fight or flee). We tend to assume that the internal experiential and physiological effects precede the external behavioral effects: I see the tiger; I am afraid; I run. Furthermore, we tend to assume that the internal effects not only precede but cause the external effects: I run because I am afraid.

The **James-Lange theory of emotion** (presented almost simultaneously by William James and Carl Lange) challenges this commonsensical view. It states that the external effects precede the internal effects: I see the tiger; I run; I am afraid. Furthermore, it states that the external effects not only precede but cause the internal effects: I am afraid because I run.

The theory appears, at first glance, to be ridiculous. However, when you meet a huge truck in your lane at the brow of a hill, you coolly swerve into the ditch and *then* break out in a cold sweat. Since a cause must precede an effect, it would seem that the external effects must cause the internal effects.

One of the physiological effects of an emotion-arousing stimulus is the secretion of adrenalin, the body's emergency fluid, into the bloodstream. Schachter and Singer injected subjects with adrenalin under the pretext that it was a new drug being tested for its effects on vision.[87] Half the subjects (informed group) were told that they would experience the various physiological effects of emotion as a side effect of the drug; the other half of the subjects (uninformed group) were not given this information. Each group was further subdivided into two subgroups, one put into a situation designed to make them happy (happy group) and the other put into a situation designed to make them angry (angry group). All the subjects were subsequently asked to rate their moods on a 9-point scale ranging from "extremely happy" through "neither angry nor happy" to "extremely angry." The informed group tended to be "neither angry nor happy"; the uninformed group deviated from this midpoint. The happy uninformed group reported that they were happy; the angry uninformed group reported that they were angry. That is, those who had no explanation for their emotional arousal interpreted it in terms of their perception of the situation they were in.

2.32   The Reticular Activating System

The **cue function** of a stimulus is to inform you of what is happening in your environment. The stimulus is transformed at the appropriate receptor (a set of cells specialized for this purpose) into nerve impulses, which are transformed at the appropriate projection area of the cortex (a set of cells specialized for this purpose) into a perception. The cue function is represented in Figure 2-3 by the solid line projecting directly onto a specific part of the cortex.

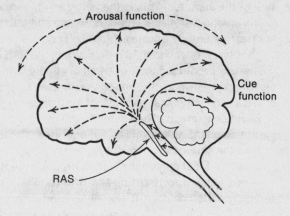

Figure 2-3. Cue and Arousal Functions of the Stimulus

Discovery of a structure in the brain called the **reticular activating system (RAS)** indicates that the stimulus has an arousal function as well as a cue function. The **arousal function** of a stimulus is to alert you to the fact that something is happening in your environment. Nerve impulses, passing along tributaries of the nerve that carries the cue function, turn on the RAS, which projects diffusely onto the cortex. The arousal function is represented in Figure 2-3 by the dotted lines that project indirectly onto the whole cortex via the reticular activating system. Indirect stimulation by way of the RAS tells you only that some information is coming in (the RAS responds in the same way to sights, sounds, smells, tastes, and touches), whereas direct stimulation tells you *what* information is coming in.

The RAS works much like a radio receiver. It has a volume control, which can be turned way down when you are asleep and way up when you are confronted by an emergency. When the volume is way down, the nerve impulses arrive at your cortex but you are not aware of them. It also has a tuning control. It can tune you in as well as turn you on. The tuning mechanism enables you to pay attention to some stimuli and not to others. Thus a mother can sleep through the snores of her husband but awaken at the slightest whimper from her newborn baby.

2.33 Emotions as Activation plus Perception

The view of emotions as negative drives (presented in Section 2.31) was based on the cue function of the stimulus. A new view of emotions as activation plus perception (presented here) is based on the cue function *and* the arousal function of the stimulus. This is the activation theory of emotion.*

The emotion-arousing stimulus, like all stimuli, has both a cue function and an arousal function. The arousal function prepares you for an emergency, whether it be necessary for you to fight or flee. When the RAS is triggered, it acts upward on the cortex, producing the experiential effects, and downward on the autonomic nervous system and the endocrine system (responsible, respectively, for the physical and chemical aspects of your internal environment), producing the physiological effects. The action on the cortex alerts you to the emergency, and the action on the autonomic and endocrine systems provides you with the energy to meet the emergency. The cue function informs you whether there is indeed an emergency. Most stimuli are not worth getting emotional about. In those cases the cortex acts downward on the RAS to inhibit the arousal function. Animals without a cortex get mad at every little thing. The cue function also informs you of the nature of the emergency so that you may respond appropriately. Otherwise, you may attack tigers and run away from rabbits.

2.34 Beyond Activation Theory

2.341 Judgment of Emotions

In considering emotions as negative drives, we focus on a very limited part of our full range of emotions. The most obvious source of information about the range of emotions of others is the face. There tends to be a one-to-one correspondence between particular facial expressions and emotions underlying them. There are, of course, exceptions. We can hide emotions that we feel—which is the skill of the poker player; we can feign emotions that we do not feel—which is the skill of the actor.† Facial expressions out of context can be misinterpreted. A crying girl

---

*Discovery of the RAS has profound implications—not only for our view of emotion but also for the problems of consciousness, wakefulness, and attention. News of its discovery is percolating through to philosophers and will provide answers to questions they have been debating for centuries. For example, the vague philosophical question "What is the relationship between body and mind?" can be translated into the more precise psychological question "How are nerve impulses transformed into perceptions?" which (since this transformation does not take place when the RAS is turned down) can be translated into the even more precise physiological question "What is the function of the reticular activating system?"

†Marlon Brando, when asked by a peasant woman in the Far East what he did for a living, replied "I make faces."

looks sad until we are informed that she is clutching a blade of grass on which Mick Jagger has just stepped. The facial expression of someone from a different culture must be interpreted in its cultural context. It is said that the Chinese stick out the tongue when they are surprised, whereas Americans raise their eyebrows. Such cultural differences cause difficulties at the United Nations.

Despite these limitations, there is a high degree of consistency between emotions portrayed by actors and judgment of those emotions by subjects. Woodworth asked an actor to portray each of six emotions: (1) love, mirth, happiness; (2) surprise; (3) fear, suffering; (4) anger, determination; (5) disgust; and (6) contempt.[112] Subjects placed the resultant facial expressions consistently within the appropriate categories. When they were wrong, they were not far wrong. That is, if we consider those emotions falling in the same order along a line, the subjects sometimes put an expression belonging in category (4) into category (5) but never into (1) or (6). The only exception was a tendency to confuse categories (1) and (6), which suggests that the categories should be placed in a circle rather than in a straight line. Schlosberg obtained even more consistent results by asking subjects to place the expressions on 9-point scales with respect to two dimensions (rejection-attention and pleasantness-unpleasantness) rather than six categories (Figure 2-4).[89]

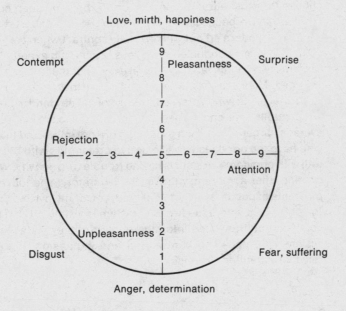

Figure 2-4. Six Categories and Two Dimensions of Facial Expressions

Subjective judgments of posed expressions on fabricated scales can be brushed aside lightly by critics. Physiological structures and states cannot be dismissed so easily. It is tempting, then, to try to anchor those two dimensions to certain concrete, underlying physiological correlates. Let's give in to this temptation.

2.342 Pupillometrics

Eckhard Hess was lying in bed one evening reading a very interesting article on perception. His wife glanced over the top of the journal and said "Eckhard, what big pupils you have!" His curiosity aroused, Hess asked his laboratory assistant the next day to look at the cards in a deck as he exposed them one by one. On two of the cards, he had pasted pictures of nudes. His assistant's pupils dilated twice—when those two cards appeared. Hess built a piece of equipment to investigate this phenomenon more formally. It consists of a 2-foot-long black box. The subject peers into one end at pictures projected onto a screen at the other end. A camera takes pictures of his eyes at the rate of two pictures a second. When a subject is looking at something that attracts him, his pupils expand; when he is looking at something that repels him, his pupils contract. Hess has been very busy since he initiated this new study of **pupillometrics.** He has helped Hugh Hefner choose the most attractive covers for *Playboy* and soap companies choose the most attractive packages for their soap. He has exposed frauds who claim an interest in modern art but whose pupils contract when confronted with a modern painting. He has conducted numerous fascinating experiments. For instance, he presents two female faces, identical except for the fact that, in one, the pupils are enlarged. Male subjects, when asked which they prefer, at first protest that they are identical but, when pressed, choose one. They tend to choose the one with the larger pupils. This choice makes sense. Girls who are interested in us have, on the average, larger pupils than those who are not interested in us. Since we like girls who have the good taste to like us, we prefer girls with big pupils. Hess is doing well with pupillometrics but is having trouble with his wife. When he got home one evening after a very busy day in the laboratory, she looked into his eyes, saw pinpoints of pupils, and said "Eckhard, you don't love me anymore!" The pupil is the only place where the nervous system is visible. "The eye is the mirror of the soul" can be translated into "the pupil of the eye is a window to the nervous system." Perhaps the contraction and expansion of the pupils reflect the rejection-attention dimension.

2.343 Pleasure and Pain Centers

Olds was poking electrodes into the brains of rats to try to find the function of a particular part of the reticular activating system.[76] He got his electrode into the wrong place and made a fascinating discovery. (This art of finding something while looking for something else is called **serendipity**.) The rat liked being stimulated in that place. Did he say "Oooh! I like that. Do it again!"? In a sense, he did. He tended to go back to the spot where he had first been shocked and, when permitted to shock himself by pressing a bar, did so. Indeed, the rat said he liked it very much. One typical rat pressed at a rate of 2,000 presses an hour for 26 consecutive hours. It would not have pressed nearly so much to get food or water or another rat. Olds had stumbled upon what has come to be called a **pleasure center.*** Complementary areas, called **pain centers,** have subsequently been discovered.† Perhaps the pleasantness-unpleasantness dimension is generated by the relative stimulation of pleasure and pain centers, just as a hot-cold dimension is generated by the relative adjustment of hot and cold taps.

*There are certain ominous 1984ish implications of this discovery. Perhaps it will soon be possible for each of us to have an electrode in our pleasure center and a battery in our pocket, to give ourselves a shot every time we get depressed. Interpersonal relations could reduce to "I'll press your button, Dear, if you'll press mine."

†This finding provides some physiological substance to the hedonistic philosophy that man is motivated by the pursuit of pleasure and the avoidance of pain.

Some village Hampden, that with dauntless breast
The little tyrant of his fields withstood;
Some mute inglorious Milton here may rest,
Some Cromwell guiltless of his country's blood.

Thomas Gray
Elegy Written in a Country Churchyard

To the classic peril of being impaled on the horns of a dilemma, we
moderns should add a new one—being split by a false dichotomy.

G. C. Homans
The Human Group

3 Genetic Approach

3.1   Genetic Determinants of Behavior

3.11   Genetics and Psychology

The most important event in your life occurred approximately nine months be-fore you were born. At that moment of conception, when the sperm of your father merged with the ovum of your mother, the basic program for your life was written. At that moment it was determined that you would talk, though not that you would talk English with an accent much like your mother's; it was deter-mined that you would walk, though not that you would walk stooped forward with hands behind your back much like your father. The amendments to your program that determined your specific styles of talking and walking were added as you developed. Since every aspect of behavior is determined by a complex interaction between genetic and environmental factors, the study of behavior as determined by genetic factors (genetics) is intimately related to the study of behavior as determined by environmental factors (psychology). It is difficult to disentangle the inherited biological constraints in the program from the ac-quired cultural constraints in the amendments, but, as geneticists clarify the former, psychologists will see more clearly the role of the latter.

Geneticists are indeed clarifying the former. The genetic code in which your basic program is written is being broken. You are composed of cells, which are composed of chromosomes, which are composed of genes, which are com-posed of DNA molecules, which are composed of strings of four chemicals—adenine, guanine, cytosine, and uracil—arranged in different orders. These four chemicals are the letters of the code, and the code is the order in which the letters are written.

3.12 Cannibal Worms—McConnell

The work of McConnell illustrates the intimate relationship between psychology and genetics. He followed his data out of his own field of psychology into the neighboring field of genetics, triggering accusations of straying from psychologists and of trespassing from geneticists. He started small in his kitchen with $3.89 worth of equipment and a supply of worms from a local pond. He became, within a few years, head of the Planaria Research Group, with a staff of 18 biologists and psychologists. They call themselves worm runners and publish a highly successful journal called *The Worm Runner's Digest*, which is devoted to the care and education of worms. Behind this lighthearted front, they are doing serious research that may revolutionize man's conception not only of worms but of himself.[68] In one experiment, a group of worms were taught to go right in a *T* maze. They were then cut in half. When the two halves regenerated, the new worms took significantly less time to learn to go right in the *T* maze than the regenerated halves of untrained worms. The tail ends retained more than the head ends. Thus the learning is not preserved, as one would expect, in the head of the worm. In an even more dramatic experiment, the worms taught to go right in the *T* maze were ground up and fed to the other worms. The cannibal worms that had fed on trained worms took significantly less time to learn to go right in the *T* maze than cannibal worms that had fed on untrained worms.* Thus the learning is not only not retained in the head end of the nervous system, but it is not retained at a neural level at all. It must be preserved at a chemical level, since that is all that survives being minced and eaten. McConnell suspects that the information is retained in the chemical **ribonucleic acid (RNA),** a biological cousin to the **deoxyribonucleic acid (DNA)** molecule, which contains the set of instructions for the development of the organism. Subsequent studies have supported this theory. RNA from an educated rat improves performance in another rat and—more surprising—in another species, the hamster. Perhaps, then, the basic program for our lives is written in our DNA molecules and the amendments are written in our RNA molecules.

*A huge mythology developed in the wake of this experiment: stories of professors who describe the experiment to their class and disappear soon after under mysterious circumstances, projects for disposing of retired professors, prospects of learning psychology by taking pills rather than courses or by injection rather than instruction.

3.2   The Nature-Nurture Controversy

The debate about the relative importance of genetic and environmental factors—the nature-nurture controversy—permeates every area of psychology. Jensen, with more crazy courage (especially for someone teaching at Berkeley, of all places) than empirical evidence, has recently caused the issue to raise its hoary head again.[51] He argues that the relative failure of programs like Head Start is due to the fact that intelligence is genetically determined and that non-white races are less well endowed. However, he has made a great contribution to egalitarianism, because the consensus on the basis of the evidence generated by the controversy that he started is that a nervous system is a nervous system is a nervous system, whatever the color of the skin it is encased in, and that any differences in IQ scores are due to cultural biases in IQ tests.

Let's focus on the nature-nurture issue as it relates to the problem of depth perception. You see the world as three-dimensional. It extends in depth as well as in length and width. You take this three-dimensional world so much for granted that it is difficult to see what the psychologist is concerned about when he talks of the *problem* of depth perception. Your perception of the world must ultimately be based on the pattern of stimulation by light on the retina of your eyes. The retina is a flat surface. How does the brain construct out of two overlapping two-dimensional patterns a three-dimensional world? The **hereditarian** would say that you are born with this capacity built into the brain; the **environmentalist** would say that you learn to see the world as three-dimensional. Let's look in turn at some evidence on each side.

3.21   Evidence for Hereditarianism

3.211   Rats and Jumping Stands

In testing depth perception, a basic research strategy is to eliminate one factor (hereditary or environmental) and, if depth perception still exists, to attribute the perception to the other factor. In one experiment the role of the environment is eliminated by raising rats in darkness. The rats are then tested for depth perception. Since it is impossible to ask rats if they perceive the world as three-dimensional, it is necessary to set up a situation such that, if they have depth perception, they can perform a certain task; if they do not have depth perception, they cannot perform the task. They are placed on a platform and persuaded to jump to another platform. The platforms are placed at varying distances apart. If the rats can consistently land on the other platform, it is reasonable to infer that they have depth perception. They can and thus they have.

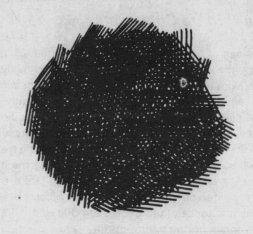

rats being reared in darkness

3.212 The Visual Cliff

Gibson and Walk set up an apparatus, called the **visual cliff,** to test whether young organisms have depth perception.[29] It consists of a glass-topped table with a board across the middle. A sheet of patterned material is placed against the underside of the glass on one side of the board (the shallow side), and a sheet of the same material is placed on the floor below the other side of the board (the deep side). The deep side is the "visual cliff," since there appears to be a sharp drop off that side of the board. Young organisms of various species—rats, dogs, goats, humans—were placed on the board, and a record was kept of the number of times they stepped off onto the shallow side and the number of times they stepped off onto the deep side. Although there is an equal probability of stepping off either side by chance, almost invariably the young animals stepped off onto the shallow side. Young children would not crawl off onto the deep side, even when their mothers treacherously called them from that side. This result does not prove, however, that organisms are born with depth perception. Since this apparatus depends on the organism's moving around, it is possible to prove only that an organism can perceive depth as soon as it can locomote.* This conclusion makes evolutionary sense, since there is no danger of falling over cliffs until one starts to move around.

*Do not, however, allow your infant to crawl around at the edge of a cliff. Since he has depth perception, he will not voluntarily crawl over; but since he is clumsy, he may involuntarily fall over. I will not be responsible for the lost children of people who don't read footnotes.

3.213 Picture Perception

A psychologist decided to raise his son without pictures. The pictures in the home were covered up, the child was never shown any picture-books, and he was screened from billboards when he went out. At 18 months he was shown pictures of familiar objects and asked to identify them. He did so in an interesting manner. The speech of an 18-month-old is not very distinct and can usually be interpreted only by intimate associates who are familiar with his particular distortion of the language. The responses to a sequence of pictures were recorded, the child's grandparents were asked to identify the sounds, and the identifications were then paired to the pictures. They were found to match. A major flaw in this experiment is the fact that it is impossible to be certain that the child never saw a picture before being tested. Perhaps some indulgent uncle had slipped him a few pictures during the first 18 months. One of the psychologist's colleagues replicated the study with monkeys under conditions in which it was impossible for some indulgent monkey's uncle to show them pictures. He got the same results. It would appear from these studies that we do not need to learn to recognize two-dimensional representations of three-dimensional objects. The fact that we can shift from three to two dimensions without experience is indirect evidence that we can shift from two to three dimensions without experience.

3.22 Evidence for Environmentalism

3.221 Sensory Deprivation

In his *Essay Concerning Human Understanding,* published in 1690, John Locke argued that the mind at birth is a blank slate on which experience writes. He is, in our terms, an extreme environmentalist. In that essay he quotes a letter from a Mr. Molyneux, suggesting that the heredity-environment issue could be resolved once and for all by conducting the following experiment. A person who was born blind and subsequently gains his sight is immediately presented with a cube and a sphere. If he can differentiate between them, the hereditarians are right; if he cannot differentiate between them, the environmentalists are right. At that time the experiment seemed impossible and was merely one of those let's-pretend exercises with which philosophers amused themselves. Since then an operation for removing cataracts has been developed, and the experiment has been conducted many times. Von Senden collected the records of all the cases he could trace in which a patient was tested for certain visual capacities immediately on gaining sight for the first time.[107] What are his conclusions? The patient does not, as in Hollywood movies, reach up immediately and embrace his sweetheart. He cannot tell his sweetheart from the nurse or from the doctor or even from the bedside table. He cannot differentiate a cube from a sphere unless he is permitted to run his hand over them. He can tell that there is something there, but he cannot tell what it is. That is, he can differentiate a figure from its background but cannot identify it. The process of learning depth is a long and laborious one. Many patients never learn. They refuse to accept the so-called blessing of sight and continue to rely entirely on the other channels of information with which they are more familiar.

3.222 Relearning Spatial Perception

A number of studies have been conducted in which the visual world is distorted by means of special goggles. Kohler equipped subjects with goggles that turned their world upside down.[56] At first they were completely disoriented. When Kohler threw a ball at them, they would reach down for a high one and up for a low one. Soon they adjusted to their new world and could not only catch the ball but ride a bicycle, fence, drive a car, and go for a walk over the mountains. When they took the spectacles off, however, and looked at the world through their normal eyes, it appeared upside down. Some years ago I spent three goggled weeks in a world distorted 30° to the right. What was it like? There were color fringes along every edge. Straight lines appeared curved, and curved lines appeared straight. When I moved my head, the world at one side rushed in and at the other side rushed away. Within a few days this bizarre world seemed perfectly normal. When the spectacles were removed, the world was distorted 30° to the left. After a few more days the world returned—fortunately—to normal. It appears, then, that our visual system can adapt to drastic changes. The fact that we can relearn spatial perception is indirect evidence that we can learn it in the first place.

3.23 A Restatement of the Issue

3.231 From Two to Five Factors—Hebb

We have been discussing the relative importance of hereditary and environmental factors in determining our perception of the world as three-dimensional. We have noted some evidence in support of both sides of the issue. None of the evidence seems particularly conclusive. The nature-nurture issue arises in many areas in psychology; in each case, as in depth perception, the results are equivocal. Often in the history of science, when we appear to be making little progress in finding answers, we discover that we have been asking the wrong questions. Hebb has suggested that the question "Is a particular behavior determined by heredity or environment?" is just such a wrong question.[43] It is based on the false assumption that behavior is determined by either heredity or environment, but these two categories are not mutually exclusive or exhaustive. He generates a five-factor classification by making certain distinctions that this simpleminded dichotomy glosses over.

We tend to think of behavior as the output of the entire organism. It is, however, the output of a subsystem of the organism: the nervous system. Part of the environment of the nervous system is the rest of the organism. It is necessary to distinguish, then, between this internal environment (chemical) and the external environment (sensory). We tend to think of genetic factors as those with which we are born and environmental factors as those operating on us since birth. The moment of birth is a convenient reference point, but it is not so meaningful as the moment of conception. We use the former rather than the latter mainly because it is easier to pinpoint. Genetic influences on our behavior are determined at the moment of conception. During the first nine months of our existence, environmental factors are influencing development as we bask in the cozy, chemical environment of the womb. Thus it is necessary to distinguish between the chemical environment before birth (chemical, prenatal) and that after birth (chemical, postnatal). We tend to think that any behavior that is universal within a species is necessarily determined by hereditary factors. However, recent studies have demonstrated that certain such universal behaviors can be changed by manipulating the environment. It seems that all members of the species behave in the same way because they are all exposed to the same environment. Therefore we must distinguish between the aspects of the sensory environment that are the same for all members of a species (sensory, constant) and those that differ from individual to individual (sensory, variable). The expan-

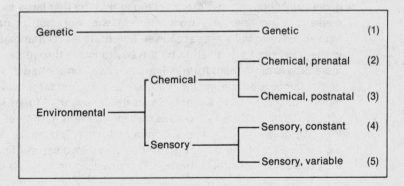

Figure 3-1. From Two to Five Factors Determining Behavior. Hebb makes three important distinctions that extend the traditional two factors on the left to the five factors on the right.

sion from two to five factors is diagramed in Figure 3-1. Factors (1) and (5) are those considered under the traditional dichotomy. Factor (1) is clearly the province of genetics, and factor (5) is clearly the province of psychology. Factor (1) was discussed in Section 3.1, and factor (5) is essentially the subject matter of this entire book. The remaining three factors are the disputed territory between genetics and psychology. Let's glance briefly at each of them in turn.

3.232 The Three "New" Factors

The effects of the prenatal chemical environment on the development of an organism are seldom noticed, unless some foreign chemical is added to it. Doses of cortisone taken by the mother during the formation of the roof of the mouth can create a cleft palate in the fetus. The chemical environment of the mother can affect the fetus, but it is doubtful that her sensory environment can. Taking Thalidomide can create a cripple; listening to Beethoven cannot produce a pianist.

The effects of the postnatal chemical environment are noticed most dramatically at puberty. Certain glands begin to secrete into the bloodstream hormones that trigger the development of the secondary sexual characteristics and correlated changes in behavior. Such events are genetically determined, even though they do not manifest themselves until well after birth. They are part of the plan laid down in the genetic code, but a part that cannot be unfolded until a certain period has elapsed. It is a time-bomb effect. The fuse is lighted at conception, but the explosion does not occur until puberty.

The effect of the constant sensory environment was discovered by changing what, under normal circumstances, was the same for all members of a species. Since all baby geese follow mother goose, it was assumed that this behavior was genetically determined. Lorenz arranged that the first large moving object baby geese saw on emerging from the egg was not mother goose but Lorenz himself.[62] These baby geese followed Lorenz. It seems that nature leaves a blank in the blueprint to be filled in by the environment through an early, rapid, and more or less permanent form of learning called **imprinting.** Nature can afford to do this, since, under normal circumstances, the first large moving object will be mother goose and the biologically useful behavior of following mother goose will be established. Lorenz got his due for interfering with nature's plans. When the baby geese grew up and sought a mate, they looked for someone like dear old Mum. Part of the courting ritual of geese involves stuffing worms into the mouth of one's intended. Lorenz was lying asleep in the grass one day, and . . . .

She makes me wash, they comb me all to thunder—the widder eats by a bell; she goes to bed by a bell; she gets up by a bell—everything's so awful reg'lar a body can't stand it.

Mark Twain
The Adventures of Tom Sawyer

Nothing we ever do is, in the strict scientific literalness, wiped out. Of course, this has its good side as well as its bad one. As we become permanent drunkards by so many separate drinks, so we become saints in the moral, and authorities and experts in the practical and scientific spheres, by so many separate acts and hours of work.

William James
The Principles of Psychology

4 Behavioristic Approach

4.1 Classical Conditioning

4.11 The Basic Model—Pavlov

4.111 Ivan P. Pavlov

It all began—so the story goes—when a great Russian physiologist walked into his laboratory and a dog salivated. Most of us would merely have been flattered and continued with our physiology. But Ivan Petrovich Pavlov was not like most of us. He recognized this reaction as an important phenomenon. Before this incident, Pavlov had already won a Nobel Prize for his work in physiology. Most of us would have been content with that. But Ivan Petrovich Pavlov was not like most of us. He began a 40-year investigation of the phenomenon and thus laid one of the cornerstones of modern psychology.[78] Have you ever heard of Twitmeyer? He was an American graduate student who stumbled on the same phenomenon before Pavlov, considered it footnoteworthy to his doctoral thesis, and went no further. Twitmeyer was like most of us.

It is ironic that Pavlov is recognized by psychologists as one of the founders of their science, for he never considered himself a psychologist and even doubted that psychology could become a science. This is only one of many contradictions in the life of this fascinating man. He defied the Soviet government from 1917 until 1933, arrogantly refusing any attempt at conciliation; yet today his work is the foundation of Soviet psychology. In his laboratory he was usually the stolid, patient, plodding researcher; but when things went wrong, he would explode and stomp around, swearing and gesticulating. In his professional life he was a stickler for detail and mercilessly attacked any slipshod work; in his private life he was indifferent to detail.*

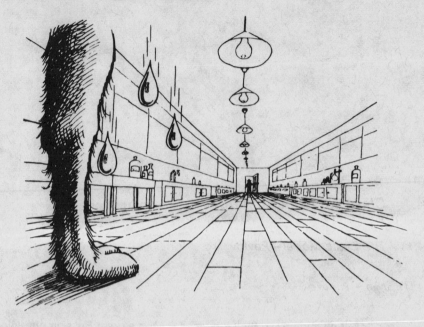

4.112 Unconditioned and Conditioned Reflexes

Environment affects behavior. This statement is true but trivial. Pavlov suggested a way to make it more precise. Representing the organism as a rather unflattering empty box, we could consider environment as the set of stimuli acting on it and behavior as the set of responses produced by it (Figure 4-1). Now we can substitute the precise statement "Stimulus x elicits response y" for the vague statement "Environment affects behavior." We are all aware that an organism can come to behave differently in the same environment. That is, it can

*For example, he arrived for his wedding in a far-off town without the money to pay for the wedding or for the return trip for him and his bride. This was just the beginning of the troubles faced by his devoted and long-suffering wife, who dedicated her life to protecting him from the world of practical affairs so he could work undistracted. Martha Bernays performed a similar function. You may never have heard of her, yet Mrs. Sigmund Freud contributed a great deal to psychology. These ladies deserve at least a footnote in the story of psychology.†

†A footnote to a footnote: Some female readers of the first edition were offended by the sexist tone of this footnote. I feebly protested that, by describing a role some women have accepted, I was not necessarily advocating it. But they are right. I leave it here as a monument to a dying attitude. Let's hope that this monument will soon be a gravestone.

learn. How does it learn? Or, more precisely, how can stimulus *x*, which was previously neutral, come to elicit response *y*?

Pavlov begins his answer by pointing out that certain stimuli are already capable of eliciting certain responses at birth. If I tap sharply below your knee, you will raise your lower leg. The tap (stimulus) is prewired to the raising of the lower leg (response). No experience necessary. Such a prewired link between a stimulus and a response is called an **unconditioned reflex** (UCR). If I blow a whistle, you will not raise your lower leg. If, however, I were to blow the whistle, tap below your knee, blow the whistle, tap below your knee, blow the whistle, tap below your knee, and so on, eventually you would raise your leg to the whistle alone. Such an acquired link is called a **conditioned reflex** (CR). It is acquired by the operation of presenting a stimulus that was originally neutral—**conditioned stimulus (CS)**—together with a stimulus that is already wired to a response—**unconditioned stimulus (UCS).** This operation is called **classical conditioning** (Figure 4–1).

Having created a conditioned reflex, it is useful to be able to say not only that it exists, but that it exists in some degree. The strength of the reflex is inferred

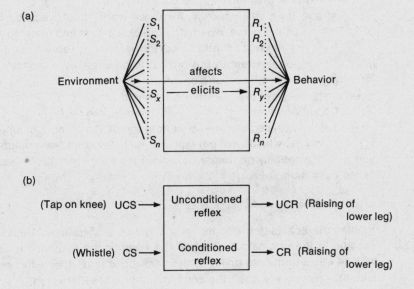

Figure 4-1. The Basic Model of Classical Conditioning
(a) The transformation of the vague statement "Environment affects behavior" to the precise statement "Stimulus x elicits response y."
(b) The establishment of a conditioned reflex by presenting a CS and a UCS together.

from the strength of the response; the strength of the response is measured as the number of drops of saliva, the angle through which the leg is raised, and so on. Response strength varies with a number of factors, three of which will be considered here.

4.113 Reinforcement and Extinction

It seems reasonable that, since the presentation of unconditioned and conditioned stimuli together produces the conditioned reflex, the more often they are presented together, the stronger the reflex will become. This is indeed the case. The more reinforcements (each presentation of unconditioned and conditioned stimuli together is called a **reinforcement**), the greater the response strength. Practice makes perfect. However, the path to perfection is characterized by diminishing returns; the gain in response strength becomes progressively less with each reinforcement. Perfection is the maximum possible response strength: the dog has only so much saliva, and you can raise your leg only so far. The relationship between response strength and the number of reinforcements is presented (a) verbally; (b) graphically, for those who prefer pictures; and (c) mathematically, for those who prefer precision (see Figure 4-2).* This particular curve, which rises quickly at first and then more and more gradually, is of interest to psychologists because it represents not only the growth of response strength but growth in general—of response strength, of forgetting, of physical size, and so on.

Unconditioned reflexes are typically wired in at birth and remain so until death. Conditioned reflexes are created and may also be destroyed. They may be "destroyed" by presenting the CS without the UCS a number of times. Thus, if I were to blow the whistle without tapping you below the knee a number of times, you would eventually no longer raise your leg to the whistle. This operation is called **extinction.**

4.114 Generalization and Discrimination

Neither the acquisition nor the extinction of a conditioned reflex is exactly specific to the original CS. That is, if a conditioned response is created to a whistle with a frequency of 360 cycles per second (cps), then whistles of 330 cps and 400 cps will also elicit the conditioned response. This tendency for condi-

---

*My apologies to the mathematically literate for being so explicit in this figure. It is necessary, however, to strip equations and curves of the awesome mystery they hold for some unfortunates who shudder with apprehension every time they appear. The reaction is so intense that it would seem that their mothers had been frightened by a logarithm while they were in the womb or that they had had a traumatic experience with a square-root sign while very young and have been irrational ever since.

(a) VERBAL

"Practice makes perfect."

(b) GRAPHICAL

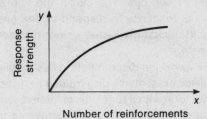

A curve is merely a picture of the relationship between two variables represented, respectively, on the x and y axes.

(c) MATHEMATICAL

$$y_x = y_{x-1} + \frac{y_{max} - y_{x-1}}{k}$$

An equation is merely a shorthand statement of the same information. It provides a recipe for finding the value of y corresponding to any given value of x. The recipe in this case for finding y_x (the response strength after reinforcement x) is:

INGREDIENTS:

k = a number that is constant for a given situation;
y_{x-1} = the response strength after the previous reinforcement;
y_{max} = the maximum possible response strength.

RECIPE:

Subtract the response strength after the previous reinforcement from the maximum possible response strength. Divide the result by the constant number. Add the result to the response strength after the previous reinforcement.

Figure 4-2. Three Statements of the Relationship between Response Strength and Number of Reinforcements

tioning to spread to stimuli similar to the original CS is called **generalization**. It seems reasonable that the response strength will be less than that to the original stimulus, and the amount less will be directly related to the difference between the test and the original stimulus.

It is possible for a dog to learn to respond to one tone (say, 300 cps) and to not respond to another tone (say, 400 cps). That is, a dog is capable of **discrimination.** This effect is achieved by presenting a tone at 300 cps followed by meat powder and a tone at 400 cps followed by nothing. The facts of discrimination can be clarified by considering it in terms of overlapping generalization curves of reinforcement and extinction. The response strength to any tone is the algebraic sum of the tendency to respond from a generalization of reinforcement of 300 cps and the tendency not to respond from a generalization of extinction of 400 cps. The closer the two stimuli, the smaller the difference between the tendency to respond to one and not to the other; the greater the difficulty in deciding whether or not to respond, the harder the stimuli are to discriminate.

Pavlov's work on discrimination has certain practical and theoretical implications. Pavlov presented a dog trained to respond to one tone and not to respond to another tone with a tone intermediate between them. It went crazy. By making dogs neurotic experimentally, he provided us with some insight as to why we become neurotic naturally. Pavlov presented a dog with the problem of discriminating between a light gray and a dark gray. It could not discriminate between them. He then taught it to discriminate between white and black, between a very light gray and a very dark gray, and so on. When it came to the original pair, it could then discriminate between them. Much of learning involves the making of subtle discriminations. Teachers can help by pointing out the endpoints of the dimensions along which the discriminations are to be made.

This algebraic summation theory used to explain discrimination has also been applied to the explanation of **displacement.** This is the take-it-out-on-someone-else—preferably-someone-smaller tendency, of which we are all aware in ourselves and others, especially others. Let's say you have built up a tendency to attack your boss over a number of trials (and tribulations). You also, however, have a tendency to not attack him because of the consequences. Fortunately for bosses and employees, the tendency to attack is usually weaker than the tendency to not attack. However, at some point along the similarity dimension, the tendency to attack is displaced to the unfortunate victim at that point (for example, a wife). Each of these operations can be represented by a graph, as shown in Figure 4-3.

4.115   Forward, Backward, and Simultaneous Conditioning

When we say that classical conditioning results from presenting the unconditioned and conditioned stimuli together, we do not necessarily mean *exactly* together. There are three alternatives: the conditioned stimulus is presented first (**forward conditioning**), the unconditioned stimulus is presented first (**backward conditioning),** or both are presented together (**simultaneous conditioning).** Research shows forward conditioning to be the most effective and the optimal time interval to be about 0.5 second. This fact makes sense in terms of the most prominent theory of the nature of classical conditioning, which considers the CS as a sign of an impending UCS. If we had to place a sign

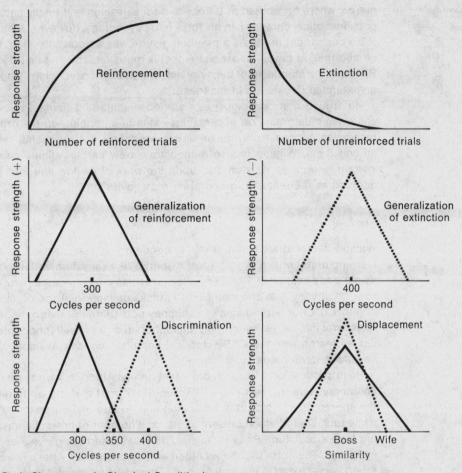

Figure 4-3. Basic Phenomena in Classical Conditioning

(CS) announcing a z curve on a highway (UCS), we would not place it after the curve or at the curve but before the curve and only a little bit before it.

4.12   The Deluxe Model—Watson

4.121   John B. Watson

Psychology was initially considered as the study of consciousness, but a dynamic young man swept onto the psychological stage and transformed it into the study of behavior. He left as abruptly as he arrived—into the world of commerce, where he worked as a door-to-door salesman and finally became a vice-president of his company. In his foray into psychology, however, John B. Watson left a permanent mark. As a psychologist he was a good salesman. He demonstrated that, at times, an overstatement is more valuable than a true statement. He wrote the manifesto of behaviorism, and much of psychology since has been an extended debate about his thesis.[110]

He argued that consciousness is unobservable and hence irrelevant to science. We must focus on observables—stimuli impinging on the organism and responses elicited from the organism—and find the functional relationships among them. Watson had to demonstrate how certain stimuli came to elicit certain responses. He stumbled upon the work of Pavlov, and thus Pavlov was adopted as the reluctant grandfather of behaviorism.

4.122 Conditioned Fear

Watson demonstrated that classical conditioning can be used to explain the learning of not only a simple, local response like salivation, but also a complex, whole-body response like fear. We have many fears, ranging from fears of specific things, like the number 13 (triskaidekaphobia), or of our wife (uxoriphobia), or of getting stuck in chimney pots (Santa Claustrophobia), to fears of general things, like everything (panaphobia) or fear itself (phobophobia). How did we learn these fears? By classical conditioning, said Watson, and he proceeded to demonstrate just how.

He introduced an 11-month-old infant named Albert to a white rat (whose age and name were not recorded).[111] When Albert first met the white rat, he made the appropriate 11-month-old reaching and cooing responses to it. Albert liked white rats. Then Watson presented the rat a number of times, fiendishly arranging for his assistant, Rosalie Rayner,* to make a terrifying noise behind Albert each time. The noise frightened Albert and made him cry. After a few repetitions, Albert began to cry at the appearance of the white rat alone. Moreover, he began to cry at the appearance of a white rabbit, a ball of cotton wool, a beard, a man with a beard, a man who accompanied a man with a beard—that is, at anything white or fluffy or anything associated with anything white or fluffy. Unfortunately, Albert's mother took him away from the hospital before Watson and Rayner could reverse their results.† They later developed a desensitization technique by which they could have cured Albert by seating him at one end of a

---

*Later to become Mrs. John B. Watson, for those who like a romantic element in the story.

†Since this experiment was conducted in 1920 Albert may still be alive today. Do you happen to know a twitchy middle-aged man named Albert?

long room, serving him his favorite dessert, and gradually bringing the white rat closer and closer until finally he could stroke it without fear. This process, you realize, must be carried out gradually, or else Albert would learn to fear his dessert.

4.123 Chain Reflexes

Behavior, however, does not consist of isolated responses, whether small or large, but of a stream of responses. Watson explained the stream of responses we call a habit as a chain of conditioned reflexes (**chain reflex**). As each response is made, a stimulus is fed back to the brain to inform it that the response has been made. The links in the chain are formed as each stimulus becomes classically conditioned to the next response. This theory may appear

to be way out, yet many of our habits are this mechanical. Many of us have gone into our bedroom to change our socks and ended up in bed. I can't type the word "ratio" without putting an "n" at the end.* A certain subset of such habits, involving the muscles in the larynx and throat, is the basis for speech. Talking is the moving of muscles of the throat, just as walking is the moving of muscles of the leg. Since talking to oneself is frowned upon, we do it in an undercover way. Thinking is simply talking to oneself so that no one else can hear. Thus Watson

*Editor's footnote: That's the truth. He really can't.

attempted to explain *all* behavior in terms of classical conditioning. He was only partly right, of course. He grasped some truth but not the whole truth. Classical conditioning determines some behavior but not all behavior. Otherwise, the story would be finished, and, as you can see, many chapters remain.

4.2   Instrumental Conditioning

4.21   The Basic Model—Thorndike

4.211   Edward L. Thorndike

Again it is necessary to reset the stage for the next character in our cast. The theory of evolution placed man where he belongs—with the other animals on the same phylogenetic scale. This discovery has two implications: humans are seen as more animal-like, and animals are seen as more human-like. The violent repercussions of the first implication have already been mentioned (Section 2.11). Let's consider briefly the less familiar repercussions of the second implication. Certain scholars began to attribute human qualities to animals. They soberly collected anecdotes from retired colonels, ministers' wives, and other animal lovers that demonstrated how ingenious animals were in solving problems. A typical anecdote describes how a field mouse got honey out of a narrow-necked jar by squatting on the rim, dipping its tail into the honey, and then licking its tail. Romanes—the leader of this movement, the father of comparative psychology, the Suzy Knickerbocker of the animal world—collected those stories in his book *Animal Intelligence*.[82] He concluded, on the basis of this anecdotal evidence, that animals are very intelligent.

Enter Thorndike, a poverty-stricken graduate student at Harvard University, arguing. Such anecdotes described the behavior of an animal *after* it had learned. If one were to study the process rather than the product of learning, the animals would perhaps not appear so intelligent. Thorndike set out to study the process of learning in animals. He collected a motley menagerie in the squalid room of his run-down rooming house. Enter Thorndike's landlady, the first villain of our story, lacking sympathy for the scientific spirit and throwing Thorndike and his animals out into the street. William James, one of the greatest and kindest figures in the story of psychology, came to the rescue by housing the menagerie in the basement of his own home and by securing facilities at Columbia University for Thorndike to continue his research. The rest of the story is history. Thorndike rounded up some stray cats from the alleys of New York City. He built a box with a door that could be opened by pressing a lever. Inside the box he placed a cat; outside the box he placed things that the cat liked (typically one or more of his famous three F's—fish, friends, and freedom). The problem was to get out, and the solution was to press the lever.

When first put in the **puzzle box,** the cat went through its repertoire of responses: clawing at bars, hissing at Thorndike, arching its back, spitting and snarling, smiling at Thorndike, purring and meowing, and so on and so on, more or less at random. Finally, by chance, it hit on the Thorndike-ordained correct response. In successive trials it took progressively less and less time to get out of the box, until, finally, it went immediately to the lever and pressed it. If Romanes had entered Thorndike's laboratory at that point and had observed the cat walking nonchalantly over to the lever and casually pressing it, he would have run off to write yet another anecdote to show how very intelligent animals are. Thorndike, who had observed the mechanical process whereby this apparently insightful product was established, knew otherwise. Romanes had written a book called *Animal Intelligence* describing how smart animals are; Thorndike then wrote his book *Animal Intelligence* demonstrating how stupid animals are.[101]

4.212 Trial-and-Error Learning

In that book Thorndike presented his now-famous description of **trial-and-error learning.** His theory of learning was somewhat analogous to the survival-of-the-fittest principle central to Darwin's theory of evolution. In a population of organisms, some are fitter to survive in a given environment; likewise, in a repertoire of responses, some are fitter to survive in a given situation. The fittest response is the one leading to reward. When a response is followed by a reward, it is more likely to occur again (**law of effect**); alternatively, the link between the stimulus situation and this reward-followed response is

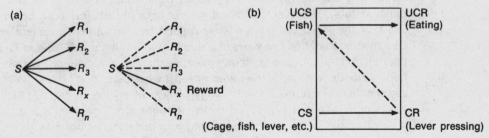

Figure 4-4. The Basic Model of Instrumental Conditioning
(a) The transformation from a state of affairs before a response has been rewarded (left) to that after a response has been rewarded (right).
(b) The establishment of a conditioned reflex because the CR permits access to the UCS.

strengthened, and the links between the stimulus situation and the other responses are thereby weakened. Thus the fittest response survives and the other responses die.

Since *all* the responses are eventually followed by the reward, the law of effect must be supplemented by its corollary, the **gradient of reinforcement.** The closer in time the reward to the response, the greater the strengthening effect. Two implications of this principle have been verified. Rats learn the last turns in a maze first and the first turns last. Rats run faster and faster on a straight runway as they approach the goal box at the end.* Thus we have a second answer to the question "How does a particular stimulus, previously neutral, come to elicit a particular response?" The response is instrumental in permitting access to a stimulus that already elicits some intrinsically rewarding response. This operation of **instrumental conditioning** is diagramed in Figure 4-4.

4.22 The Deluxe Model—Skinner

4.221 B. F. Skinner

As the most famous living exponent of pure behaviorism, Skinner is seen by many laymen as a sinister ogre scheming to manipulate their behavior. They see him as Big Brother—watching them. The publication of his novel, *Walden Two,* enhanced this reputation.[94] He described a utopian society—a sort of benevolent Brave New World—based on his conditioning techniques. In today-the-community-tomorrow-the-world fashion, he has argued convincingly in his later book, *Beyond Freedom and Dignity,* that the problems of our planet can be alleviated by application of the principles of conditioning.[95] There are persistent rumors that Skinner, retired from Harvard, is embarking on a great social experiment using human material bequeathed by a South American dictator. The rumor is false. However, some individuals have indeed formed a community based on the principles expounded in *Walden Two,* and one of the members has documented their first five years of triumphs and tribulations.[54] *Walden Two* was possibly written more as a literary exercise than as a social program (Skinner frankly admits to being a frustrated novelist who found that he had nothing to say and therefore turned to psychology). Any twinkle you may catch in Skinner's eye is more likely to be caused by the thought of his next witty and incisive article than by the thought of controlling your behavior. He defends his extreme position against many critics with vigor and charm. We have nothing to fear from this courtly and responsible man.

Skinner transformed Thorndike's puzzle box into what has come to be called,

---

*Just as lovers run faster and faster when they run toward each other across a bridge in innumerable foreign movies. Fortunately, both rats and lovers learn to slow down just before they reach the goal.

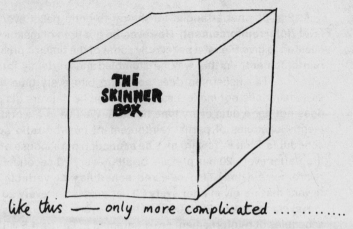

like this — only more complicated............

in his honor and to his dismay, the **Skinner box.** It contains a lever and a tray arranged so that pressing the lever permits a pellet to drop into the tray. The index of learning is the number of times the lever is pressed, rather than the time taken to get out of the box. Originally, the rewards were dispensed and the responses were recorded by Skinner himself. Now, however, the Skinner box has become completely automated, and the rat can run its own experiment without the aid of an experimenter. When the bar is pressed, two metal surfaces make contact, a circuit is completed, a disk turns, and a pellet drops into the tray. Thus the rewards are dispensed. When the bar is pressed, a pen moves up one notch against a tape, moving horizontally at a constant speed and leaving a **cumulative record** of the number of presses in each unit of time. Thus the responses are recorded.

4.222   *Reinforcement*

The only factor preventing total automation is the fact that the rat must be taught to press the lever. This is done by a process called **shaping,** using the **method of successive approximations**. The rat glances toward the lever. Give it a pellet. It looks at the lever. Give it a pellet. It takes a step toward the lever. Give it a pellet. It sniffs at the lever. Give it a pellet. It raises its paw in the direction of the lever. Give it a pellet. Each response that is a successively closer approximation to the desired response is rewarded, until the rat is pressing the lever and supplying its own pellets.*

*The method of successive approximations is used in advertising. There was a time when women did not smoke. A cigarette manufacturer started a campaign showing a man smoking and a woman beside him saying "Blow a little smoke my way." As the campaign progressed, the cigarette moved imperceptibly across the page until it was in her mouth, and women were smoking. The next logical step in this campaign is underway today. Just watch that cigar move!

At first Skinner arranged for the rat to get a pellet every time it pressed the lever **(total reinforcement)**. However, he got tired of making so many pellets and decided to give the rat a pellet only some of the times it pressed the lever (**partial reinforcement**). In this way he stumbled inadvertently into a more true-to-life situation. The fisherman does not get a bite every time he casts his line, the salesman does not make a sale every time he delivers his pitch, and the wooer does not get a date every time he asks. We live in a world of partial reinforcement. Schedules of partial reinforcement may be **ratio schedules** or **interval schedules**. That is, reward may be a function of response or of time; a pellet may drop after every 20 bar presses or after every 20 seconds. Schedules of partial reinforcement may also be **fixed schedules** or **variable schedules**. That is, reward may be given after every 20 bar presses or every 20 seconds or after, *on the average*, every 20 bar presses or every 20 seconds. The four resultant schedules of reinforcement are diagramed in Figure 4-5 with the typical cumulative record for each. The slope of the line is an index of the rate of responding, and the shape of the line is an index of the regularity of responding. Ratio schedules tend to produce higher rates of responding than do interval schedules, and variable schedules tend to produce higher rates of responding than fixed schedules. Thus rats work better on piecework than on salary and when they are paid sporadically rather than regularly. The most powerful schedule, the variable ratio, is used in gambling casinos to produce a high rate of feeding coins into one-armed bandits and in homes to produce a high rate of crying in babies. The peculiar scalloping effect in the fixed-interval schedule makes sense if you ratomorphize a little and imagine yourself as a rat in a world that rewards you regularly and independently of your responses. In the early stage you work hard, get no pellets, become discouraged, and slow down, until the next pellet starts you working hard again. In the late stage you have learned that the pellet will come only after *x* seconds, regardless of what you do. After getting a pellet, therefore, you relax until about *x* seconds have passed, and then you go back to work.

Just as classical conditioning can be extinguished by presenting the CS without the UCS, so instrumental conditioning can be extinguished by permitting the response without the reinforcement.* When the mechanism for dispensing pellets is disconnected so that the rat never gets a pellet when it presses the lever, the rat eventually stops pressing. It stops pressing sooner when it has been trained on total reinforcement than when it has been trained on partial

*Skinnerians, by the way, prefer to refer to classical and instrumental conditioning as respondent and operant conditioning, respectively. I point this out in case you are confused on coming across those terms. But I cling stubbornly to the less modern terminology so that all the work in this area does not become subsumed under the Skinnerian part of it, even if that part is admittedly the most interesting part.

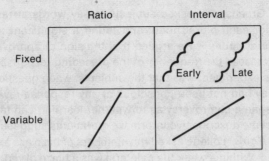

Figure 4-5. Schedules of Reinforcement

reinforcement. This greater resistance to extinction of a partial as opposed to total schedule **(partial paradox)** is surprising, since Thorndike would have predicted that, the more often a response is followed by a reward, the greater the response strength and thus the harder it would be to extinguish. The partial paradox probably results because a schedule in which one is rewarded some of the time is more similar to that in which one is rewarded none of the time than it is to that in which one is rewarded all of the time. In other words, it is more difficult to recognize that the schedule has changed.

4.223   Some Implications and Applications

Skinner once left a number of pigeons overnight, each in its private Skinner box on a fixed-interval schedule.[92] The mechanism broke, so that a pellet was released periodically regardless of what the pigeon did. The next day he found one pigeon standing on one leg, another with its head under its wing, a third pecking the floor of the box, and so on. How had this effect come about? Let's consider the pigeon standing on one leg. By chance, it had happened to be standing on one leg when a pellet was released. This chance juxtaposition of a response and a reward increased the frequency of the response, hence the probability that it would be standing on one leg when rewarded later, hence once again the frequency of the response. After a number of repetitions of this cycle, the pigeon was finally standing all the time on one leg. After all, this was the way to get pellets. Skinner called this phenomenon **superstitious behavior** and suggested that perhaps this is the mechanism by which human superstitions are born. Primitive men chanced to be dancing when the much-desired rain fell. The frequency of dancing increased, hence the probability that they would be dancing when it rained again, hence a further increase in dancing. Finally the rain dance was established. Since a partial schedule is more resistant to extinction, superstitious behavior persists because of (rather than in spite of) the fact that it is rewarded infrequently and irregularly.

Greenspoon asked subjects to say words at random, muttered "mm-hmm" after each plural noun, and found a significant increase in the frequency of plural nouns.[35] He argued that the sign of approval served as a reward, which increased the frequency of the preceding response. The most startling aspect of his experiment was that the subjects, when questioned afterward, reported that they had not been conscious of any response-reward contingency. Thus there began a controversy as to whether learning can take place without awareness. Let me describe two informal experiments suggesting that it can. A psychologist at a girls' college asked the members of his class to compliment any girl wearing red. Within a week the cafeteria was a blaze of red. None of the girls were aware of being influenced, although they did notice that the atmosphere was more friendly. A class at the University of Minnesota is reported to have conditioned their psychology professor a week after he told them about learning without awareness. Every time he moved toward the right side of the room, they paid more attention and laughed more uproariously at his jokes, until apparently they were able to condition him right out of the door. This phenomenon has certain practical implications. A skilled interviewer can very easily regulate the rate of verbal output by judiciously placed mm-hmms, nods, smiles, and so on, providing cues so subtle that we are not aware of them.* Indeed, such cues are so subtle that perhaps the interviewer as well as the interviewee may not be aware of them. Psychoanalytic theory may be influenced by such a mechanism, since the psychoanalyst may unconsciously reward talk of sex and thus produce an overemphasis on the importance of sex in neuroses.

Skinner boxes have been adapted to a number of purposes. There is the gigantic Skinner box to contain all Skinner boxes—the utopian society painted by Skinner in *Walden Two*. There are Skinner boxes for babies—in which they may be raised in a well-regulated environment (untouched, add Skinner's critics, by human hands). There are Skinner boxes for schizophrenics; a bare room is fitted with a cup and a lever arranged so that, on pressing the lever, a reward (cigarette, candy, and so on) falls into the cup. Hopeless schizophrenics, who haven't done anything for themselves for decades, have been brought back a little bit toward contact with reality by this device. There are Skinner boxes for students—the much-discussed **teaching machines**.† Since none of us are

*The cues used by students to stop the verbal output of a lecturer toward the end of the lecture are not so subtle. Glancing at one's watch is not bad, but glancing at the watch, frowning, holding it to the ear, and shaking it can be most disturbing.

†When the teaching machine first appeared, there was some fear that the teacher would become a victim of automation. The general sentiment today, however, is that a teacher who could be replaced by a machine should be replaced by a machine and a teacher who could not be replaced by a machine can use it to free himself from the mechanical aspects of teaching so he can concentrate on the human aspects of teaching.

babies, only a few of us are schizophrenics, but all of us are students, let's focus on the teaching machine. More specifically, let's focus on the program, since the teaching machine is merely a device for presenting, in order, the set of frames of which the program is composed. We are interested in the radio script rather than the radio. The program consists of a series of statements and questions to which the student makes some response. He then turns to the next frame, where he can check to see if his answer is correct and can read the next set of statements and questions. The situation is analogous to that of the rat in the Skinner box. The response is writing the answer rather than pressing the lever; the reward is confirming that the correct response has been made rather than receiving a pellet. The various principles in designing a program are derived from work with rats in the laboratory. The principle that the reward should follow as soon as possible after the response is a direct application of the gradient of reinforcement. The principle that each frame should go only a short step beyond the last is a direct analogue to the method of successive approximations.

4.224 Verbal Behavior

One day Skinner found himself at a banquet sitting next to the great philosopher Alfred North Whitehead and launched into an enthusiastic exposition of his project to explain all human behavior in terms of conditioning. The calm old philosopher listened benignly to the brash young scientist and agreed that perhaps he could handle nonverbal behavior within this framework. But Whitehead baulked at verbal behavior, arguing, by way of example, that Skinner would never be able to explain why he, at that moment, said "No black scorpion is falling on this table." Skinner began his book *Verbal Behavior* the next morning and published it several decades later.[93] In this book he presented the following response to Whitehead's challenge. Verbal behavior is behavior reinforced through the mediation of other people. There are two ways in which you can get a glass of water: by nonverbal behavior (getting it yourself) or by verbal behavior (asking someone else to get it for you). We use words, then, to gain reinforcement through the mediation of other people. How do we acquire them in the first place? Skinner proposed the three mechanisms diagramed in Figure 4-6. The child utters an imitation of a word in the presence of the word, and the mother gives him approval **(echoic response)**; the child utters the name of an object in the presence of the object, and the mother gives him the object **(tact)**; the child utters the name of a satisfier of a need in the presence of the need, and the mother gives him the satisfier of the need **(mand)**. This answer would appear to be very far from meeting Whitehead's challenge. Skinner argues, however, that the scientist is not required to explain each specific event within his province, but only the general principles underlying the specific events. The physicist is not expected to predict the order in which leaves will fall from a tree or the pattern they will form on the ground; he is only expected to provide the general laws governing falling bodies. Thus Skinner attempted to explain *all* behavior in terms of instrumental conditioning. He, like Watson, is, of course, only partly right. He too has grasped some truth but not the whole truth. Instrumental conditioning determines some behavior but not all behavior. Otherwise, the story would be finished, but, again, many chapters remain.

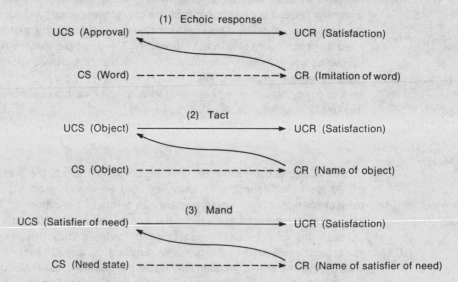

Figure 4–6. Skinner's Three Mechanisms for Acquisition of Speech. Note that the CR is always a word, that it permits access to the UCS only through the mediation of another person, and that approval is assumed to be intrinsically satisfying.

We may, of course, strike a balance between what a living organism takes in as nourishment and what it gives out in excretions; but the result would be mere statistics incapable of throwing light on the inmost phenomena of nutrition in living beings. According to a Dutch chemist's phrase, this would be like trying to tell what happens inside a house by watching what goes in by the door and what comes out by the chimney.

Claud Bernard
Introduction a l'Étude de la Médecine Expérimentale

5

Mediational Approach

5.1 Intervening Variables and Hypothetical Constructs

It is impossible, of course, to write a history of psychology in one page. A condensation of a summary of the history would, however, read something like this: The philosopher focused on processes and structures within the organism, such as "will," "consciousness," and "soul." He did not get very far along the road to understanding. The introspectionist varied the stimuli impinging on the organism and observed the effect of this variation on processes within the organism. He got a bit farther. The behaviorist varied the stimuli impinging on the organism and observed the effect of this variation on the responses emitted by the organism. He got considerably farther. Each step toward understanding has been characterized by less emphasis on what is going on inside the organism and more emphasis on what is going on outside the organism. The final product is the by-now-familiar, unflattering portrait of you and me as an empty box. The task of the psychologist is seen as manipulating stimuli, observing responses, and establishing the relationship between them. Whatever is going on within the organism between the stimulus and the response is unobservable and therefore irrelevant.

Most psychologists recognize the progress made by the pure behaviorist but feel that he has gone just about as far as he can go. Most psychologists accept with gratitude the nice, clean, empty box but recognize that the time has come to put something back into it. That certain "something" that mediates between the stimulus and the response may be either an **intervening variable** or a **hypothetical construct**. In this mediational approach we will consider two sets of intervening variables—Osgood's meaning and Hull's habit strength and drive—and two sets of hypothetical constructs—Tolman's cognitive map and Hebb's cell assembly and phase sequence. Since none of these mediators are observable, it would appear superficially that we are right back where we started. Man has lost his "soul" only to gain "meaning." Man has lost "consciousness" and recovered to find himself equipped with an equally obscure "cognitive map." "Meaning" and "cognitive map" differ from "soul" and "consciousness," however, in that, although they are not observable themselves, they are tightly tied to observables. "Meaning" is defined purely in terms of observed stimuli and responses, and "cognitive maps" are reasonably inferred from the observed structure of the nervous system. *Intervening variables* are inventions, whereas *hypothetical constructs* are potential discoveries. Since intervening variables are defined in terms of stimuli and responses, they tend to be used by theorists attempting to extend the behavioristic approach; hypothetical constructs tend to be used by theorists who are reacting against the behavioristic approach.

5.2   Intervening Variables

5.21   Meaning—Osgood

5.211   Classical and Instrumental Conditioning as Complementary

In the last chapter we posed the question "How do we learn?" Or, in the more prosaic but more precise language of psychologists, how does a particular stimulus come to elicit a particular response? In Section 4.1 we proposed one answer: because it is presented together with another stimulus that already elicits that response. This is the phenomenon of classical conditioning. In Section 4.2 we proposed a different answer:* because the response permits access to a stimulus that already elicits a response. This is the phenomenon of instrumental conditioning. The two processes are diagramed in Figure 5-1. The processes are similar in that they both explain the basic fact of learning—that a particular stimulus can come to elicit a particular response. They both explain this fact with reference to a stimulus-response bond already wired into the organism. They differ with respect to the manner in which the newly acquired bond is related to the previously wired one. Classical conditioning attributes learning to the fact that the CS and UCS are presented together; instrumental conditioning attributes learning to the fact that the CR permits access to the UCS. They could be considered in a simpleminded way as complementary pro-

*This is not a different answer in the sense implied by the wry undergraduate comment that the questions in a psychology examination are always the same but every year the answers are different. Sometimes we learn by classical conditioning, and sometimes we learn by instrumental conditioning.

cesses. Classical conditioning involves the same response to different stimuli; instrumental conditioning involves different responses to the same stimulus. Classical conditioning is associated with the involuntary responses of the autonomic nervous system (that is, the part of the nervous system responsible for dealing with the internal environment); instrumental conditioning is associated with the voluntary responses of the central nervous system (that is, the part of the nervous system responsible for dealing with the external environment).

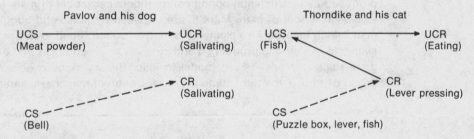

Figure 5-1. Classical and Instrumental Conditioning

5.212   Classical and Instrumental Conditioning in Combination

Section 4.1 concluded with an attempt by Watson to explain verbal behavior in terms of classical conditioning; Section 4.2 concluded with an attempt by Skinner to explain verbal behavior in terms of instrumental conditioning. It was implied in each case that the attempt was a failure. Osgood agrees that neither classical nor instrumental conditioning can explain verbal behavior, but he suggests that perhaps a combination of the two can.

The central problem of verbal behavior (and, say some, of psychology) is that of meaning. How can a word come to represent a thing? How can an arbitrary sequence of sounds or pattern of lines come to elicit responses related to the thing they represent? Osgood and his co-workers attempted to explain these phenomena in terms of conditioning.[77] The word, being a previously neutral stimulus that comes to elicit a response, can be considered as the CS. The thing, being a stimulus that is already linked to a particular response, can be considered as the UCS. The inadequacy of either conditioning model alone can be demonstrated clearly by the case in which the UCS is Raquel Welch and the CS is the words "Raquel Welch." The classical-conditioning model will not do, since the UCR and the CR do not even remotely resemble each other. Your response to the words "Raquel Welch" would be entirely different from your response to their referent. The instrumental-conditioning model will not do either, for the CR does not permit access to the UCS. Your response to the words "Raquel Welch" cannot—alas—gain you access to their referent. Osgood suggests, however, that the two models in combination can explain meaning. (See Figure 5-2.) The contiguous presentation of the word and the thing produces a response within the organism that is some part of the response to the thing (classical conditioning), and this response is instrumental in producing a stimulus within the organism that is linked to the CR (instrumental conditioning). Meaning is thus the internal (r_m-s_m) bond that acts as mediator between the CS and the CR. One-stage behaviorism is replaced by two-stage behaviorism, in which input is provided by classical conditioning and output is produced by instrumental conditioning. Kiddie-car model of man, Mark I, and kiddie-car model of man, Mark II, are replaced by horse-and-buggy model of man, which incorporates elements of both. Osgood found even this model too simple to explain the production and perception of sentences and developed a three-stage, or Model-T Ford, model, in which the first stage involves the organization of stimuli, the third stage the organization of responses, and the second

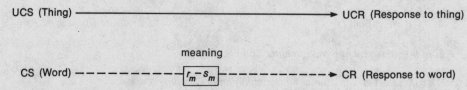

Figure 5-2. Osgood's Model of Meaning

stage the mediation between the first and third. If this is found inadequate for certain phenomena, must we continue to a four-stage, or Ford Mustang, model? Will the ultimate model of man be a further development along those lines, or are we on the wrong track? Will psychology progress through evolution or revolution?

5.22 Habit Strength and Drive—Hull

Hull used intervening variables in pursuit of a dream.[48] He hoped to do for behavior what Euclid had done for two-dimensional space. Euclid, you will remember from high school geometry, deduced from a few simple axioms the many complex facts about two-dimensional space. Hull wished to uncover the few simple axioms from which he could deduce the many complex facts of behavior. His strategy was to observe facts of behavior, derive intervening variables to account for them, and develop axioms stating relationships between those variables. Do you remember the fact that "practice makes perfect" (Section 4.113)? Hull describes this fact in terms of an intervening variable, called habit strength and written sHr, which increases with practice and thus produces an improvement in performance. Do you remember the fact that, when there is no reinforcement, practice does not make perfect (Section 4.212)? In Hull's terms there is an increase in habit strength with no improvement in performance. Hull describes this fact by adding a second intervening variable, called drive and written D, which increases with reinforcement and thus produces an improvement in performance. How are his two intervening variables related? Hull reasoned that, since there is no improvement in performance unless there is both practice and reinforcement, the tendency to respond, sEr, is the *product* of habit strength and drive ($sEr = sHr \times D$). Thus, if either of them is zero, there will be no tendency to respond. In a similar manner, Hull added more and more intervening variables to describe more and more facts of behavior. For 40 years he pursued his dream of accommodating all the facts of behavior in this way. Although most of the psychologists of his day helped on his vast project, his dream died with him. The project was premature rather than impossible. The dream is still with us. The vacancy for the Euclid of psychology is still open. Will the ultimate model of behavior take this form of a few simple axioms from which necessarily flow the many complex facts of behavior?

5.3   Hypothetical Constructs

5.31   Cognitive Map—Tolman

5.311   Place Learning—Tolman

A rat learning to run a maze, according to behaviorists,* is having a chain of responses stamped in. This position has been challenged by a number of observations. A group of rats is taught to run a maze. Rats with their spinal cord cut, so that there is no sensory feedback, waddle to the goal. Rats with their cerebel-

---

*"Behaviorist" is used here to refer to a psychologist who aspires to explain all behavior in terms of conditioning. If such a person exists today (or ever did exist), he is certainly in the minority. Indeed, he is a straw man, and his theory is a dead horse. It is useful, however, for heuristic purposes, to set up a straw man and knock it down again, to resurrect a dead horse and kill it again. The synthesis emerging from a strong thesis and a hearty antithesis is clearer than the synthesis presented directly.

lum removed, so that there is no control of balance, waltz to the goal. Rats with one leg broken wobble to the goal. Rats with all legs broken roll to the goal. If the maze is flooded, the rats swim to the goal. Since, under each of these conditions, the rat is not making the same sequence of responses it made when it initially learned to run the maze, it must have been learning something different. It must have been learning to go to a particular place (**place learning**) rather than to make a particular response (**response learning**), and it struggled gamely to get to that place with whatever sequence of responses it could muster.

Tolman and his associates designed an elegant experiment in which the response- and place-learning theories would predict different outcomes.[104] Rats were taught to turn right in a *T* maze. The maze was then turned through 180° (see Figure 5-3). When a rat came to the intersection, it had to make a decision. Should it turn right, or should it turn left? Should it make the same response, or should it go to the same place? Should it be a Watsonian rat, or should it be a Tolmanian rat? Most of the rats most of the time decided to support Tolman rather than Watson.* When the maze was covered, however, the rats tended to turn right again. This result suggests that learning to go to a particular place implies learning the relationship between two stimuli; that is, the rat learns to go to the goal box next to the window.

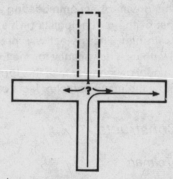

Figure 5-3. Place versus Response Learning

5.312   Latent Learning—Blodgett

Behaviorists argue further that, for learning to take place, a response not only must be made, but it must be followed by reinforcement. Blodgett demonstrated that reinforcement is *not* necessary for learning.[10] Two groups of rats were run

*After all, it was Tolman's experiment and Tolman was supplying the pellets. Rats tend to mirror the theoretical preferences of their runners. They even take on their personalities. Bertrand Russell once observed that rats run by American psychologists run frantically through a maze, whereas those run by German psychologists sit in the center of the maze and ponder.

in a maze. Group *A*, which got pellets every time they reached the goal box, showed considerable improvement in performance. Group *B*, which got nothing every time they reached the goal box, showed little improvement in performance. On a certain trial for group *B*, pellets were introduced into the goal box. On the next trial there was a tremendous improvement in performance. (See Figure 5-4.) It is unreasonable to assume that all this learning had taken place in a single trial. It is much more likely that learning had been taking place during the previous unreinforced trials but had not manifested itself until reinforcement was provided. The rats had learned without reinforcement.

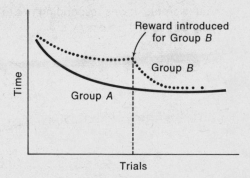

Figure 5-4. Latent Learning

Such learning that does not manifest itself in performance (**latent learning**) highlights an important distinction. We have to use performance as an index of learning. As you are reading this book, you are (it is hoped) learning. That is, certain changes are taking place somewhere in your nervous system. Those changes cannot be measured directly. We don't know what they are, and, even if we did, you would probably be unwilling to have us operate in order to measure them. They must be measured indirectly by presenting you with an examination question, which (it is presumed) you will answer correctly if you have learned a certain principle and will answer incorrectly if you have not. Although your performance on the examination may be a reasonable *index* of learning, it is not learning. Thus injustice is possible. There may be cases in which learning has taken place but is not reflected in performance. There may be some justification for the perennial student wail "I knew it, but your exam didn't test what I knew."

5.313   Depression and Elation—Crespi

An experiment by Crespi suggests that rats are capable of learning the relationship between two stimuli. First, however, an informal experiment by

Tinklepaugh[103] may help to clarify the formal experiment by Crespi. Tinklepaugh placed two flowerpots upside down in front of a monkey and, while the monkey watched, put something it liked under one of them. A barrier was lowered between the monkey and the flowerpots. When it was raised again, the monkey was required to lift the correct flowerpot and pick up his reward. When grapes were used as a reward, the monkey worked very hard to learn this task; when lettuce was used, it worked, but not so enthusiastically. Grapes are presumably more of an incentive than lettuce. On one trial, when the barrier was lowered, Tinklepaugh treacherously substituted lettuce for grapes. The monkey, which had previously worked quite happily for lettuce, threw temper tantrums, lettuce leaves, and flowerpots. It was responding not to the lettuce but to the relationship between lettuce and grapes.

Crespi performed the identical experiment with less charm but more rigor.[16] Two groups of rats were taught to run a maze. One group received two pellets and the other group received ten pellets every time they reached the goal box.

Both groups demonstrated the typical learning curve, with the ten-pellet-group curve steeper, since the reward was greater. On a certain trial, Crespi substituted two pellets for ten pellets (just as Tinklepaugh had substituted lettuce for grapes). This group now performed much worse than before and, more significantly, worse than the group that had been getting two pellets all along. If both groups are now getting two pellets, why does one group do worse? Those rats are responding not to the two pellets now but to the relationship between two pellets now and ten pellets then. They have known better times. This **depression effect** and the parallel **elation effect** are diagramed in Figure 5-5.

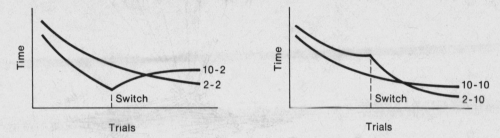

Figure 5-5. Depression and Elation

Humans also tend to respond to the relationship between what they get and what they expect, rather than to what they get. Two students get a C in a course. One is depressed because he expected an A, and the other is elated because he expected an F. Most people expect what they can reasonably get, but some set their expectations unreasonably high. We all know someone pushing a pen in some office and dreaming of being a film star or teaching English in some school and dreaming of being a novelist. They are highly susceptible to depression, because achievement usually falls short of aspiration. A similar fate may haunt those whose once-reasonable expectations are no longer so. The fading beauty who still expects to be complimented and the tiring athlete who still expects to win are often depressed and seldom elated. Some persons set their expectations unreasonably low: nothing ventured, nothing lost. We all know someone who advises us constantly not to expect anything in case we may be disappointed, not to love because we may lose, not to live because we will die.

5.314 Insight Learning—Köhler

A German psychologist named Köhler happened to be on an island when World War I broke out. Unable to return home, he was marooned on this island for four years. On the island with him was a bunch of apes. He decided that, since he was going to be there for some time, he might as well do something useful. He began studying the apes.[57] He built a cage. Inside the cage he placed an ape; outside the cage and outside the ape's reach, he placed things that apes like. So far, the situation is very much like that of Thorndike and his cat, substituting ape for cat and banana for fish. The solution, however, is not to press a lever to get out of the cage to get the fish; the solution is to pick up a stick, which happens to be

CONTENTS:
6 APES
1 LARGE CAGE
800 BANANAS

SURVIVAL KIT

TO KEEP
PSYCHOLOGISTS
AMUSED ON DESERT
ISLANDS DURING
WORLD WARS.

lying in the cage, to pull in the banana. The ape tried various responses: pulling at the bars, reaching through the bars, beckoning to Köhler to pass him the banana, and so on and so on. Finding that none of those tactics worked, he sat and pondered for a bit and then suddenly leaped up, grabbed the stick, and pulled in the banana. A high point of apish ingenuity was reached when Sultan, the genius of the group, joined two sticks together to reach a banana that was out of reach to either stick alone. This sudden type of learning is called **insight learning.**

How does the type of learning exhibited by Köhler's apes differ from that exhibited by Thorndike's cats? The most obvious difference is the suddenness of the solution in insight learning in contrast to the gradualness of that in trial-and-error learning. Insight has been called the **aha phenomenon** in animals and the **eureka effect** in humans.*

A second difference is the extent to which this type of learning can be transferred to other situations. The apes had grasped not only a stick and a banana, but a principle. The arm can be extended by means of sticks. They were able to apply this principle to other situations. Köhler tested for transfer to a situation in which the banana was suspended out of reach overhead. Most apes transferred the principle of extending the arm horizontally to extending it vertically. One ape had a better idea. It defied both Köhler and gravity by planting the stick below the banana and scrambling up it to grab the banana before the stick fell. This solution was better, since it got an unbruised banana. The apes also transferred from extending the arm to extending the leg. They learned to pile up packing cases that were lying around the cage to get at the banana. One ape had a better idea. It led Köhler by the hand to a position underneath the banana and used the great Herr Professor Doktor Köhler as it would a pile of packing cases.

A third difference is the evidence that one ape can be involved in the learning of another. Two apes worked together to pile the packing cases, although there was an obvious reluctance to place the last case, since the other ape would immediately clamber up and get the banana. Baby apes watching their elders working to get the bananas were obviously, by their expressions and gestures, empathizing. Such cooperation and empathy suggest that the apes understood what was going on.

5.315 *Subjective Map of Objective World*

All these experiments suggest that even the lowly rat, and certainly the ape, is responding not to the objective world per se but to its subjective map, however sketchy, of the objective world. Tolman called such a subjective representation of the objective world a **cognitive map** and used this hypothetical construct to explain the behavior of animals and humans. Thus he argues that even the behavior of a rat cannot be explained in terms of the world-as-it-is but must be explained in terms of the world-as-the-rat-sees-it. It is obviously true in the case of our species that our behavior is determined by the world-as-we-see-it rather than by the world-as-it-is. An actual tree can have no effect on our behavior unless we become aware of it; an imaginary enemy lurking behind the tree can have an effect on our behavior even though he is not there.

*The latter term, of course, comes from the story of Archimedes, who suddenly recognized the principle of specific gravity while lowering himself into a bathtub and ran naked through the streets shouting "Eureka!" This is Greek for "Good God, that water's hot!"

Hebb also wishes to put something between the stimulus and the response, but something based on the known structure of the nervous system rather than on the relationships between stimuli and responses external to the nervous system.[41] He couches his theory in terms of hypothetical constructs, which refer to things within the nervous system that haven't been found yet but may be found in the future. His hypothetical constructs are **cell assemblies,** or circuits of neurons around which impulses may continue without external stimulation, and **phase sequences,** or chains of cell assemblies linked such that the firing of one triggers the firing of the next.

Hebb's theory can explain both perceptual and conceptual phenomena, whereas many theories in psychology tend to specialize in one or the other. Let's look at a perceptual phenomenon (reversible figures—Section 9.212) and a conceptual phenomenon (mass action—Section 18.312), each of which will be discussed at more length later in this book.

Look for a moment at the right-hand diagram in Figure 9-2, on page 127. The phase sequences necessary to explain the phenomenon of reversible figures are presented in Figure 5-6. The firing of phase sequence *CDE* underlies one perception (say, the young woman), and the firing of phase sequence *XYZ* underlies the other perception (the old lady). External stimulation from the reversible figure along neurons *A* and *B* can trigger either phase sequence. Since there is not sufficient energy to fire both, the firing of *C* inhibits the firing of *X* and vice versa. This explains why both perceptions cannot be experienced simultaneously. If one phase sequence is already firing, the resistance is lower and thus this one is more likely to refire. This explains why those previously exposed to the young woman tend to perceive the young woman first. After the phase sequence has been firing for a time, fatigue increases the resistance and the

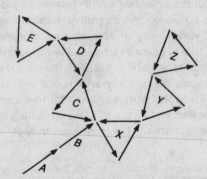

Figure 5-6. Phase Sequences Underlying Reversible Figures

impulse will thus switch to the other phase sequence. This explains why the two perceptions alternate as you stare at the reversible figure.

Lashley removed varying amounts of the brains of rats and discovered that the decrement in their memory was a function not of the location but of the extent of the brain damage.[60] That is, the more he removed, the greater the decrement, regardless of where he removed it from. Lashley concluded that the brain works as a whole (mass action) and that information must be somehow stored throughout the brain, but he could not imagine how this could be accomplished. Hebb suggests that the information is stored in the form of cell assemblies and phase sequences. Since they are replicated many times throughout the brain, damage to any cell assembly does not destroy the memory but merely reduces its strength. The discovery of two qualitatively different types of memory —short-term and long-term—also fits within Hebb's theory. You use short-term memory when you hold a strange phone number in mind long enough to dial it; you use long-term memory when you retrieve a familiar phone number from memory and dial it. Hebb suggests that short-term memory corresponds to the firing of a nerve impulse through a neural circuit and that long-term memory corresponds to the permanent structure (cell assembly) that is created when the nerve impulses pass around the neural circuit often enough to close the gaps between the neurons of which it is composed.

"But 'glory' doesn't mean 'a nice knockdown argument,' " Alice objected.

"When I use a word," Humpty Dumpty said, in rather a scornful tone, "it means just what I choose it to mean—neither more nor less."

"The question is," said Alice, "whether you *can* make words mean so many different things."

"The question is," said Humpty Dumpty, "which is to be master—that's all."

Lewis Carroll
Through the Looking-Glass

6 Approach through Verbal Response

6.1 Behavioristic Analysis

6.11 Associations

6.111 Francis Galton

The systematic study of verbal responses began, as so many things have begun, with a remarkable Englishman named Francis Galton. He was the cousin of Charles Darwin and the father of word-association studies, the questionnaire, the normal distribution, the meteorological charts, and the high-frequency whistle dog caller—to name but a few of his innovations. He searched the world for interesting phenomena, and, when he found them, he measured them. He stood on street corners in every major city in the British Isles. He was not idly watching the girls go by. He was rating them on a scale to devise a beauty index for each city. (Scotsmen have never quite forgiven him for rating Glasgow and Edinburgh low on that scale.) He tied threads to the shoulders of guests at a banquet, with the other ends tied to a delicate machine overhead that measured the inclination of the guest. In this way he was able to determine that, even when ostensibly bolt upright, a guest would unconsciously be inclined in the direction of the person he preferred. He walked along Pall Mall and fixed his attention on each successive object that caught his eye until it suggested one or two thoughts to him. He was amazed to notice that those thoughts included samples of his entire life. He repeated his walk several days later and found that his associations were very much a repeat performance. He was disappointed, since it reduced his faith in the teeming activity of his mind, but also pleased, because it revealed certain consistencies, and, where there are consistencies, one can measure. He set out to study associations more systematically. He would write words on slips of paper, put them in a hat, draw one out, and record the first word that occurred to him and the time between seeing the stimulus word and emitting the response word. This technique, with minor variations, is the design of the thousands of association experiments that have been conducted since Galton's time. Let's look at some products of those experiments.

6.112   *Products of Association Studies*

Tables have been compiled listing the frequencies of different responses to particular stimuli. The most famous of these tables is the **Kent-Rosanoff list,** which was compiled by presenting 100 familiar English nouns and adjectives to 1,000 normal adult subjects and recording their first responses. Thus the Kent-Rosanoff list for the word "needle" is as follows.

NEEDLE	160	thread
	158	pin(s)
	152	sharp
	132	sew(s)
	107	sewing
	53	steel

⋮

    1   blood, camel, wire, woman, and so on

Such lists have been used as diagnostic devices. Many eccentric (that is, low-frequency) responses may indicate schizophrenia or creativity. The lists can also be used for theoretical purposes. Responses may be classified as **paradigmatic responses** (those that are of the same part of speech as the stimulus—for example, thread) or **syntagmatic responses** (those that might naturally occur in the same sentence as the stimulus—for example, sharp). Adults tend to give paradigmatic responses, whereas children tend to give syntagmatic responses. This tendency may provide some insight into changes in the manner in which words are stored as one gets older.

Word-association tests are used in the detection of guilt in criminals. The suspect is presented with a list of words that includes certain words of emotional significance only to someone acquainted with the facts of the crime. Let us pretend that a housewife has been hit over the head with a frozen leg of mutton, chopped up with a breadknife, ground through a mincer, and stuffed down an incinerator. The innocuous words "mutton," "breadknife," "mincer," and "incinerator" would produce no reaction in an innocent suspect but could produce some unusual reaction in one who had just performed such dastardly deeds. Typical unusual reactions would be eccentric responses and long reaction times. Those reactions, by the way, tend to go together. **Marbe's law** states that the association reaction time is inversely proportional to the number of people who give that response. Thus the average reaction time for those who gave "thread" as a response to "needle" would be low, whereas the reaction time for those who gave "blood" as a response would be high. More direct evidence is often provided by associations relating to a crime (for example, mutton—club) and by signs of emotion to the significant stimulus words. Jung, one of Freud's early disciples, has used the same technique to uncover complexes in his clinical work. By noting unusual reactions to certain classes of words, he got clues about the particular areas of life in which his patients had problems. He could then focus attention on those areas.

6.113 Critique

Considering the vast amount of time, money, and effort devoted to word-association studies, they have not been—and may never be—very fruitful. The associations of each individual are products of his own unique life experience and promise little hope of providing insights into the behavior of man in general. The approach may, however, give some insight into the stream of consciousness that underlies the stream of behavior. Have you ever tried to follow your stream of consciousness back upstream? You find yourself thinking of something and trace back to find the series of associations that led up to it. You often find that your stream of consciousness has been diverted by a clang association, or what is familiarly known as a pun. You are thinking about "tree," then "bough," then "wow," then "dog." In his novel *Ulysses,* James Joyce tried to simulate the stream of consciousness and used 5,000 puns. Perhaps the woolly thought processes of English-speaking people are partly caused by the fact that they have such a punny language, and the logical thought processes of German-speaking people are caused by the fact that it is relatively difficult to pun in German.*

Such association studies as have been described deal with associations that have already been formed. It is always easy to *post*dict those associations. That is, after the association is given, one can easily find an explanation for it. "Camel," for example, in response to "needle" is explicable in terms of the Biblical reference to the difficulty of pushing a camel through the eye of a

*Especially if one can't speak German.

needle. The aim of science, however, is to *predict*—to call the shots before they are played. Perhaps it would be more productive to study the formation of associations rather than associations that are already formed.

6.12 Acquisition of Associations

6.121 Herman Ebbinghaus

A very methodical German named Ebbinghaus was the first person to be present at the birth of an association. He decided not to use familiar words in the study of the formation of associations, because any two familiar words could already have some association between them. He therefore made up words by putting any vowel between any two consonants and thus created the first **nonsense syllables.** He created 2,300 such nonsense syllables, wrote them on slips of

paper, drew them out of a hat in pairs, and memorized them. Practically every day for 20 years he worked on his nonsense syllables, memorizing, it is said, 8 lists of 12 pairs before breakfast. The conclusions he reached with such simple equipment (a hatful of words on slips of paper) and one subject (himself) have not been seriously challenged or substantially augmented by the legions of researchers with elaborate equipment and many subjects who have mined this area since then.

6.122 Rote Learning

Mechanical learning is called **rote learning.** There are two forms: in **paired-associates learning,** pairs of nonsense syllables are presented, after which the subject is given the first and required to provide the second; in **serial learning,** a series of nonsense syllables is presented in order, after which the subject is given the first and required to anticipate the second, given the second and required to anticipate the third, and so on. Serial learning may therefore be considered as a special case of paired-associates learning in which the response word for one pair is the stimulus word for the next pair. Learning vocabulary in a foreign language is paired-associates learning; learning a poem is serial learning.

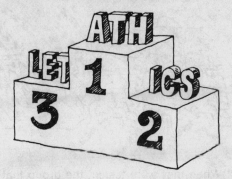

Studies of this type have yielded some useful generalizations. Let's look by way of example at the **serial position effect.** Consider a case in which 50 subjects are tested on a series of 15 nonsense syllables. If we were to plot the average number of trials the subjects took to learn each syllable, we would get a curve, as indicated in Figure 6-1. This curve means that we tend to learn the first, last, and middle syllables, in that order. If you have ever tried to learn a poem by reading it over and over, you will know this to be true. When the national anthem is played, the Lord's Prayer is intoned, or popular songs are sung, a group tends to start out strong, fade in the middle, and come in strong again—but not quite so strong—at the end.

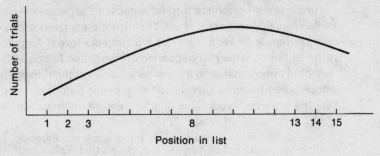

Figure 6-1. Serial Position Effect

An experiment was conducted in which two groups of college students learned some material.[50] One group slept for 8 hours, and the other group wandered about doing whatever college students do for 8 hours. When they were tested on what they had learned, the group that had slept retained significantly more than the group that had stayed awake. In a parallel experiment, two groups of cockroaches learned to run a maze.[73] One group was put in a refrigerator, and the other group wandered about doing whatever cock-

roaches do. When they were tested, the group that had been refrigerated retained significantly more than the group that had not been refrigerated. Thus, if you want to retain what you are learning in this chapter, go to sleep or go sit in a refrigerator. Why do those who sleep retain more? Mueller and Pilzecker phrased the question better: why do those who stay awake retain less? They performed a classic experiment in which two groups were taught a list of nonsense syllables and then were tested for retention.[74] In the interval between training and testing, group 1 learned another list of nonsense syllables and group 2 did nothing. Group 1 retained considerably less than group 2.* Those who stayed awake retained less because they had learned other things before being tested. This interference with previous learning by subsequent learning is called **retroactive inhibition.**

Underwood performed a great number of experiments on learning nonsense syllables using volunteers from the introductory psychology class at Northwestern University.[105] He found that his subjects forgot 75 percent of the material after 24 hours. What had happened during those 24 hours? Surely they were not learning things similar to nonsense syllables at the university. He found that the more experiments a student had taken part in before learning the original material, the more he forgot. This interference with subsequent learning by previous

---

*Group 1, by the way, was Mueller, and group 2 was Pilzecker. The great Ebbinghaus had pioneered studies of memory with one subject: Ebbinghaus. Mueller and Pilzecker went one better. Mueller studied Pilzecker, and Pilzecker studied Mueller.

learning is called **proactive inhibition.** The reason why the first and last parts of a series are learned before the middle part is clear. The middle has both proactive and retroactive inhibition acting on it, whereas the beginning has only retroactive and the end has only proactive. Why is the first easier than the last? It seems to stem from a certain principle built into our culture—that one should begin at the beginning when presented with any task. This is substantiated by the fact that subjects presented with the same task as a test of pronunciation rather than of learning do better on the last than on the first syllables. Young children show the same pattern as those incidental learners and only slowly take on the typical adult pattern. They have to learn the principle of beginning at the beginning.

6.123 Critique

Behaviorists have attempted to explain paired-associates learning in terms of the gradual strengthening of the link between the stimulus (first word) and the response (second word). This interpretation was challenged by Rock.[81] He had two groups of subjects learn pairs of nonsense syllables. In one group, each pair that was not learned in a trial was replaced by another pair on the next trial. If the link was being strengthened a little bit on each trial, as the behaviorists claim, that group should have done worse than the other group. They did equally well. Rock concluded that on any trial each link either is established or is not. Such an all-or-none principle is the basis of his concept of **one-trial learning.**

When learning a sequence of nonsense syllables, subjects have the inconvenient habit of twisting them into meaningful words. This tendency is frowned upon by experimenters, since they are concerned with the learning of new associations rather than with the clever manipulation of old associations. They are concerned with behavior rather than misbehavior. This striving to make the meaningless meaningful in terms of past experience is an important aspect of human learning and very worthy of study. Psychologists have tended to ignore it because it is difficult to investigate. They are like the drunk who drops his key while trying to get it into the keyhole and goes down the street to look for it under the streetlight because the light is better there. We tend to study what is convenient rather than what is. One way in which the meaningless can be made meaningful is through the use of mnemonics. We all use "Thirty days hath September . . ." and other such techniques for organizing isolated propositions into a system to help us recall those propositions. Psychologists have left this important area to stage magicians and authors of self-help books. Only recently have they conducted a few studies in this area. In one such study subjects were asked to associate pairs of words by making some bizarre mental image. Thus for rhinoceros-ribbon, they would visualize a rhinoceros with a ribbon tied in a bow around its tusk. By this method, ordinary subjects off the street have memorized 500 pairs of familiar words with 99 percent accuracy. The only limit to the experiment was the patience of the experimenters.

6.2 Linguistic Analysis

6.21 Language

Only an imbecile would attempt to discuss such an important topic as language in half a chapter. The remaining half of this chapter is on language. Such a short account of such an important subject is perhaps justified. There appears to be a law in psychological research that the more important a topic, the less we know about it. Language is perhaps the most important and least understood aspect of psychology. We know so little about it because it is so complex that we have feared to approach it with our as-yet-underdeveloped instruments. We have contented ourselves with studies of the single word, as described to date, and have stayed away from the study of the complex system of words that we call language. Recently, however, some psychologists met some friendly linguists who assured them that they had developed a description of language that made research in this area possible. An exciting discipline, called psycholinguistics, has grown up, in which linguists, who study the structure of language, and psychologists, who study the function of language, cooperate. Let's look first at the work of the linguists on the structure of language and then at the work of the psychologists on the function of language.

6.211 Hierarchical Structure

Language, the linguist tells us, consists of a hierarchy of units and a set of rules for combining units at one level to form units at the next level. What was that? Linguists don't talk too clearly. Let me say it again more slowly. The raw material of a language is obviously sounds. Of the approximately 10,000 sounds man can emit, he selects a set of about 30 as the basis for his language. These sounds are called **phonemes.** A phoneme is a group of sounds, any one of which can be exchanged with any other within a language without it making any difference. Your "r" and my "r" are different sounds but the same phoneme. They are different sounds in that a picture of the sounds would be different, but they are the same phoneme in that you could trade my "r" for your "r" without any change in meaning. My "r" and my "l" are different phonemes: "lift" and"rift" have different meanings. Those two phonemes are only one phoneme in Chinese. That is why the Chinese who learn English as adults offer us "flied lice." They have not learned to distinguish "r" and "l." Phonemes may be combined to yield morphemes. A **morpheme** is the smallest language unit that has meaning all its own. Most, but not all, morphemes are words. The suffix "-ed," for example, is a morpheme (it means past tense) but is not a word. Morphemes may be combined to yield sentences, and sentences may be combined to yield discourses. This is what the linguist means by a hierarchy of units. This chapter consists of thousands of phonemes in order. They are grouped into morphemes, which in turn are grouped into sentences, which in their turn are grouped into the total chapter. Not all strings of units are meaningful within any given language. The acceptable strings are determined by the rules for combining the units at the lower level. The study of the rules for combining phonemes to yield morphemes is morphology, for combining morphemes to yield sentences is grammar, and for combining sentences to yield discourses is logic.

6.212 Design Features

A linguist named Hockett has listed for us 13 design features of language.[46] Rather than enumerate all 13 design features, let me discuss briefly the three features that, he concluded, are characteristic of human but not of animal communication. They are: (1) **duality of patterning,** (2) **displacement,** and (3) **productivity.**

1. Duality of patterning. I don't understand this one.*

2. Displacement. Most animal communication is initiated in response to a particular stimulus. Thus, for instance, a baboon smells danger and emits its danger call to warn the other baboons. Often, unfortunately, the source of the danger also hears the cry, and the baboon dies an unsuspecting martyr. Humans have the capacity to withhold their danger cry for a more opportune moment. When a human smells danger, he can creep furtively over to the others and whisper his danger cry in their ears: "Let's get the hell out of here." This capacity to retain vocalization until times other than immediately after the relevant stimulus enables man to talk of things not here and not now, to consider the past, and to contemplate the future.

3. Productivity. No form of animal communication permits the combination of elements to yield meaningful new elements. Thus, for instance, jackdaws have four sounds by which they communicate: they can say "kaaa" (let's fly South), "kiii" (let's fly North again), "keee" (let's attack our enemies), and "kooo" (let's make love). This is their entire vocabulary. What else do jackdaws have to talk about? They cannot combine those elements as we can combine words to create sentences. They cannot say "kaaa, keee, kiii, kooo," which means "let's fly South, make war, then fly North again, and make love." Because of the

*Footnote to second edition: I still don't understand this one.

hierarchical structure of human language, humans can combine elements to yield meaningful new elements. This capacity enables them to say something new. I can state something that has never been said in the entire history of the human race since the dawn of time. I just have. In case you are not convinced, here is another: two weeks ago, on Thanksgiving Day, within the walls of my classroom, there lay, in various stages of decomposition, the mutilated corpses of at least 100 turkeys.

There is a form of animal communication that, in a sense, has the last two design features. When bees find a source of pollen for making honey, they go back to their hives to tell their buddies where it is. Von Frisch found that they do this by means of a dance, in which the direction of the dance indicates the direction of the source and the number of wiggles per turn indicates the distance from the hive.[106] This form of communication exhibits displacement, in that the bees are communicating about something not immediately present, and exhibits productivity, in that a bee can say "the pollen is on a line 35° 24' from due North 327 yards from the hive," which can be novel in the sense that those precise figures have never been used before. Communication between bees is, however, qualitatively different from communication between humans. It is built in at birth and remains fixed until death. It cannot be changed to adapt to changing circumstances. This becomes clear in von Frisch's later work on dialects in bees. When he introduced African bees to North American bees, they could not communicate —one was wiggling where the other was waggling—but they could procreate. The products of those matings—the sons of bees—had difficulty communicating with either of their parent species, since they had adopted some compromise between the two dialects.

6.213 *Sequential Presentation*

After we acquire language, we use it. We speak. Watch your psychology professor lecture. Whatever your feelings may be about the content of the lecture, you must admire the form. You are observing the most magnificent feat of the most exciting species in the universe. Behaviorists attempt to explain speaking in terms of a chain of conditioned reflexes. The feedback from the utterance of one phoneme becomes linked to the next phoneme, and so on. A psychologist named Miller and a linguist named Chomsky have criticized this theory. They point out, among other things, that it would take more than 100 years, with no time for eating and sleeping, to learn every possible string of words up to 20 words with perfect retention after only one presentation. It would be like learning the number system by memorizing all the possible sequences of digits. The alternative suggested by Miller and Chomsky is that we should start with the intention of uttering a sentence and then apply, in appropriate order, a number of rules. The sentence must contain a noun phrase and a verb phrase. The noun phrase must contain an article and a noun. The verb phrase must contain a verb and noun phrase. The noun phrase must contain an article and a noun. By applying the appropriate vocabulary rules, the sentence is then churned out (see Figure 6-2). There are, then, rules of transformation by which this **kernel sentence** ("the boy hit the ball") may be made passive ("the ball was hit by the boy"), negative ("the boy did not hit the ball"), or interrogative ("did the boy hit the ball?"). I emphasize this explanation because a model such as this may become a model for all behavior. Whereas behavior is sequential (that is, one response after another), the structures underlying behavior may be hierarchical.

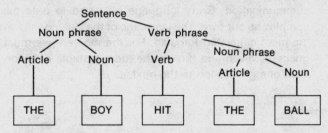

Figure 6-2. *The Hierarchical Structure Underlying the Sequential Generation of a Sentence*

6.22 Acquisition of Language

6.221 In Species

There has been a great deal of speculation about how we—the species *Homo sapiens*—first acquired language. Since speaking—unlike the comparatively recent trick of writing—leaves no permanent trace, the investigation of the beginning of language is very difficult. There are more theories in this area than facts.

Some argue that language developed through imitation of the sounds of nature (the ding-dong theory); some argue that it arose out of automatic interjections (the oof-ouch theory); some argue that it developed from sounds to accompany group work activities (the yo-he-ho theory); and so on. Some approaches seemed promising. Hockett's design features were created to differentiate animal and human communication with a view to seeing how one could evolve out of the other. It was hoped that a primitive language could be found—a sort of linguistic missing link—that would bridge the gap between animal and human communication. Every language observed to date has been found to be as complex as our own. The language of the Bushman is as sophisticated as that of the most cultivated Parisian. For the moment we must reluctantly accept language as given and turn to the more testable question of how it is passed on from one generation to the next.

6.222 In Individual

All babies babble. All babies, whether Chinese, English, or Hottentot, babble in the same way. They all have the same vocal equipment and thus are capable of the same range of sounds. All adults talk to, at, or in the presence of babies. They talk, however, using the phonemes of their particular language. When we coo at babies, we coo in English phonemes; when we baby-talk, we baby-talk in English phonemes. The child imitates the sounds he hears, hears the sounds he imitates, and repeats the sounds over and over again. The feedback from one's own voice is essential to learning speech. Deaf and dumb people are originally only deaf but cannot learn to speak because they cannot hear themselves speaking. Devices are now being marketed to provide feedback through sensory channels other than hearing to overcome this difficulty. Having learned to make some distinctive sound, such as "da-da," the child must now learn to associate it with the appropriate object. He may begin by uttering it on hearing any sound and then gradually narrow it down to any male voice or deep female voice, to any male figure (milkman, postman, and so on—an embarrassing stage), to two or three males who have something in common with father (wear glasses, embrace mother, and so on), and then, finally, to the single sociologically if not biologically appropriate male. The child learns the rules for combining phonemes to yield meaningful morphemes, and so on up the hierarchy. (A Martian arriving on our planet would have to go through the same long process—he would not immediately say, "Take me to your leader.")

Having learned to speak, the child now can begin to learn to read. English has an advantage over some other languages in that its morphemes are formed by

Phoneme	Grapheme
	though
	mow
O	go
	beau
	doe
bough	
tough	
cough	OUGH
though	
thought	

Figure 6-3. Failures of Grapheme-Phoneme Correspondence in English

combining a relatively small group of phonemes. In Chinese, every word has a corresponding visual pattern. In the modern whole-word method of reading, we teach the child to associate the configuration "dog" with the object. We lose our advantage. We teach English as if it were Chinese. The rationale for the whole-word approach is the many peculiarities of pronunciation in our language (see Figure 6-3). A more promising approach is the ITA system, in which an alphabet with perfect correspondence between sounds (phonemes) and letters (graphemes) is learned and used until the child has a grasp of it; then the shocking news is broken to him that adults have a number of strange exceptions to those rules. Children tend to be not at all surprised—it's almost as if they expect such things from crazy adults.

The shrewd guess, the fertile hypothesis, the courageous leap to a tentative conclusion—these are the most valuable coins of the thinker at work. But in most schools guessing is heavily penalized and is associated somehow with laziness.

Jerome Seymour Bruner
The Process of Education

7 Approach through Novel Response

7.1 Definition

Behavioristic theory explains learning in terms of a response from the repertoire of an organism that is followed by reinforcement, which increases the probability of that response. Thus the theory cannot explain the response that the organism has never made before. Such novel responses are the focus of psychologists studying creativity. The psychological study of novel responses has been confused by considerations creeping in from the sociological level of analysis. Since psychology focuses on the individual, a novel response is simply a response that a *particular* person has never made before. You are no less creative in making an inference from a statement in a book than the author who makes the same inference on the following page. The eccentric hermit who independently invented the alarm clock 30 years too late was no less creative than the original inventor. Both are cases of psychological but not sociological novelty. Sociological considerations are involved only in evaluating which novel responses are useful. Here we depend on the consensus of critics. Keep in mind, however, that the consensus has often been wrong. A critic of Freud's once said "There is much that is new and there is much that is true, but what is new is not true and what is true is not new." He was wrong about Freud, but he was right about the criteria of novel responses in sociological terms: they must be both new and true.

A rigorous adherence to the psychological level of analysis can help counteract the smug definition of creativity as the exclusive domain of the artist. One tends to talk of the creative painter but not of the creative plumber. Maslow has suggested, however, that a good pie is better than a poor poem. Koestler has argued that the creative process is the same whether the product is a painting or a postulate or a pun. The capacity to make novel responses is a characteristic of all members of species *Homo sapiens*. Some of us generate more novel responses than others, and some of us generate better novel responses than others. (Indeed, the quantity and quality of novel responses may very well be correlated, since, if you emit many novel responses, some of them are likely to be good.) But all of us generate novel responses.

Perhaps creativity tends to be considered as the province of art rather than of science because of poor training in science. The scientist is taking the universe apart to see how it works, and the science student is shown the pile of parts. If he were encouraged to look over the scientist's shoulder and understand what he was doing, the student would appreciate the art at the heart of science. Scientists are playing a game with nature: they ask questions to which she must answer "yes" or "no." The questions must be clear so that they force an unequivocal yes-or-no answer. To a vague question Mother Nature merely shrugs a "maybe." The scientist can ask as many questions as he can manage before nature calls time. Since nature must respond, the answer to a good question is inevitable. Albert Einstein, one of the masters of the game, said lovingly of his competitor: "Nature is subtle but never whimsical." It is in the asking of the questions, then, rather than in the setting up of the means of answering them that the master of science is set off from the apprentice. This was more blatant than usual in the case of a brilliant chemistry professor at Cornell University who was reputed to sit in an armchair in the lounge tossing out hypotheses while his less creative colleagues scurried off to test them. Many professors view graduate education as a process whereby the professor asks questions, in the laboratory and in the classroom, and the student seeks the answers. Even courses that focus on the process rather than the product of science tend to emphasize the logical thinking involved in testing hypotheses rather than the creative thinking involved in finding hypotheses. The instruction manuals on how to do science in five easy lessons are like recipes for hippopotamus pie that begin "First, catch a hippopotamus." Once you have your hippopotamus, the pie can easily be created by following a series of clearly stated steps. The first step of catching the hippopotamus cannot be easily described. That is, there are rules for logical thinking, but there are no rules for creative thinking.

However, certain factors are known to influence the probability that productive hypotheses will be generated. Awareness of those factors will increase the likelihood that you will be creative. You are more likely to catch hippopotamuses if you know their habits and hang around their habitats. The novel response, like all responses, is determined by stimuli from the environment and by states of the organism. Let's look, then, in turn, at two environmental and two organismic factors that affect creativity.

7.2 Environmental Determinants

7.21 Zeitgeist

Since it is difficult to produce novel responses in the laboratory, much of the evidence for environmental determinants of creativity comes from observations in natural settings. The history of science suggests that the most important determinant is the total intellectual climate, the spirit of the times, the **zeitgeist**. The times seem to be ripe at a particular period for a particular discovery. Just as an individual or a species must be ready for the next innovation, so must a science. The pieces of the jigsaw are available, and it requires only the creative person to put them together. The many instances of simultaneous discovery point to the influence of the zeitgeist. The calculus was invented independently by three people at about the same time. Darwin and Wallace presented the theory of evolution almost simultaneously. The times were ripe for the theory, and it would have developed—if not by Darwin, then by Wallace, and, if not by Wallace, then by someone else. Further evidence for the zeitgeist comes from the neglect of important discoveries because they were ahead of their time. The inventor of the can opener had to await the inventor of the can. Mendel's princi-

ples of genetics languished in an obscure journal until the climate was right for them to flourish. Watson is one of the prime examples in psychology of the right man in the right place at the right time with the right idea. You and I are too late to discover the theory of evolution or the basic principles of genetics, but there are many undiscovered principles awaiting us. Of course, we don't know what they are, but we can be certain that, after the shock of their novelty wears off, they will appear obvious to those who have assimilated the zeitgeist. The principle always seems so inevitable in retrospect. This ease of postdiction compared with the difficulty of prediction is further evidence for the zeitgeist.

7.22   *Serendipity*

Anecdotes from the history of science relate, again and again, that a chance event can trigger a novel response. The most famous, if apocryphal, are the rising of the water in Archimedes' bathtub and the falling of the apple on Newton's head. Psychology has its own favorite anecdotes. Skinner runs out of pellets, decides to reward the rats only some of the time, and stumbles on partial conditioning. Olds drops an electrode into the reticular formation, misses, and finds the pleasure center. This art of finding something while looking for something else is called **serendipity**, after Walpole's *Three Princes of Serendip*, who wandered around the world finding things they weren't looking for. It is found art, for the art lies in recognizing the significance of the unplanned event.

7.23   Zeitgeist and Serendipity

The zeitgeist can be identified with the accumulated body of information that constitutes a science. You assimilate the zeitgeist by reviewing the literature. Serendipity can be identified with your own unique life experience. To gain maximum benefit from both your personal experience and the collective experience of the scientific community, it is more productive to consider a problem in the light of your personal experience first. In this way you are less likely to be blinkered against alternative viewpoints by the official consensus. Also, you may find that the traditionally dull ritual of reviewing the literature will be very exciting. Neutral facts acquire an emotional charge and leap off the page because you are sensitized to the problem to which they are relevant. They will be exciting because they provide evidence for one of your hypotheses or threatening because they contradict one of your hypotheses or tantalizing because they could be explained by your hypotheses if you made some slight change. You will experience mixed emotions as you encounter theories you have formulated— joy that you are on the right track and sorrow that you are so far behind.

7.3   Organismic Determinants

The spirit may hover and accidents may happen, but, in the absence of a creative mind to take advantage of them, no novel responses will be produced. Necessity is not the mother of invention but the father. Creative minds are the mothers of invention. Let's look at two characteristics of the creative mind: perseverance to assimilate the zeitgeist and flexibility to take advantage of serendipity.

7.31   Perseverance

The zeitgeist manifests itself only through the prepared mind that has assimilated it. The times were ripe for the theory of evolution, but only Darwin and Wallace were ripe with the times. Both had the perseverance to "review the literature" in order to be imbued with the spirit of the times. Darwin is honored above Wallace, however, because he had the further perseverance to develop and document his novel idea. Remember the success story of Pavlov and the sad tale of Twitmeyer?

Don't be discouraged by the giants who have gone before you. Newton said he could see so far only because he stood on the shoulders of giants. You in turn can stand on Newton's shoulders and see even farther. Don't be discouraged if you initially appear to be limited in novel responses. Every new idea is a product of two old ideas. Every new idea must have a mama and a papa. As the number of old ideas increases linearly, the number of potential new ideas increases exponentially. As you assimilate more and more old ideas, you will suddenly hit the steep slope of the exponential curve and be off on that exhilarating, and sometimes terrifying, roller-coaster ride of creativity.

7.32 Flexibility

Serendipity likewise strikes only the prepared mind. Serendipitous findings may be accidents, but some of us are more accident-prone than others. Ever since Adam plucked an apple, countless people have seen them fall. It took a Newton to transform this trivial, specific event into the significant, universal law of gravitation. If Adam's apple represents man's fall from grace, then Newton's apple represents man's rise to wisdom. A fallen apple, in the absence of a creative mind, remains simply a fallen apple. Archimedes had pondered his problem for some time before he sat down in his bathtub. It is futile to sit around in bathtubs waiting for inspiration to strike without shedding the preliminary perspiration. I once saw Hebb turn up the edges of a 3 × 5 card to hold his ashes when he couldn't find an ashtray. A friend of a friend once saw Einstein lick his finger to write on a blackboard when he couldn't find a piece of chalk. Little things, but little things mean a lot. To most of us, a 3 × 5 card is for writing on and an index finger is for pointing at. It is difficult for us to see them as ash holders and blackboard writers. Our peculiar susceptibility to set is the deadly enemy of creativity.

The traditional educational system "prepares" our minds for the zeitgeist but not for serendipity. Perseverance is encouraged, but flexibility is discouraged. As a small counterbalance, here are some exercises to encourage flexibility.

1. List unfamiliar functions of familiar objects: (a) wire coathanger, (b) brick, (c) magnet, (d) wine bottle.

2. Solve mysteries like the following:
   (a) A man is found hanging from a light fixture in the middle of a room with nothing in it but a pool of water. What happened?
   (b) Two drinkers order Scotch on the rocks and are served from the same bottle. The fast drinker downs five glasses in the time it takes the slow drinker to finish his first. The slow drinker falls dead. What happened?

3. Invent Tom Swifties. For example:
   "Where is my register?" asked the teacher listlessly.
   "No, I won't tell you which is my hotel room," she exclaimed forthrightly.

The best strategy is to find an adverb with a double meaning and then invent an appropriate quotation. Try: (a) weakly, (b) callously, (c) gravely, (d) pregnantly.

4. Make up captions for cartoons. Cover the original caption and list a series of appropriate alternatives. Compare your efforts with the original.

5. Provide your own dialogue for movies. While watching a late movie on television with a group of friends, turn off the sound and distribute the major roles among the audience.

7.33   Perseverance and Flexibility

This apparently incompatible pair of characteristics—perseverance and flexibility—must be augmented by a subtle, impossible-to-describe-or-teach sensitivity to be able to differentiate situations in which one should be persistent from situations in which one should be flexible.* Skinner suggests: "When you chance on something interesting, drop everything else and follow it." But only a man of Skinner's sensitivity to what is potentially productive in his area can decide what is "interesting." We lesser mortals tend to persevere too much as we lumber along dead-end streets or to be too flexible as we flit from street to street getting nowhere. We tend to be drudges or dilettantes. It is difficult to be persistent but not pig-headed and flexible but not flighty. Perhaps the issue is not so much whether to be persistent or flexible but *when* to be. We could consider the creative process as a one-man brainstorming session. In stage 1 the critical faculty is suspended and ideas are allowed to flow freely; in stage 2 the critical faculty is clamped down again and the ideas are evaluated. Stage 1 generates many responses, and stage 2 selects from them the good responses. First you gather the wheat, and then you winnow the chaff from the grain. The types of thinking in each stage are complementary, but, since they are also mutually inhibitory, you engage first in one and then in the other. Flexibility is important in the first stage, and perseverance is important in the second stage.

De Bono suggests ways in which we can combine the perseverance to accumulate many old ideas with the flexibility to recombine them in new ways to generate new ideas. Children have the capacity to recombine ideas in new ways, as he charmingly illustrates in his book *Dog Exercising Machine*.[19] But they do not have many old ideas to recombine. As we grow older, we accumulate more and more old ideas but get less and less flexible. De Bono offers an escape route

*With apologies to Alcoholics Anonymous, a prayer for the creative person: "Give us persistence to build what cannot be changed, flexibility to change what should be changed, and wisdom to distinguish the one from the other."

from between the horns of this dilemma. He describes ways in which we can integrate the perseverance of the adult with the flexibility of the child.

Some nervous systems, he argues, are designed to link stimuli directly to responses.[18] This set-up has the advantage of permitting an immediate and appropriate response to a stimulus. Other nervous systems, like ours, for example, are designed to permit the process of thinking to intervene between the stimulus and the response. This set-up has the advantage of permitting a variety of possible responses to a stimulus. After a particular response has become established, however, we lose this advantage and gain the advantage of the other type of nervous system. Thinking, that "waste of time" between the stimulus and the response, has obsolescence built in—that is, when the nervous system is operating normally under natural circumstances. De Bono recommends that we create abnormal circumstances and perform unnatural acts. He suggests that we use our brains as they are *not* supposed to be used. I pointed out earlier that every new idea must have a mama and a papa. De Bono organizes orgies so that two old ideas unlikely to meet under "normal" circumstances can get together and perhaps be fruitful and procreate a new idea. I also stated that serendipity strikes only the prepared mind. De Bono creates accident-prone environments to increase the probability that serendipity will strike. All he is saying is "Give chance a chance."

You can find specific examples of de Bono's techniques within his spate of recent books. Let me add a few of my techniques.

1. *Messing around in the matrix.* Draw a matrix, and write anything you like as headings for the columns and the rows. Flit through the cells of the matrix, and consider each combination of column and row. For instance, let's say that you have headed the columns with the various sensory modalities (sight, hearing, touch, smell, taste) and the rows with various relevant categories (receptor, human versus animal, entertainment, privacy, and so on). As you flipped along the "entertainment" row, you would notice that the silent film utilized sight, the talkies added hearing, the feelies described by Huxley in one of his futuristic books added touch, the smellies in which appropriate smells are pumped into the movie theater added smell, and so on. As you can see, the creativity of Huxley and the "smelly" inventors, although impressive, is a simple mechanical matter of examining the implications of cells in a matrix. You, too, can be a creative genius by introducing tasties, in which each customer is given a bag of assorted foods and drinks so that, by eating and drinking them at the appropriate times, he or she may share the taste experiences of the characters in the movie. Or, more prosaically, you could list the various pieces of apparatus in your psychology laboratory on one axis, list various psychological problems on the other, and ask yourself, as you plod methodically through the cells, how each piece of apparatus could be used to help solve each problem. You needn't,

of course, go through all the cells. If you have a particular problem you wish to solve, you need only go down that column; if you have a favorite apparatus you enjoy playing with, you need only go along that row. You don't even need to consider a whole row or a whole column. You can simply pin your matrix on a wall, throw a dart at it, and consider the combination represented by the cell in which it lands. This is an effective randomizing process, if you happen to be as skillful with darts as I am.

2. *The analogy game.* Make two columns on a sheet of paper, and head each column with the name of a system. List as many elements, relationships between elements, events, and processes within the first system as you can think of, and then try to fill in alongside the corresponding concept with respect to the second system. Repeat starting with the second system. (Throughout this book this strategy is used as the nervous system is placed alongside the digestive system, the internal-combustion engine, the computer, and the thermostat.) Perhaps we would be more creative if we were trained as generalists rather than as specialists, because we would have more systems to work with in this creative analogizing. Out-of-school systems (chess, football, gambling, gardening, dating, and so on) are valuable sources of analogies once the rigid categories of "in-school systems" and "out-of-school systems" are allowed to merge. Miller's Analogies, consisting of a series of items of the form "a is to b as c is to ?," is the best predictor of success in graduate school.

3. *Table of random ideas.* Collect a list of operations (reverse, negate, equate, subsume, and so on), and, every time you have a problem, go through your list and think of how each operation could be applied to help solve it. The list of approaches in this book could be used in the same way. Consider in turn how each of these approaches has been applied or could be applied to solve the problem you have in mind. Indeed, this is essentially what I have been doing while writing this book. The problem in mind is, of course, that basic problem of understanding ourselves.

Each of these techniques, as well as each of de Bono's and those of others who teach creativity, is essentially a variation of "Messing around in the Matrix." They differ merely in the strategy for choosing names for the rows and columns and for choosing cells on which to focus. Thus, when de Bono recommends that you open a dictionary at random and free-associate to the first word on the page, he is suggesting how to name one of the rows; when he recommends that you wander around Woolworth's looking at objects with a particular design problem in mind, he is suggesting how to run along a row of cells. Because of previous experience, we tend to get imprisoned within certain cells in each matrix. The solution is to become not less mechanical but more mechanical. Perhaps the unconscious mind earns its reputation for creativity with sudden solutions after a period of incubation because it mechanically plods through cells in a matrix until it hits one that creates a "Eureka!" in a mind sensitized to this solution.

What is matter?—never mind.
What is mind?—no matter.

Punch
Volume XXIX, page 19

8

8

Psychophysical Approach

8.1 Behavior and Experience

In the preceding chunk of this book (Chapters 2-7) we focused on behavior; in this chunk of the book (Chapters 8-10) we will focus on experience. The distinction between behavior and experience was stated in the prologue. This important and difficult distinction is elaborated here for the intelligentsia who like to see how everything hangs together. Psychology is the science that studies the nervous system. This system is unique among all the systems studied by scientists in that it may be studied from the inside as well as from the outside. The manifestation of the functioning of the nervous system as seen from the outside is behavior; the manifestation of the functioning of the nervous system as seen from the inside is experience. The two views overlap but not completely. Let's imagine that you are watching me now as I write. You are viewing the functioning of my nervous system from the outside, and I am viewing the functioning of my nervous system from the inside. You are observing my behavior, and I, in my exclusive ringside seat, am experiencing. Your observation that I am writing has a counterpart in my awareness that I am writing. There are, however, some aspects of one view that have no counterpart in the other view. You may observe certain unconscious mannerisms from out there that I do not experience from in here, and I may experience certain unwritten thoughts from in here that you do not observe from out there.* Thus a complete picture of the nervous system

---

*Indeed, "unconscious" could be defined as referring to those aspects of behavior with no counterpart in experience. If you want to have a stab at changing our language, perhaps you could coin a much-needed word to refer to those aspects of experience with no counterpart in behavior.

requires both views. Let's now take the inside perspective to round out the picture constructed so far from the outside perspective.

8.2 Sensory Psychophysics—Fechner

8.21 Gustav Fechner

If you believe, as many scientists do, that a science begins when the phenomena it studies can be measured, then keep October 22 open to celebrate the birthday of psychology. For it was on the morning of October 22, 1850, that an eminent physicist named Gustav Fechner woke up and cried "aha!," "Eureka!," or whatever. At the same moment a celebrated mystic named Dr. Mises also woke up and cried "aha!," "Eureka!," or whatever. It was no coincidence. The objective scientist and the subjective mystic were the same person. Gustav Fechner led a double life. Since he published his scientific work under his own name and his mystical work under the pseudonym Dr. Mises, it would appear that he considered the scientist in him as his Mr. Hyde. Historians, however, tend to view him as a mystic who accidentally advanced a science while trying to prove a theology. What was his insight? A prerequisite to the scientific study of a phenomenon is the measurement of that phenomenon. Sensation is difficult to measure, whereas energy is easy to measure. If one could find the relationship between sensation and energy, then one could measure that which is difficult in terms of that which is easy. The dimensions of energy have corresponding dimensions of sensation. By varying a dimension of energy and observing the effect on the corresponding dimension of sensation, the relationship between them could be

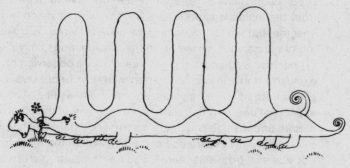

"—an absolute limen grazes
    alongside a terminal limen."

found. In this way Fechner-Mises hoped to integrate the two disparate aspects of his personality; to reconcile the objective scientist interested in the physical world and the subjective mystic interested in the psychological world; to demonstrate the relationship between the physical aspect of man—his body—and the psychic aspect of man—his mind—and thus solve a problem that had haunted philosophers for centuries. His moment of insight marked the beginning of the study of the relationship between the psychological world and the physical world. Psychophysics was born.

8.22 The Psychological Dimension

8.221 Absolute and Terminal Limen

The human organism is sensitive to a number of forms of physical energy: heat, light, sound, and so on. Let's focus on sound. Sound energy varies along three dimensions (wavelength, amplitude, and complexity), and each of these dimensions has a corresponding dimension of sensation (pitch, loudness, and timbre) (see Figure 8-1). Now let's focus on amplitude and loudness. The measurement of amplitude presents no difficulty. The zero point is 0 millicentimeters, and the unit is 1 millicentimeter. The measurement of loudness is more difficult. What is zero loudness? What is the unit of loudness? Fechner defined zero loudness as

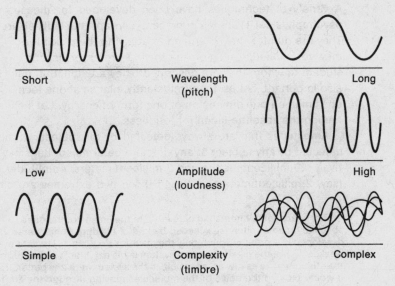

Figure 8-1. The Three Dimensions of Sound Energy and the Corresponding Dimensions of Sensation

the smallest amplitude that can be detected and the unit of loudness as the smallest difference in amplitude that can be detected. He called the former the **absolute limen** and the latter the **difference limen**. Although there is no upper limit in amplitude, there is an upper limit in loudness. The largest amplitude that can be detected is called the **terminal limen**. Thus the psychological scale has a lower limit (absolute limen) and an upper limit (terminal limen), with the dimension between them chopped up into units (difference limen).*

8.222   Weber's Law

The difference limen is not the same in terms of millicentimeters at all points on the scale. The smallest difference that can be detected is obviously dependent on that value from which the difference is detected. Very little would have to be added to a 1-pound bag of sugar for the difference to be detected, but a great deal must be added to a 300-pound husband before it would become obvious that he had been indulging in the sugar. Stated more precisely, the ratio of the difference limen (ΔY) to the stimulus from which the difference is measured (Y) is a constant (k), or, more succinctly, $\Delta Y/Y = k$. This relationship is **Weber's law.**

8.23   The Psychophysical Methods

A variety of techniques have been developed for measuring limens. These **psychophysical methods** represent perhaps the dullest area in psychology. They are dull for the experimenter applying them and for the subject to whom they are applied. They are dull for the professor describing them and for the student to whom they are described. They are dull, but, unfortunately, they are also important. Let us, then, reluctantly, glance at one technique for measuring one limen on one dimension of one form of energy. Let's consider a method of finding the absolute limen for loudness.

Amplitudes that are always detected by all subjects at all times and never detected by any subject at any time are determined. Let's say they are, respectively, 20 millicentimeters and 2 millicentimeters. Amplitudes at small intervals (say, 2 millicentimeters) between those two extremes are chosen. These am-

---

*There are some interesting sidelights to the limens of the dimensions of sound. Man's absolute limen of pitch is exceeded by that of his dog. Some stereo equipment has been developed to a point at which only the master's dog can appreciate the improvement. The weakest link in the master's sound system is his ear. Man's absolute limen of loudness, on the other hand, is as low as is feasible. If the system were any better, it would be worse, for it would pick up the noise of the molecules moving through the air. Rock groups sometimes push amplitude up over the terminal limen until the sensation of loudness changes quality to that of pain.

plitudes will be detected some of the time and not detected some of the time. Each amplitude is presented to each of the subjects 100 times (see what I mean about those methods being dull?). The percentage of times that each stimulus is detected may be plotted in a graph, such as that in Figure 8-2. The absolute limen is arbitrarily defined as the stimulus that is detected 50 percent of the time.

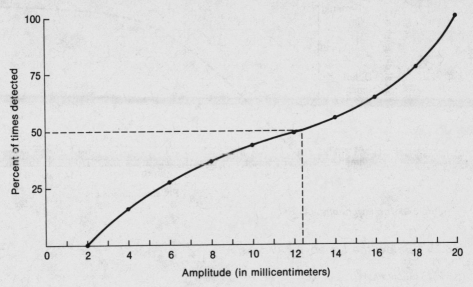

Figure 8-2. A Psychophysical Method for Determining the Absolute Limen for Loudness

8.24 The Psychophysical Relation

In Figure 8-3 a physical dimension is represented on the x axis and the corresponding psychological dimension is represented on the y axis. Now that a zero point and a unit on the psychological scale have been established, it is possible to find a point on the y axis corresponding to each point on the x axis. The curve created by joining all those points represents the relationship between the physical and the psychological dimensions. What is the equation of this curve? Fechner suggested that it is $y = a \log x$ **(logarithmic law)**, where a is a constant; Stevens has more recently suggested that it is $y = bx^c$ **(power law)**, where b and c are constants. These two theoretical curves derived by reason are designed to fit as snugly as possible with the empirical curves derived by observation. As a child, you probably played a game in which coins were thrown toward a wall and the person whose coin came closest won all the coins. Stevens is claiming that his coin is closer to the wall than Fechner's. Unfortunately, in this case, it is not so easy to measure which is closest. Fechner's curve fits the data better for some dimensions, and Stevens' curve fits the data better for other dimensions. The debate continues.

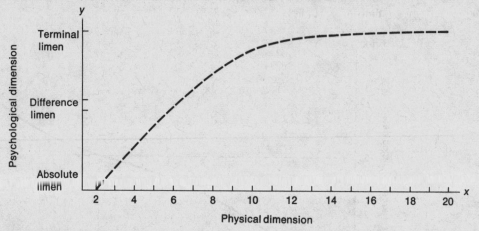

Figure 8-3. The Psychophysical Relation

8.25 Below the Limen

8.251 Subliminal Perception

A few years ago a cinema manager flashed the words "Drink Coke" on the screen at intervals during the showing of the movie *Picnic*. He reported a tremendous increase in the sale of Cokes. This would not have been surprising, except that the presentations were so brief that the audience was not aware of the message. Such a stimulus normally affects behavior through the mediation of an experience, but in this case it was affecting behavior directly. This subliminal advertising produced a violent public reaction, with cries of being hit below the psychological belt and scares of murder epidemics if the message "Kill your wife" flashed on the TV screen during the late-late show. A close look at the experiment, however, revealed that one of the basic principles of experimental procedure had been violated. The demonstration that one event (flashing the message "Drink Coke") is cause and another event (buying a Coke) is effect requires a strict control over any other event that could possibly have been the cause of the observed effect. In this case the increase in Coke sales could have been caused by a number of other factors. It could have been the heat: the experiment was conducted during a long, hot summer, and the air conditioner was not working. It could have been heat of another sort: with Kim Novak and Bill Holden cavorting around, one could use something cool. It could have been suggestion: the movie was *Picnic*, and Coke is consumed at picnics.* It could have been the absence of any other kind of drink, the extra salt in the popcorn, and so on and so on. More controlled experiments subsequently conducted by investigators who were more sophisticated in experimental method have failed to demonstrate any effect of subliminal stimulation. We have nothing to fear from subliminal advertising. Indeed, one prominent psychologist has expressed the wish that more advertising were subliminal—supraliminal advertising bothers him.

8.252   *Perceptual Vigilance and Defense*

Certain states of the nervous system may have the effect of lowering **(perceptual vigilance)** and raising **(perceptual defense)** the limen. Here is a typical demonstration of perceptual vigilance. A group of graduate students in law and a group of graduate students in divinity are presented with a list of randomly mixed legal and religious terms. The words are presented with a **tachistoscope** for progressively longer and longer intervals until they are recognized. The law students recognize the legal terms significantly sooner than the religious terms, whereas the divinity students recognize the religious terms significantly sooner

than the legal terms. Here is a typical demonstration of perceptual defense. A group of subjects is presented with a list of randomly mixed "dirty" and "clean" words.† The clean words are recognized significantly sooner than the dirty

*It is no secret that more cold drinks were sold during the showing of *Lawrence of Arabia* than during the showing of *Scott of the Antarctic*.

†Some psychologists who had been graduate students at Cornell during this epoch of dirty-word experiments assured me that their group used the dirtiest words of all. Their work was never published, they claimed, because the words were so dirty that journal editors refused to print the reports of their experiments.

words. The first dirty-word experiment was criticized on the ground that the dirty words were not recognized later but *uttered* later. It was conducted at a girls' college by a young, good-looking male psychologist. A nice, well-brought-up, middle-class girl will say a clean word like "brush" as soon as she recognizes it but will hesitate about saying a dirty word like "penis" for all sorts of reasons. She may doubt that a professor would know such a word, much less show it to a sweet young thing like her. She may also worry about what this nice young man would think if she said "penis" when presented with "piano." The experiment was replicated later, however, with a group of male students as subjects and another male student as experimenter. The effect persisted.

This effect caused great excitement. In order to raise the limen to block an undesirable stimulus, one would have to unconsciously perceive the stimulus. This mechanism of **subception** was postulated by Freud but had not yet been demonstrated. Such a spooky explanation is, however, not necessary, for both perceptual vigilance and perceptual defense can be explained more satisfactorily in terms of familiarity. The more familiar a word, the easier it is to perceive. Legal words are more familiar to law students, and religious words are more familiar to divinity students. Clean words (at least written clean words) are more familiar to everyone (except perhaps devotees of pornographic novels or washroom graffiti) than dirty words.

8.3   Perceptual Psychophysics—Gibson

8.31   Higher-Order Variables

In two brilliant books, Gibson has applied the psychophysical approach first to the visual system[30] and then to all our perceptual systems.[31] Let's consider two of the ways in which Gibson's perceptual psychophysics differs from Fechner's sensory psychophysics.

Whereas Fechner approaches the visual system from the outside in, Gibson approaches it from the inside out. We will see in Section 9.122 that, as we move from the outside in, from the retina to the visual cortex, individual cells respond to increasingly complex aspects of the physical world. They respond to points and then to circles and then to lines and then to moving lines. This does not mean, however, that our experience is built up that way. We experience from the inside out. Thus, whereas sensation may precede perception neurologically, perception precedes sensation experientially. Perception is primary; it is not constructed out of sensations. The sophisticated phenomenon of sensation is possible only in the artificial setting of a laboratory. We should be looking, then, for the physical correlates of perceptual phenomena, not for those of sensory dimensions. Gibson calls such physical correlates **higher-order variables,** since they are not simple dimensions of energy like wavelength and amplitude but complex ratios between variables.

For example, the perceptual experience of surface slant has a corresponding physical variable of **texture gradient**. Texture gradient is the rate of change of the distance between lines on a surface and varies from zero (for a vertical surface) to some maximum (for a horizontal surface). This higher-order variable of texture gradient helps solve the problems of size and shape constancy, which have puzzled thinkers for centuries. Why are the two rectangles in Figure 8-4a interpreted as being of the same size but at different distances rather than as being of different sizes at different heights (size constancy), and why is the block in Figure 8-4b interpreted as a horizontal rectangle rather than as a vertical trapezoid (shape constancy)? Gibson answers both questions in terms of texture gradient. In the former case both rectangles cover the same number of units of texture; in the latter case the far and near sides of the rectangle cover the same number of units of texture.

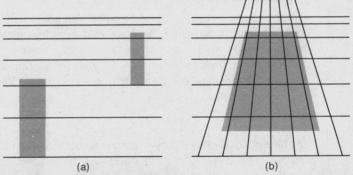

(a)   (b)

Figure 8-4. *Explanation of Size and Shape Constancy in Terms of Texture Gradient*

Whereas Fechner focuses on the light that falls on the retina, Gibson focuses on the light that is emitted or reflected by the object. The light that falls on the retina is only that sliver of the light emanating from the object in all directions that is arbitrarily determined by the position of the observer. To get to know the object, the observer must view it under different illuminations, at different distances, and from different orientations. This is, indeed, how you get to know objects in your everyday environment. If you were a subject in a laboratory, however, the illumination on the object, your distance from it, and your orientation to it would be kept constant. This makes sense within the experimental setting, since these are extraneous variables that must be controlled in a psychophysical experiment. Unfortunately, the experimenter will never get to know how you get to know an object outside the laboratory, because you get to know it by varying the illumination, distance, and orientation and by observing what remains constant despite those variations. The experimenter not only distorts the phenomenon by observing it under the controlled conditions of the laboratory but also creates pseudoproblems (like that of object constancy), which are problems only in the artificial environment of the laboratory.

8.32 Post-Gibson Man

To read Gibson is to be introduced to future man. Paradoxically, however, in order to meet future man, we must take a trip into the past. A puckish Peter Pan of a person ushers us aboard the Gibsonian time machine. Fasten your seatbelts and adjust your headsets. Service will be resumed only when you can see the world through the innocent eyes of your ancestors. We are off on a trip up the stream of consciousness, going back to a time when our species was very young.

We are back before the comparatively recent tricks of reading and writing. Our eyes have not been tamed to make that artificial left-to-right scanning motion line after orderly line. We have wild eyes that make staccato surveys of a hostile environment in search of things that we eat and things that eat us. We have not read the learned volumes that assure us, time after pompous time, that our perceptions are built up from our sensations. We have not yet had the disadvantage of an education.

We are back before the trick of using instruments to expand our sense organs. Since we have not yet seen the world through the microscope or through the telescope, we have not yet conceived of the world in atomic or cosmic terms. We see solid surfaces in a flat world. Our simple perceptual map of the world is not cluttered with the complex conceptual map superimposed on it.

We are back before the trick of simulating the objective world by sculpting and painting. The artist and the artisan have not yet conned our eyes into accepting their art and artifact as representations of reality. We have not yet fallen prey to that double-dealing delusion whereby artists and psychologists have provided one another with evidence for their practices and theories. The flora and fauna of nature are not yet cluttered with the flotsam and jetsam of man. We do not yet enjoy the cultural luxury of perceiving the beauty of things but only the biological necessity of perceiving the utility of things.

We have, in short, gotten rid of the accumulated artifacts and anachronisms that distort our perception of perception. We have not yet donned our linguistic and cultural blinkers. We are now ready to meet post-Gibson man—our future model of man—who is, paradoxically, prehistoric man.

The visual world of post-Gibson man is not the traditional mosaic of points of varying hue, brightness, and saturation out of which he constructs a perception (the eye was developed long before newsprint and pointillistic painting); it is a pattern of overlapping surfaces of varying texture gradients from which he differentiates out a perception. The visual system of post-Gibson man is not the traditional retina/camera projecting an image onto the occipital-lobe/screen; it is a filter sifting from his environment the information relevant to his survival. Post-Gibson man is not the traditional robot sitting passively with locked eyes and neck and legs, having stimuli impinging on him; he is an active organism, moving his eyes with respect to his head, his head with respect to his body, and his body with respect to his environment as he moves around and looks around to squeeze information out of a rich objective world. He may not talk, but he can walk. He is an R-S rather than an S-R organism. His perceptual world is simple, but his life is difficult. He must survive in a hostile environment. He needs a hearing system and a seeing system to help him approach things that he eats and avoid things that eat him. He needs a tasting system to sample what he eats and a smelling system to sample what he breathes. He needs a skin sensitive to noxious stimuli. He needs to explore to anticipate danger.

After this trip forward into the past, let's now return to the future. As we pass the present in our time-ship trip from past to future, we get a glimpse of pre-Gibson man, according to traditional psychophysics. He is imprisoned in a laboratory with his body, his head, and his eyes fixed on an impoverished environment. He is permitted to talk but not to walk, since it is not convenient for him to wander around in the enclosed space of the laboratory. We chuckle at this quaint image, but we shudder at the cruel picture of pre-Gibson child imprisoned in a classroom with his body fixed in an immobile chair, his head fixed facing the front of the class, and his eyes fixed on the impoverished environment of the blackboard.

As we move into the future, we see that the Gibsonian revolution has taken place. The 1970s' interest in the environment has caught up with the 1950s' capital of Gibson's theory. Revolutionaries, who recognize a real revolution as a change in man's view of himself rather than as a shoddy shift in political personnel, have worked out much of Gibson's program of finding the higher-order variables corresponding to the various aspects of perceptual experience. They know that they need a theory as well as a conscience—that there is nothing as practical as a good theory. Traditional textbooks have become obsolete, although some have been salvaged for supplementary reading in the history of psychology. The revolutionaries have not only filled out the Gibsonian foundation but have built on this solid base. "I perceive, therefore I am" has replaced the traditional "I think, therefore I am" and provided a strong perceptual foundation on which the conceptual superstructure was built.

What appeared to be problems have melted into phenomena. The pseudo-problem of depth perception is seen as a mistaken conception of two-dimensional viewing as primary and three-dimensional viewing as secondary. Misperceptions are seen not so much as facts but as artifacts created by artificial situations. The few true cases of misperception are due to a lack of specificity in a system that, under natural conditions, provides a remarkably accurate view of the world. The nature-nurture issue in perceptual development reduces to the determination of the stage at which the organism is able to move so as to create the transformations that provide it with the information contained in the environment.

"Tell me," says Micromegas, an inhabitant of one of the planets of the Dog Star, to the secretary of the Academy of Sciences in the planet Saturn, at which he had recently arrived in a journey through the heavens—"Tell me, how many senses have the men on your globe?" . . . "We have seventy-two senses," answered the academician, "and we are every day complaining of the smallness of the number . . . in spite of our curiosity, and in spite of as many passions as can result from six dozen of senses, we find our hours hang very heavily on our hands, and can always find time enough for yawning." "I can very well believe it," says Micromegas, "for, in our globe, we have very near one thousand senses, and yet, with all these, we feel continually a sort of listless inquietude and vague desire, which are for ever telling us that we are nothing, and that there are beings infinitely nearer perfection."

Voltaire
Micromegas

Psychophysiological Approach

9.1 Between the Object and Its Perception

9.11 Psychophysics and Psychophysiology

In the psychophysical approach we considered the relationship between the public world of objects and the private world of perception of those objects. In the psychophysiological approach we will consider the series of transformations that mediate between the object and the perception of the object. (The psychophysiological approach is to the psychophysical approach as the mediational approach is to the behavioristic approach.) The various forms of physical energy to which our nervous system is sensitive are transformed at the appropriate receptor, by some as-yet-not-fully-understood process, into a pattern of nerve impulses, which are in turn transformed at the appropriate projection area of the cortex, by some not-at-all-understood process, into perceptions. That is, the physiological world of nerve impulses mediates between the physical world of objects and the psychological world of perceptions. These nerve impulses are the only currency that the nervous system accepts. The perception of light cannot be produced by shining a flashlight directly onto the cortex. In addition, these nerve impulses are qualitatively the same for all modalities. Different qualitative experiences (sights, sounds, smells, tastes, touches) are produced from the same nerve impulses at the appropriate projection area of the cortex. If the optic nerve and the auditory nerve were crossed, you would hear the lightning and then see the thunder.

9.12   The Visual System

9.121   Traditional View

Let's consider the two transformations (physical energy to nerve impulses and nerve impulses to perceptions) in more detail with respect to light energy. The receptor for light energy is the eye. More precisely, it is the photosensitive surface at the back of the eye called the **retina**, the eye being merely a device for focusing light on the retina. The eye is traditionally compared with the camera, with retina as film, pupil as aperture, iris as diaphragm, and so on. Presumptuous psychologists (including my first-edition self) proceed to point out how poorly constructed the eye-as-camera is. The film is in backward, it has a hole in it, and shadows cast over it; the image is upside down; the entire camera constantly wobbles up and down. The projection area of the cortex for light energy is the occipital lobe. The occipital lobe is traditionally compared with a screen onto which the image is projected. This model of eye/camera projecting a point-by-point image of an object onto occipital-lobe/screen implies a little person in the head looking at this image in order to interpret it. This little person would, in turn, require another littler person in *his* head to interpret *his* image, and so on through an infinite regress of nested little people. The early Egyptians, who had a similar notion that we are controlled by a little person in the head, avoided this problem by angrily and arbitrarily cutting the regress short at the seventh little person and calling him God. You cannot deny that you have a little person in your head. Look into someone's eyes or, if you do not have someone handy, look into a mirror. You will see the little person looking out at you. You cannot deny that this little person has wonderful powers. Switch your attention from one eye to the other, and you will notice that the little person has moved, quick as light, to the other eye. Since the evidence for our traditional view of the visual system is of this order, let's continue to a new view, which may be more soul-satisfying.

9.122   A New View

It has long been recognized that there is not a single set of neurons stretching all the way from the retina to the occipital lobe but rather a sequence of neurons with synapses between them. It has, however, been tacitly assumed that this was a simple bucket brigade with information being passed on essentially unchanged from one neuron to the next. We ought to have known better. Nature never evolves a complex system when a simple system would perform the same function. It is now clear that the neurons at each level within the visual system respond to qualitatively different aspects of the stimulus. That is, there are changes taking place at each synapse. There is a great deal of organization of the information before it arrives at the visual cortex. The message at the visual cortex is a coded rather than a projected representation of the image at the retina. This revolution in our view of the visual system has been triggered by the evolution of a technique for picking up impulses from a single neuron. A visual display is presented to the fixed retina of an organism, and an electrode is dropped into a single neuron within the visual system to record whether or not it is firing. The area of the retina that, on stimulation, produces a response from a cell is called the **receptive field** of that cell. Let's look at some studies using this technique at various points on the phylogenetic scale.

Hartline dropped electrodes into the retinal cells of the frog and found that there were essentially three types.[40] One fired when a light was turned on **(on-cells)**, one fired when a light was turned off **(off-cells)**, and one fired when a light was turned on or off **(on/off-cells).** The off-cells and the on/off-cells projected to one part of the brain and the on-cells to another part. (These parts happen to be called the optic tectum and the dorsal thalamus, respectively, but the names are not important—the frog can see and you can see how the frog sees without knowing the names.) Dropping his electrodes now into the optic-

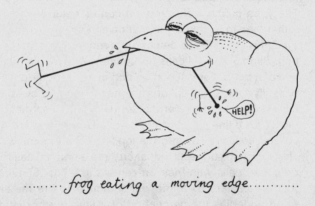

.... *frog eating a moving edge* ....

tectum cells, Hartline found that there were four types. One fired to sharp edges, one fired to moving edges, one fired to small, dark, moving objects, and one fired when a light was turned off. Dropping his electrodes into the dorsal thalamus, another investigator found cells that were differentially sensitive to light of different wavelengths. Most of the cells tended to be most sensitive to blue light. As we move from the periphery to the center of the visual system, we see that the cells respond to more complex aspects of the stimulus. In general, the cells that project to the optic tectum provide the frog with information about form and the cells that project to the dorsal thalamus provide the frog with information about color.

This information is not a projection of the objective world but a selection from it. The retina is not a film but a filter. It selects the information from the environment that is relevant to the survival of the organism. Moving edges and small, dark, moving objects are important to the frog because they represent, respectively, things that eat it and things that it eats. Because of the greater sensitivity to blue light, the frog tends to jump into the safer blue water when danger looms—a move that makes good Darwinian sense. The fact that the visual system of the frog is functional (designed for its survival) rather than veridical (designed to provide an accurate map of the world) raises interesting questions about our visual system. Perhaps our visual system selects only that limited aspect of the "real" world that we must see in order to survive. Perhaps our perception of the world is limited not only by our culture, as many anthropologists argue, but by our biology as well.

There are six sets of cells in the visual system of the cat between the retina and the occipital lobe, as illustrated in Figure 9-1. Hubel and Wiesel dropped electrodes into the ganglion cells of cats and found that there were two types.[47] One fired to a particular region in the retina but not to the surrounding region, and the other fired to the surrounding region but not to the particular region. These **on-center cells** and **off-center cells** are responsive, then, to relative rather than to absolute stimulation and give substance to the view that the visual system is designed to detect differences rather than simply to pick up illumination. Simple cortical cells fire to lines. A particular simple cortical cell fires to a line of a particular orientation and in a particular position. The receptive field is typically a narrow slit of on-regions surrounded by off-regions. Complex cortical cells fire to lines of a particular orientation regardless of position. Since a moving line is a line of a particular orientation in a sequence of positions, complex cortical cells provide information about movement. Study of the structure of the visual system suggests that each simple cortical cell receives input from a set of on-center cells with their on-centers in a line. Simultaneous illumination of all their on-centers by a line will summate to fire the simple cortical cell whose firing underlies the perception of a line. Further study of the structure of the

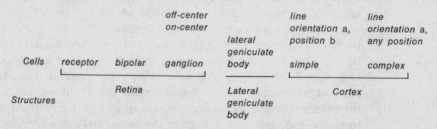

Figure 9-1.   Six Sets of Cells in Visual System of Cats

visual system suggests that each complex cortical cell receives, in turn, input from a set of simple cortical cells with their lines of a particular orientation but in different positions. Successive illumination of all their receptive fields by a moving line will summate to fire the complex cortical cell whose firing underlies the perception of a moving line.

The apparent mechanical defects pointed out earlier by eye-as-camera advocates demonstrate the limitation of the metaphor rather than the limitation of the visual system. Our visual system is a beautifully designed visual system rather than a poorly constructed camera. The Leica is a lousy eye. What appears malfunctional when considered as a camera turns out to be functional when considered as an eye. Let's look at **physiological nystagmus**—the fact that the eye wobbles up and down.

Pritchard discovered the function of physiological nystagmus by eliminating it.[80] He fitted subjects with mirrors fixed to the eye so that an image projected onto the mirror always fell in the same position on the retina. He found that, when the image falls continuously on the same region of the retina, that region fatigues and the image fades and disappears. The function of physiological nystagmus appears, then, to be to preserve a continuous image by continuously changing the region of the retina on which it falls. Since the complex cortical cells respond in the same way regardless of position, the perception remains constant even though the eye moves up and down. Further light is thrown on the function of the visual system by the manner in which the image fades. It does not fade evenly. One part fades and then another and then another, until the entire image is gone. Meaningful parts tend to disappear as a whole. Thus, in a face, the mouth may disappear, then the nose, then the eyes, and so on. Moreover, the parts do not disappear randomly. Thus, in a word, parts will fade to leave meaningful wholes. A meaningless figure will fade randomly at first, but, as it acquires meaning, it fades systematically. It would appear, then, that the visual system not only organizes the mosaic of points on the retina into more and more complex units on the way to the visual cortex but also incorporates the effects of learning.

9.2   Form Perception

9.21   The Facts

9.211   Ganzfeld

Your visual experience must ultimately depend on the millions of mind pictures taken by your eyes between your first moment and your present moment. Stop and consider the picture being taken by your eyes right now. Note that it is an oval.* Note that it is highly complex. It contains a variety of colors and textures, of shapes and surfaces, of objects loaded with association and symbols saturated with meaning. Since it is much too complex to begin our study of perception, let us simplify it. Move close to a blank wall so that its surface fills your

entire visual field. There are still complications because of the texture of the surface. Imagine the wall to be perfectly uniform. There are still complications because the parts of the surface in the periphery of your visual field are farther from the retina than the part in the center. Imagine the surface curved so that each part is equidistant from the retina. You now have the simplest possible visual experience in which all parts of the retina are equally stimulated. You now have the **ganzfeld**. The first ganzfeld, consisting of a 6-foot sphere with the subject placed in the center, was constructed in Germany. A pocket ganzfeld, consisting of half a Ping-Pong ball taped over each eye, was subsequently constructed with typical American ingenuity in the United States.[45] The simplest possible perceptual experience is also an uncomfortable experience. Try it sometime.

9.212 Figure and Ground

This simplest possible perception is, in a sense, no perception. You do not perceive stimuli per se but relationships between them. When sitting in the bathtub, you perceive neither the hot on the bottom nor the cold on the top, but the ring around the middle. When the country boy goes to the city, he can't sleep—not because it is too noisy but because it is too different. When the city boy goes to the country, he can't sleep either. Since perception is a relative

*It's not exactly an oval, since your nose breaks the symmetry. Gibson once whimsically suggested that the nose is the basis for the ego, since it is the only constant in the varying visual fields that constitute our experience. When asked if we would have a big ego if we had a big nose or no ego if we had no nose, he switches off his hearing aid and smiles his charming smile.

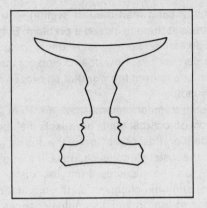 

Figure 9-2. Two Examples of Reversible Figures

rather than an absolute experience, the visual field must contain two surfaces. A dot on the ganzfeld, then, would constitute the simplest possible perception. The dot is perceived as **figure**, and the rest of the visual field is perceived as **ground**. This is apparently a very basic experience, since you will remember (Section 3.221) that von Senden's patients reported it on first perceiving the world after their cataract operations. In certain cases it is not clear what is figure and what is ground. **Reversible figures** (Figure 9-2) have been designed in which figure and ground alternate. In the diagram on the left, we perceive alternately two heads and a goblet; in the diagram on the right, we perceive alternately a young woman and an old woman. In these reversible figures, the identical retinal pattern produces two very different perceptual experiences—a clear illustration that man does not live by retina alone.

9.213 Object Constancy

A further step in complexity takes place when we turn from the perception that there is something there to the perception that there is a certain something there—from the perception of figure-ground to the perception of an object. One of the most remarkable facts about object perception is the amazing correspondence between our perception of an object and the object itself.* Let's consider

*Gleitman held the specter of his grandmother over our heads throughout his course. She represented common-sense wisdom, which haunts psychologists with the uncomfortable reminder that hundreds of hours and thousands of dollars of research may yield results that are nothing but common sense. The character was so well drawn that every member of the class could sense her gloating in the background at every obvious or apparently obvious finding and could share the psychologist's joy at her discomfort over every counterintuitive finding. Can you hear her now? "So what's the problem? You see things as they are because that's the way they are. You psychologists are always making with the problems."

this problem of **object constancy**. Having read the last section, you are now sophisticated enough to recognize that there is indeed a problem. Between the object and the perception of that object there is a series of transformations from light energy to nerve impulses to perceptions. How does the object maintain its integrity despite those dramatic changes from the world of physics to the world of physiology to the world of psychology?

Consider only the least drastic transformation: from *distal* to *proximal* stimulus—that is, from the physical object that emits or reflects the light energy **(distal stimulus)** to the projection of this object onto the retina **(proximal stimulus)**.*As the illumination on the distal stimulus changes, the brightness of the proximal stimulus changes; as the distance from the distal stimulus changes, the size of the proximal stimulus changes; as the orientation to the distal stimulus changes, the shape of the proximal stimulus changes. Yet, despite variation in illumination, distance, and orientation, perception of the brightness, size, and the shape of the distal stimulus remains constant. These are the facts, respectively, of **brightness, size,** and **shape constancy**. Check these facts for yourself. Look at some convenient door. Shine a light on it. It does not appear any brighter. Move away from it. It does not appear any smaller. Open it. As it opens, its shape changes from a rectangle to a trapezoid to a wedge, yet you still perceive it as a rectangle. A door is a door is a door, even when it is ajar.

Let's state the fact of constancy more formally with respect to brightness constancy. The fact can be demonstrated experimentally by presenting a sub-

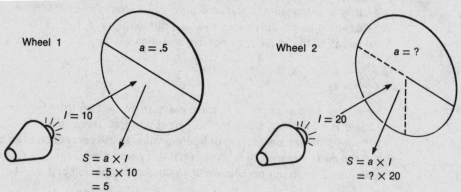

Figure 9-3. *Demonstration and Statement of Fact of Brightness Constancy*

*We cannot know the distal stimulus directly but only indirectly through the proximal stimulus. Whether the object continues to exist when no one is looking at it is a question we will leave for philosophers. Psychologists prefer to concentrate on questions with potential answers.

ject with two color wheels under different illuminations, as depicted in Figure 9-3, and asking him to adjust one until it is the same shade of gray as the other. The subject will adjust it until it is objectively the same rather than until the amount of light entering the eye is the same. That is, if S represents the amount of light entering the eye, I represents the illumination on the object, and a represents the percentage of light that this surface reflects, he adjusts in terms of a rather than in terms of S. In this particular case, he adjusts the percentage of black in wheel 2 to 180° (giving the same a as wheel 1) rather than to 270° (giving the same S as wheel 1). The fact of brightness constancy may now be restated as the fact that, when all a subject knows directly is S, he can solve for a without knowing I or, alternatively, keep a constant despite variation in I.

9.22 Explaining the Facts

Theorists with the traditional view of the visual system attempted to explain brightness constancy in terms of learning. You perceive a swan under dim illumination as white and a raven under bright illumination as black—even though there may be less light entering the eye from the swan than from the raven—because you have learned that swans are white and that ravens are black. This argument breaks down on both logical and empirical grounds. There must have been someone somewhere who saw some swan before he was prejudiced as to the color swans should be. Besides, the phenomenon is demonstrated with color wheels, even when subjects have never seen color wheels before. Gelb showed that learning has no effect on the subsequent perception of brightness.[27] He presented a gray with a strong light behind it and no background surrounding it. The subject reported white. Gelb held a piece of white paper in front of the gray. The subject reported gray. Gelb took away the white paper. The subject reported that he knew it was gray but saw it as white.

A clue to the correct solution is provided by an extension of the experiment described above for demonstrating brightness constancy. If the two color wheels are looked at through **reduction screens** (devices for eliminating the background, such as paper cylinders), brightness constancy is lost. The subject adjusts in terms of the proximal, rather than of the distal, stimulus. Brightness

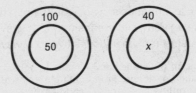

Figure 9-4. Explanation of Brightness Constancy—Wallach

constancy must depend, then, on the relationship between the figure and the ground. Wallach demonstrated exactly what that relationship was.[109] He presented the concentric circles indicated in Figure 9-4 through reduction screens and requested subjects to adjust *x* until it was equal in brightness to the center of the other circle. They adjusted it not to 50, so that it would be objectively equal, but to 20, so that the ratios between figure and ground would be equal. This response makes sense. Since the sun shines democratically on figure and ground alike, the ratio remains constant despite variations in illumination.*

9.3 Color Perception

9.31 The Facts

9.311 Brightness

Many of the psychological facts of brightness perception can be observed on the standard date. You go to an early movie. As you move suddenly from the bright illumination outside to the dim illumination inside, you are temporarily blind. After a few minutes you can see relatively well, and the invisible legs you stumbled over on the way to your seat can now be seen without any trouble. You get into your car after the movie and notice that, in the dim illumination of evening, your red car is relatively duller, whereas the blue car next to it is relatively brighter. You drive to a quiet spot to look at the stars and notice that it is easier to see a dim star by looking at it indirectly than by looking at it directly.

The physiological facts of brightness perception are not so easily observed. If, however, you were able to look closely into the eyes of your date, you would observe that the receptor cells in the retina are of two types. There are short fat cells concentrated at the center and long thin cells concentrated at the periphery. Let us call them, respectively (because of their shapes), **cones** and **rods**. If you were to look closely into the eyes of a chicken, you would see only cones; if you were to look closely into the eyes of an owl, you would see only rods. If you were to grind up cones (from humans or chickens), you would obtain one chemical, **iodopsin**; if you were to grind up rods (from humans or owls), you would obtain another chemical, **rhodopsin**. If you were then to pass light through those chemicals, you would find that they both decomposed, with iodopsin being maximally sensitive to a wavelength of 560 millimicrons and rhodopsin being maximally sensitive to a wavelength of 510 millimicrons.

*Characters on the stage can be made to appear saintly or ghostly by tampering with this natural state of affairs. Frontlighting creates a bright figure by shining light on the figure but not on the background, and backlighting creates a dim figure by shining light on the background but not on the figure.

Imagine that you had a huge pile of chips representing all the possible colors: the familiar reds, blues, greens, yellows, blacks, whites; the esoteric indigos, chartreuses, rusts, fuchsias, vermilions, avocados; the uncountable, unnamed shades in between. If you were to pick out all the achromatic colors (that is, all the blacks, whites, and grays as seen in a black-and-white movie), you would be able to arrange them in a line ranging from white through the various grays to black, such that each chip would be just noticeably different from the chips next

to it. If you were to pick out all the blues, you would be able to arrange them in a line ranging from the most vivid blue to the dullest blue, such that each chip would be just noticeably different from the chips next to it. If you were to pick out all the most vivid colors—all the vivid reds, blues, greens; all the colors of the rainbow—you would be able to arrange them in a line ranging from blue to red, such that each chip would be just noticeably different from the chips next to it. These three dimensions are called, respectively, brightness, saturation, and hue. The relationship among the three dimensions may be represented by the **color cone** (see Figure 9-5), with brightness as the axis, saturation as the radius, and hue as the circumference. All the myriad colors in our colorful world fit somewhere within this space. The location of each color may be pinpointed by finding its position on each of the three dimensions.

The color cone helps clarify our thinking about color sensation, not only by reducing a myriad of experiences to three dimensions, but also by providing a means of visualizing the result of mixing colors. To find the result of mixing any two colors in any proportions, represent each of the colors by points at the appropriate places on the color cone, and divide the line between the points inversely in the ratio of the two colors in the mixture. Thus, in Figure 9-5, point *C*

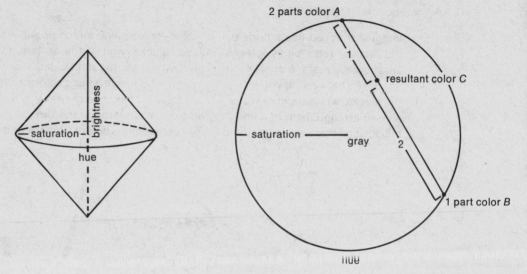

Figure 9-5. The Color Cone. The figure on the right represents the hue-saturation surface obtained by cutting the cone on the left across the middle and turning it through 90 degrees. The center of the circle is the midpoint of the brightness dimension and thus represents gray.

represents the result of mixing two parts of color *A* and one part of color *B*. It follows, then, that a mixture of equal amounts of two colors opposite each other on the hue dimension will yield gray. Such colors are called **complementaries**.

A few people see the world as if it were a black-and-white rather than a Technicolor movie. They are totally **color-blind**. Many people (about 1 in 10 males and about 1 in 100 females) can perceive some colors but cannot differentiate all the colors within the color cone. They are partially color-blind. You may have taken the **Ishihari test** for color blindness while being tested for a driving license. It consists of numbers composed of dots in one color superimposed on a background composed of dots in another color. Someone who is red-green color-blind cannot identify the number, since he cannot differentiate the red dots that form the number from the green dots that form the background.

A gray on a blue background looks yellowish and on a yellow background looks bluish; that is, a color tends to take on the complementary of its background. This effect is called **simultaneous contrast**. If one fixates on a blue surface and then looks at a white surface, he sees yellow. That is, after fixating on a color, he sees its complementary on being stimulated by white light. This effect is called **successive contrast**.

9.32 Explaining the Facts

9.321 Duplicity Theory

Had you observed the psychological facts of your date (which is unlikely under the circumstances), and had you been sufficiently puzzled by them to seek an explanation (which is even more unlikely under any circumstances), you might have reasoned as follows. Different structures suggest different functions. Perhaps we have not one visual system but two: one, involving the cones, is for bright illumination; the other, involving the rods, is for dim illumination. Congratulations on rediscovering the **duplicity theory**. Diurnal organisms like chickens need only cones; nocturnal organisms like owls need only rods; but organisms like us, who prowl around both day and night, need both. The period of **dark adaptation** in the movie theater represents the time required to switch from the bright to the dim system.* The relative brightness of the blue car and the relative dullness of the red car under dim illumination are caused by the fact that the rods are more sensitive than the cones to the lower end of the spectrum.

*This effect is not noticed under natural circumstances, because, although the falling of night and the breaking of day *sound* sudden, they are actually gradual, allowing time for the switch from one system to the other. This dual system fails to function perfectly only because man has created unnatural circumstances in which the switch from bright to dim or from dim to bright illumination is sudden.

The apparently incongruous fact that dim stars can be seen better by looking at them indirectly now becomes congruous, since indirect observation permits the light to fall on the periphery of the retina, where the rods are.

9.322 Young-Helmholtz and Hering Theories

The duplicity theory would be adequate to explain color perception if the world were seen as in a black-and-white movie. However, since we see the world in Technicolor rather than in black and white, it is necessary to go beyond the brightness dimension to the brightness, hue, and saturation dimensions of the color cone—to go beyond the duplicity theory to a supplementary theory.

The duplicity theory divided the visual receptors into rods and cones. The **Young-Helmholtz theory** adds that the cones are further subdivided into three types, maximally sensitive, respectively, to blue, green, and red (see Figure 9-6). When your blue receptor is stimulated, you perceive blue; when your green receptor is stimulated, you perceive green; when your red receptor is stimulated, you perceive red; when your blue and green receptors are stimulated equally, you perceive blue-green; when your green and red receptors are stimulated equally, you perceive yellow; when your red and blue receptors are stimu-

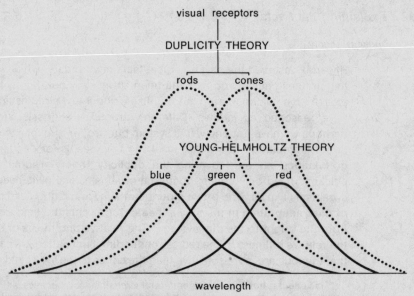

Figure 9-6. Duplicity Theory and Young-Helmholtz Theory.
*Duplicity theory divides visual receptors into rods and cones;
Young-Helmholtz theory further divides cones into blue, green, and
red receptors. The curves represent the sensitivity of the receptors
to different wavelengths.*

lated equally, you perceive purple; when your blue, green, and red receptors are stimulated equally, you perceive gray. The manner in which the Young-Helmholtz theory explains the fact that all colors may be represented by the color cone can perhaps best be described in terms of the three physical dimensions of light and the corresponding psychological dimensions of visual sensation. As you move from left to right along the wavelength dimension in Figure 9-6, you will note that you generate, in order, the hues of the spectrum—blue, blue-green, green, yellow, and red. By varying from a light of unmixed wavelengths, which maximally stimulates one receptor and minimally stimulates the other two, to a light of mixed wavelengths, which stimulates all three receptors equally, we generate the corresponding psychological dimension of saturation. By varying light of low amplitude, which stimulates all three receptors minimally, to light of high amplitude, which stimulates all three receptors maximally, we generate the corresponding psychological dimension of brightness.

A mixture of two vivid noncomplementary colors would be produced by a mixture of the lights producing each of the constituent colors. Thus (according to the Young-Helmholtz theory) it will be between the two constituent colors on the hue dimension and lower than both on the saturation dimension. This statement may be verified by using the procedure described above for finding the result of mixing colors by using the color cone. The special case of two complementary colors producing gray would also be anticipated by the theory as explained here in the case of blue and yellow. Since blue light stimulates the blue receptors and yellow light stimulates the green and red receptors, the combination of blue and yellow light stimulates all receptors and thus produces gray.

Persons who are color-blind possess all three types of cone receptors, but the sensitivity curves overlap—all three in the case of those who are totally color-blind and two in the case of those who are partially color-blind. Thus the individual who is red-green color-blind has overlapping sensitivity curves for his red and green receptors, which permits him to perceive both red and green but not to differentiate between them.

An explanation of the contrast effects requires additional assumptions about physiological processes within the receptors. Simultaneous contrast can be explained by assuming that the firing of some receptors inhibits the firing of the neighboring receptors of the same type. Thus a blue ground inhibits the neighboring blue receptors on the gray figure, and gray light, which stimulates all three equally, stimulates the green and red more to produce a yellowish tinge. Successive contrast can be explained by assuming that receptors tire after being stimulated for some time. Thus fixating on blue inhibits the blue receptors, and gray light, which stimulates all three equally, stimulates the green and red relatively more to produce yellow.

The **Hering theory** aspires to explain the same set of facts in terms of two rather than three types of cones. These cones are responsible, respectively, for the perception of blue-yellow and red-green, with one color being perceived as a result of a chemical change in the receptor and the other being perceived when this change is reversed. When your blue-yellow receptor is in one state, you perceive blue; when your blue-yellow receptor is in the reverse state, you perceive yellow; when your red-green receptor is in one state, you perceive red; when your red-green receptor is in the reverse state, you perceive green; and when both receptors are in their neutral state, you perceive gray.

Since the two theories are designed to explain the same set of facts, it would appear that one must be wrong and the other must be right. The debate as to which is which has raged for decades. As an example of the give-and-take, the assumption making and counterexampling, the fact and counterfact, let us consider the debate about color blindness. Advocates of the Young-Helmholtz theory originally conceived color blindness in terms of the absence of receptors. Thus red-green color-blind people lacked either red or green receptors. Advocates of the Hering theory discovered that red-green color-blind people can perceive yellow.* This fact was somewhat embarrassing to the Young-Helmholtz theory, since it explained the perception of yellow in terms of equal stimulation of red and green receptors. How can they be equally stimulated when one is missing? (One point for Hering.) Hecht, an advocate of the Young-Helmholtz theory, came to the rescue by suggesting that color blindness was due not to missing receptors but to overlapping sensitivity curves. Thus red-green color-blind people can perceive yellow at any point along the wavelength dimension in which the red and green receptors are stimulated and the blue receptor is not. (One point for Young-Helmholtz.) Furthermore, at one point on the wavelength dimension, at the point where normals perceive blue-green, the red-green color-blind should perceive gray. Indeed, they do. (Touché.)

Recently a reconciliation of the two positions appeared.[65] It has been made possible by the new view of the visual system and the new method of studying it described in Section 9.122. When electrodes are placed in single cells in the visual system, three types of neurons, maximally sensitive to blue, green, and red, respectively, can be identified among the cones, and two types of neurons, associated with blue-yellow and red-green, respectively, can be identified among the ganglion cells. Thus visual sensation involves at least two stages,

*How did they know that what red-green color-blind people call yellow is the same experience as that which noncolor-blind people call yellow? The Hering disciples fiendishly sought out the few people in the world who are red-green color-blind in one eye and normal in the other. Thus the impossible task of comparing experiences in two private worlds is replaced by the simple task of comparing two experiences in one private world. Cunning?

with the Young-Helmholtz theory correct at one stage and the Hering theory correct at the other. They each had a little bit of the truth. As is so often the case, two apparently incompatible theories turn out to reflect different perspectives on the same phenomenon.*

*One is reminded of the story of the blind men and the elephant. The one who held the tusk conceived of the elephant as solid and smooth, the one who held the tail conceived of the elephant as soft and stringy, and so on.

Still thou are blest, compared wi' me!
The present only toucheth thee:
But och! I backward cast my e'e,
    On prospects drear!
An' forward, tho' I canna see,
    I guess an' fear!

Robert Burns
To a Mouse

10 Phenomenological Approach

10.1 Behavior and Experience

10.11 Thesis—Introspection

The first, and often the last, approach to self-understanding by the layman is typically the introspective approach. It was the first approach used by the psychologist, too. Wundt, who founded the first psychological laboratory, was an **introspectionist.** His laboratory was the "in" place at the end of the last century.* Students converged from around the world to sit at Wundt's feet and diverged again to spread the gospel. What was the gospel? That psychology is the study of experience. How is it studied? By submitting oneself to a particular stimulus and observing one's experience. What is the aim of the study? To analyze experience into its constituent elements: sensations, feelings, and images. If I were to give you the instruction "Add . . . two and three," you would probably respond "five." What was your experience during that pause between "add" and "two and three"? If I had said "multiply" rather than "add," you would have responded immediately with a different answer. Something must have happened in your brain, then, between "add" and "two and three" to set you to respond "five." What was your experience between the instruction "two and three" and your response "five"? If you observed images, you are a Titchenerian; if you observed nothing, you are a Kulpian. Titchener and Kulpe were two of Wundt's students who got involved in a controversy after Titchener had

*You are a student of Gardiner, who was a student of Ryan, who was a student of Bentley, who was a student of Titchener, who was a student of Wundt. Thus you are only five generations away from the beginning of scientific psychology.

returned to the United States and Kulpe had returned to Würzburg. Kulpe claimed that it was possible to have thoughts without images, but Titchener disagreed. There are images, said Titchener. There are not, said Kulpe. There are so. There are not. There are so. There are not. There was no way in which this transatlantic argument could be resolved. Titchener was the world's foremost authority on Titchener's experience, and Kulpe was the world's foremost authority on Kulpe's experience.

10.12 Antithesis—Behaviorism

Watson headed the introspectionists off at this impasse. He wrote the manifesto of behaviorism, and, since then, almost all psychologists have been behaviorists or postbehaviorists or neopostbehaviorists or antibehaviorists.[110] What was *his* gospel? That psychology is the study not of experience but of behavior. One's experience is not observable by others and thus is not amenable to scientific study. How is behavior studied? By observing the behavior of others rather than the experience of oneself. What is the aim of the study? To discover the functional relationships between the stimuli impinging on other people and the responses emitted by them. Hebb has suggested further that introspection, in the sense of "looking inward," is not only unscientific but impossible.[42] We are not conscious of our consciousness. Our experience of ourselves is simply fedback information from our own behavior. All mental processes, not just the subset Freud focuses on, are unconscious. Just as we infer the mental processes of others from what they do, we infer the mental processes of ourselves from what we do.

10.13   Synthesis

A synthesis of the introspective and behavioristic approaches is possible by considering that peculiar interpersonal relationship between an experimenter and a subject. To make the illustration more intimate, let's assume that you are the experimenter and that I am the subject. We are dealing in our relationship with two nervous systems, yours and mine. The manifestation of the functioning of each nervous system can be viewed from the inside and from the outside. You observe the functioning of your nervous system from the inside (your experience) and the functioning of my nervous system from the outside (my behavior). I observe the functioning of my nervous system from the inside (my experience) and the functioning of your nervous system from the outside (your behavior). A complete consideration of our relationship must include your experience, my experience, your behavior, and my behavior.

The introspectionist and the behaviorist both limit themselves to a consideration of only one of those four aspects of our relationship. If you were an introspectionist, you would aspire to explain only your experience; if you were a behaviorist, you would aspire to explain only my behavior. The introspectionist and the behaviorist both aspire to explain their chosen aspect by experimentally eliminating the other aspects. If you were an introspectionist, you would eliminate my experience and my behavior by serving as your own subject, and you would eliminate your behavior by ignoring it. The former strategy of putting experimenter and subject within the same epidermis causes problems when your experience conflicts with my experience, as we have seen in that sad impasse between Kulpe and Titchener. The latter strategy of ignoring your behavior fails too, since your behavior continues to influence your experience. For instance, your behavior of focusing on simple stimuli with a set to analyze them into their elements places strict constraints on your experience. If you were a behaviorist, you would eliminate your behavior and your experience through various scientific strategies to ensure "objectivity," and you would eliminate my experience through the less scientific strategy of ignoring it and hoping it would go away. A spate of recent experiments on the experimenter effect have demonstrated that my behavior is influenced by your behavior. And the fact that my behavior is determined by my experience is so assumed in perception experiments that a case in which it was apparently not resulted in great excitement. Who would have been interested in my behavior of buying a Coke when subliminally stimulated by the message ''Drink Coke'' if my experience of that stimulus had intervened? You as a behaviorist may think that you are studying my behavior, but you are actually studying your experience of my behavior, which is determined by your behavior and my experience. Criticism of introspection and behaviorism has focused mainly on their attempts to analyze your experience and my behavior, respectively, into their elements. But the basic error of both is to analyze the experimenter-subject relationship into its elements and focus on only one of them.

10.2 Perceptual and Conceptual Maps

10.21 Perceptual Map—MacLeod

MacLeod has been arguing eloquently for decades that we must consider all four aspects of the experimenter-subject relationship and be alert to the intimate interactions among them.[64] He argues further that the most fruitful initial focus for you is your experience. He would appear to be bringing us right back to where we started from. However, his phenomenological approach differs in a number of ways from the introspective approach. Although both views focus on your experience, the phenomenological approach is not committed to analyzing it into its elements. Indeed, the essence of phenomenology is the suspension of any commitments. The behaviorist attempts to attain objectivity by treating the subject as object. The phenomenologist attempts to achieve objectivity by eliminating his built-in biases so that his subjective map is an accurate representation of the objective world.

A second difference is that you as a phenomenologist go beyond your experience to my experience. It is obvious that your behavior and my behavior can become part of your experience, but there is no direct way in which my experience can become part of your experience. The behaviorist assumes that he and a fellow behaviorist will share the same experience if they perform the same experiment under the same conditions. The phenomenologist extends this faith to his subject, recognizing that his subject is another phenomenologist for whom he is the subject. Together we two phenomenologists can work toward building accurate subjective maps of the objective world. Discrepancies between our subjective maps alert us to a bias in at least one of them. By a careful examination of our prejudgments, we each try to perceive the world directly rather than through our distorting mirrors of interpretations. A perfect match between our subjective maps does not guarantee that those maps will be accurate representations of the objective world; it is, however, a necessary, if not sufficient, condition.

A third difference is that you as a phenomenologist go beyond your perceptual map of the objective world to your conceptual map. Your subjective map consists of a **perceptual map,** based on percepts, and a **conceptual map,** based on concepts. A percept in your subjective map corresponds to a thing in the objective world, and a concept in your subjective map corresponds to a word in the objective world, as diagramed in Figure 10-1. The relationship between the percept and the thing is determined by the structure of the nervous system and is thus primary. The relationship between the concept and the word is determined by the arbitrary link between percept and concept in the subjective map and the arbitrary link between thing and word in the objective world and is thus secondary. Phenomenologists recognize that perception is primary but proceed to consider conception as based on perception.

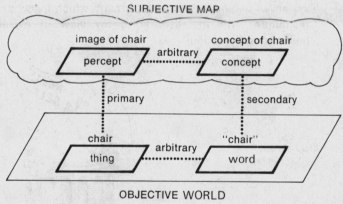

Figure 10-1. The Objective World and the Subjective Map

10.22   Conceptual Map—Kelly

It is easy to see how your perceptual map and my perceptual map would match if both of them were accurate. Since our conceptual maps involve the different meanings you and I assign to things and events in the objective world, it is difficult to see how our conceptual maps could match. However, if your conceptual map can become part of mine and my conceptual map can become part of yours, they can match in the sense that, for each of the conceptions in your conceptual map, there is a corresponding awareness in my conceptual map that you have that conception. Like Richard Nixon and Chou En-lai, you and I can agree to disagree. Our conceptual maps can match not like print and reprint but like print and negative. In his **personal construct** theory, Kelly provides a means of making your conceptual world part of mine and my conceptual world part of yours.[53]

Each of us, in trying to make sense of the objective world, constructs a subjective map of it. The personal construct is the basic unit of this subjective map. It is a dichotomy by which we can categorize the other people and things in the objective world. We differ from one another in terms of the sets of constructs that we use. These constructs are not merely means of labeling persons and things but means of understanding and predicting events. Constructs are established when predictions based on them are validated and may be changed when predictions based on them are invalidated. Thus, contrary to reinforcement theory, development occurs when predictions are *not* validated. Your behavior is not a reaction to a stimulus but an experiment to test a hypothesis; my behavior influences your behavior in the sense that I validate or invalidate your hypotheses. Kelly provides you with an objective method for teasing out the system of personal constructs through which I view the world (**repertory grid technique**) and for discovering my view of myself within this system (**self-characterization**).

Kelly suggests, contrary to behavioristic theory, that you act to produce a stimulus rather than react to a stimulus. You are your own invention. You should be not so much discovering your "real" self (whatever that is) as inventing a desirable self. If you are dissatisfied with your present self, you should invent the self you want to be. The traditional psychotherapist, by focusing on discovery of the present self, tends to ingrain that unsatisfactory self that the client came to him to change. If your self is in your "lacking-confidence" category and you are unhappy about this, transfer your self into the "confident" category and conduct a series of experiments to validate your new hypothesis. That is, act the role of the confident person. The self-fulfilling prophecy (if you expect something to happen, it will happen) may work on your behalf so that you do indeed become a confident person. If you have me in your "stupid" category, switch me to "smart" and watch me smarten up. Rosenthal and Jacobson produced dramatic gains in the academic performance and IQ of children by telling their teachers that the children were intelligent.[84]

The reflexive nature of the experimenter-subject relationship has already been mentioned: one person is thinking about another person thinking. Kelly points out the discrepancy in psychology texts between the description of the first "thinking" and the description of the second "thinking." The experimenter is developing theories, creating hypotheses to test those theories, designing experiments to validate the hypotheses, and changing the theories to accommodate the facts generated by the experiments. Meanwhile, back at the laboratory, the subject (an obviously much less endowed organism) is emitting responses to stimuli and having them stamped in and out by positive and negative reinforcement.* A theory in psychology is inadequate unless it can explain its own creation. Psychology is a metascience—that is, it is a theory about theories. Psychologists should be able to use the same language to describe the thinking of the experimenter that they use to describe the thinking of the subject. Since the traditional subject language is so obviously inadequate to describe the thinking of the experimenter, Kelly uses the traditional experimenter language to describe the thinking of the subject.

10.3 Past, Future, and Present

There is considerable controversy within psychology as to whether behavior should be explained in terms of the past (historical explanation), the future (teleological explanation), or the present (contemporaneous explanation). Let's see how the phenomenological approach may cast some light on this issue.

*In the few cases in which an experimenter has used the subject language to describe his own behavior, he has done so in a whimsical manner. Skinner refers to a collection of papers as his "cumulative record," and refreshments at psychology conventions are advertised as "reinforcements dispensed." The autobiographies in A History of Psychology in Autobiography are noteworthy for the fact that so few psychologists even attempt to use their own theoretical language to describe their own behavior.

10.31 Historical Explanation

Watson's little Albert was afraid of rats because he had been conditioned in the past to fear rats. Freud's little Hans was afraid of horses because he had had a traumatic experience in the past involving a horse.* We are as we are today, say the behaviorists, because of our conditioning in all our yesterdays. We are as we are today, say the psychoanalysts, because of our traumas in all our yesterdays. Behaviorists and psychoanalysts make strange bedfellows, but the bed of historical explanation they must share. It is a crowded bed, for the vast majority of psychologists have couched their explanations of present behavior and their predictions of future behavior in terms of the past.

Our behavior today, however, is influenced by tomorrow as well as by yesterday. We are pulled by the future as well as pushed by the past. This fact is obvious to the psychologist in his living room and his bedroom but is apparently preposterous to him in his office and his laboratory. His theories and experiments overwhelmingly emphasize the past over the future, and he scolds the few brave theorists who dare to talk in terms of the future with names like "teleologist," "mystic," and other dirty words.

Reasons for the preference for historical over teleological explanation are not hard to find. At first glance, the conception of the future influencing the present would seem to imply that a future event is the cause of a present event as effect. Psychologists, self-conscious in their shiny new lab coats, recoil from what would appear to violate a basic prescription in the dogma of science: thou shalt not put effect before cause. The use of the rat as the prototypic organism is perhaps a second contributory factor. Many a Pied Piper has tried to clear out the rat-infested laboratory by condemning the rat as an inadequate model for human perception and human learning. Such a criticism is even more valid when directed at the rat as a model for human planning. The rat may be short in sight and low in insight, but it is particularly limited in foresight.

10.32 Teleological Explanation

Philosophers talked unapologetically about behavior in terms of purposes and goals. Such futuristic terms were some of the proverbial babies behaviorists threw out with the bath water. However, a group of scientists working on the border of psychology and engineering are now beginning to make teleology respectable again. They advocate that we turn for our inspiration from the rat to

*Little Hans was the son of a colleague of Freud's. His father sent Freud regular observations on the behavior of Hans and, on the basis of those observations and one interview, Freud cured the phobia. This was the first instance of psychoanalysis by correspondence.

the thermostat, from the study of the rat in the Skinner box to the study of the Skinner box, from the comparative psychology of man and beast to the comparative psychology of man and machine. They point out that the goal-directed behavior of the thermostat (its goal being to maintain a constant temperature) can be explained in purely mechanical terms. The teleologist can look the

mechanist straight in the eye and say "Consider ye the thermostat, how it works. It intends not; neither does it have purpose. Yet Solomon in all his glory was not so directed as one of these." He can build a machine that is a concrete embodiment of his teleological model and make it work. Many scientists have claimed this as the true mark of understanding. It certainly makes one confident of understanding and is a powerful means of silencing critics. Such subjective satisfactions contribute not only to the well-being of the psychologist but to the progress of psychology. No longer timid about investigating the obvious effects of the future on the present, the teleologist has built a more powerful model of man.

10.33 Contemporaneous Explanation

The fear of teleology may partly account for the peculiar neglect by psychologists of the phenomenon of death. This is puzzling, because, whether you believe that "the aim of life is death" or "death is what makes life worth living," you recognize that death has a profound effect on life. Writers have demonstrated this point by chronicling the dramatic changes that take place in the behavior of a person who discovers that his death is imminent. The fact that we are aware of our mortality may be one of the important distinctions between us and the other animals. Could it be that one of the reasons for neglecting death is that the event of death comes after all the events of life and thus death as a causal factor in life would smack of teleology? This consideration of death illuminates the irrationality behind teleophobia. It is not the fact that we die later that influences our lives now but the fact that we know now that we are going to die later. It is not an event in the future that is the cause of our present behavior but some representation of that event within the nervous system at present. Thus teleological explanations are no more mystical than historical explanations, since they both refer simply to present representations within the nervous system of future and past events, respectively. Lewin makes this brilliantly obvious statement in his **contemporaneity principle:** only present facts can influence present behavior.

When you focus on the objective world (the world-as-it-is), you see it as stretched out over time, with past, present, and future influences on behavior. However, when you focus on the subjective map of the objective world (the world-as-you-see-it), as recommended by phenomenologists, you realize that past, present, and future are all embodied in the present. You are not restricted in your subjective map, as you are in your objective world, to be in a particular place at a particular time. You can roam around the world and explore the planets while sitting in your armchair. This morning you can walk along the shore of the Sea of Galilee with Jesus Christ in the year 30, and this afternoon you can talk to HAL in the year 2001. The infinity of space and the eternity of time are potentially here and now. Your behavior can be determined by things not here and not now if they have become part of your subjective map. The present is saturated with the past and pregnant with the future.

An unlearned carpenter of my acquaintance once said in my hearing: "there is very little difference between one man and another; but what little there is, is very important." This seems to me to go to the root of the matter.

William James
The Will to Believe, The Importance of Individuals

11

Psychometric Approach

11.1 One Intelligence—Binet

11.11 Measuring Intelligence*

11.111 The Intelligence Quotient (IQ)

The story began, as so many stories begin, in Paris. The Minister of Public Instruction had a problem. Many children in the Paris school system, for which he was responsible, were not benefiting from instruction. In some cases a child lacked the potential to benefit from instruction; in other cases the potential was there but was not being developed. The solution to his problem in the former cases would be different from the solution in the latter cases. It was necessary, then, for him to find some means of separating the former from the latter, the dull from the lazy, those who couldn't learn from those who wouldn't learn. It was necessary for him to develop a means of measuring the capacity to benefit from instruction.

He presented his problem to a versatile young man named Binet, who was already a psychologist, hypnotist, lawyer, and playwright, among other things. He asked Binet to become also a psychometrician. Indeed, he invited Binet to

---

*The psychometric approach involves administering tests to subjects and placing the subjects along dimensions on the basis of their responses. There are tests available to place you on dimensions of authoritarianism, Machiavellianism, and tolerance for ambiguity, among a thousand others. Intelligence is only one such dimension, but I prefer to focus on it (and even then only skim the surface) rather than attempt to survey the myriad means of measuring your interest in, aptitude for, and attitude toward practically everything.

become the world's first psychometrician. Binet tackled the problem in a manner that was brilliantly obvious. He constructed a large number of problems that appeared intuitively to test the capacity to profit from instruction (for example, items testing memory, discrimination, vocabulary, and so on) and presented the problems to a large number of children of all ages. On the basis of their solutions, he selected the good items. What is a good item? Assuming that this capacity, whatever it is, increases with age, a good item is one that is solved more easily as children get older. Figure 11-1 provides some representative good and poor items. He then placed the good items in groups, according to the age at which 50 percent of the children solved the problem correctly. Thus good item 1 in Figure 11-1 would be placed in the 8-year-old group and good item 2 would be placed in the 14-year-old group. This original test, constructed by

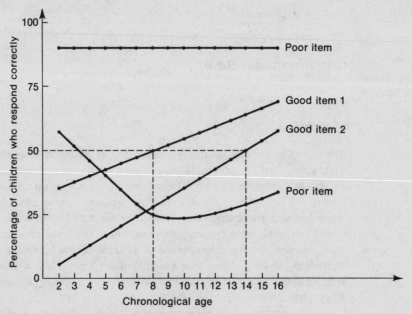

Figure 11-1. The Basis for Selection of Items for Binet's Test

Binet and revised periodically at Stanford University (**Stanford-Binet test**), is still one of the most familiar and most frequently used intelligence tests today. Binet constructed his test by selecting six good items for each age from 2 to 16. Figure 11-2 provides a few illustrative items.

How may this instrument be used to derive an index of intelligence? Let's say the test is administered to 10-year-old Bob, and he solves all the problems up to and including the 8-year-old group, four problems in the 9-year-old group, three

50% OF CHILDREN OF:

Age 5   define two of the following three words: ball, hat, stove; fold a paper square twice to make a triangle after a demonstration by an examiner.

Age 8   distinguish between such words as airplane and kite, ocean and river; know what makes a sailboat move; know what to do if they find a lost 3-year-old baby.

Age 12   see the absurdity in such statements as "Bill Jones' feet are so big that he has to pull his trousers on over his head"; repeat five digits reversed.

Figure 11-2. Some Representative Items from the Stanford-Binet Test

in the 10-year-old group, two in the 11-year-old group, and none in the 12-year-old group. We are concerned with the range between the age at which he gets all the items correct and the age at which he gets none of the items correct. Within this range he gets two months' credit for each item correct. Bob's total credit, then, is 9.5 years, as shown in Figure 11-3. This is called his **mental age (MA)** and is defined as the average chronological age of the children who pass the same number of items as he does. Since Bob is 10 years old, he is about average for his age. However, if 7-year-old Joe gets the same score, he would be above average for his age, and if 14-year-old Sam gets the same score,

(a) CALCULATING MENTAL AGE FOR BOB

		Credit	
Age Level	Items Correct	Years	Months
8	all	8	0
9	4	0	8
10	3	0	6
11	2	0	4
12	none	0	0
		9	6

(b) CALCULATING INTELLIGENCE QUOTIENT FOR BOB, JOE, AND SAM

	Mental Age	Chronological Age	Mental Age / Chronological Age	Intelligence Quotient
Bob	9.5	10	0.95	95
Joe	9.5	7	1.36	136
Sam	9.5	14	0.68	68

Figure 11-3. Calculation of Mental Age and Intelligence Quotient

he would be below average for his age. An index that takes chronological age into consideration would therefore be useful. An obvious index is the mental age divided by the chronological age. An obvious refinement is to multiply this index by 100 to get rid of the awkward decimal point. The resultant index is the famous **intelligence quotient (IQ).** The IQs of Bob, Joe, and Sam are calculated in Figure 11-3.

11.112 *Distribution of IQs*

The mean is, by definition, 100, and the distribution of scores about that mean is, as would be expected, normal. For convenience, the distribution may be cut into slices with descriptive labels attached to each slice. One such schema is presented in Figure 11-4. The descriptive terms at the lower end of the scale get progressively more and more insulting.* Fortunately, few people reading this book will fall very far along into the lower regions of the normal distribution. Perhaps it is unfortunate. Since it is difficult to imagine what life is like down there, educators, who tend—believe it or not—to live on the other side of the peak, set unrealistic standards for people with such limited potentiality. The upper end of the scale needs less discussion, since you have all come in contact with genius—if not in yourself, at least in others. We tend to think—or, better, we want to think—that nature is democratic in her distribution of talents. An arsenal of aphorisms ("Genius is to madness near akin," "A healthy mind and a healthy body—take your pick") reflects this tendency. Mort Sahl points out, however, that "God did not create all men equal. Jefferson did." Genius is not necessarily close to insanity. For each torrid genius like Van Gogh and Dostoyevsky, there is a quiet genius like Einstein and Darwin. Indeed, a study by Terman of children in the California school system with IQs over 130 revealed that they were also above average in emotional stability and physical health. Discouraging, isn't it?

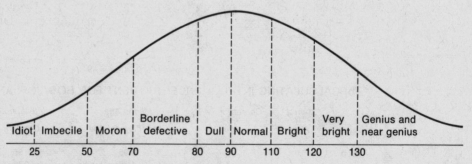

Figure 11-4. Distribution of IQs and Descriptive Categories

*These terms have been replaced recently by less insulting ones: 50-69, mildly retarded; 35-49, moderately retarded; 20-35, severely retarded; under 20, profoundly retarded. It will take a few years, said one of my reviewers, for these terms to become insulting.

The IQ is one of the most maligned concepts in the history of psychology. Let's examine the case against it. The mere title of the book *How to Raise Your Child's IQ* implies that a child's IQ is not quite so stable as the color of his eyes. Few psychometricians would, however, claim to be measuring some innate and unchangeable trait. They see IQ rather as the measure of the cumulative effects of

genetic and environmental factors up to the moment of administration. Practice in taking tests can raise the IQ score, since the content can become more familiar. Psychometricians hope to cancel out this source of error by making everyone testwise. That is, if everyone has had practice in taking tests, then no one has an advantage. Despite some dramatic changes reported because of changes in the environment, the IQ remains surprisingly stable under normal conditions. There is some evidence that it drops after about age 20, but not enough to justify the claim of some student activists that they should thus take over the country.* The tremendous increase in experience gained more than compensates for the slight reduction in the capacity to gain from experience.

A second criticism focuses on variation in IQ from group to group rather than from administration to administration. The average IQ score for lower-class

*The drop has been attributed to the fact that many brain cells die daily and are not replaced. I worried about this for a bit, until I discovered that the lost cells are an infinitesimal proportion of the total. Scientists often initiate such unnecessary worries. Who has never glanced apprehensively to the north after hearing about the galloping glaciers or felt insecure after hearing about the expanding universe? They forget to mention that these processes will have no effect on man until billions of years from now. Billions? Phew, I thought you said millions!

children is lower than that for middle-class children; the average IQ for foreign children is lower than that for North American children; the average IQ for minority-group children is lower than that for white Anglo-Saxon Protestant children. This difference stems partly from the fact that the tests are designed by middle-class, North American, white Anglo-Saxon Protestant psychologists. That bias is unconsciously built into them is illustrated by the cases in which an item inadvertently favors minority groups. Lower-class kids did consistently better than middle-class kids on an item that involved the principle of the siphon. The difference also stems partly from the fact that the early environment of less privileged children tends to be less stimulating. Sensory-deprivation studies (Section 2.252) suggest that early sensory deprivation can stunt intellectual growth. Those of you who had the good fortune to be born into a home saturated with good music and good conversation may be smart because you are rich rather than rich because you are smart.

Despite its shortcomings, the IQ index is extremely useful. Put yourself into the shoes of the registrar of your university. He is required to select, say, 1,000 freshmen from 5,000 applicants. He could select those with blue eyes and blond hair or those from a particular district or those of a particular nationality. This is obviously unfair. He could list the names alphabetically and select every fifth name. This seems very fair and democratic. It would, however, result in the acceptance of many who would not benefit from university instruction and the rejection of many who would. It would be better to derive an index of the capacity to benefit from instruction and select those high on this index. Such an index is the IQ. This procedure is, of course, not perfect. It rejects many whose low potentiality is overcome by hard work and accepts many whose high potentiality is destroyed by emotional instability. It must be evaluated, however, not against some mystical, ideal selection procedure, but against the alternatives available. Selection by test is certainly better than selection by whim or by chance or by crystal ball.

11.12 Defining Intelligence

"Yes, Mr. Binet," the Minister of Public Instruction could reasonably have said, "you have provided a means of placing individuals along a dimension in terms of their capacity to benefit from instruction, or, as it has come to be called, intelligence. This has solved my practical problem, and I thank you. However, I am curious as to precisely what this mysterious commodity is. What exactly is intelligence?"

"Intelligence," Binet might have replied, "is that which my intelligence test measures."

"Don't put me on! Surely you're being flippant. This would mean that there was no intelligence until you came along to measure it and that there will be as many intelligences as there are measures of it."

"I am merely giving you an **operational definition.** Rather than attempting to define a vague concept in terms of other concepts, I am providing a series of precise instructions for arriving at the concept. Just as a Zen master, asked to define Nirvana, could reasonably say 'I cannot define the indefinable but will teach you the steps to attain it.' Just as a housewife, asked for a definition of haggis, could reasonably say 'I cannot define the inedible but will give you a series of instructions for obtaining it.' "

"Very well, I'm convinced. But now that I know how to obtain it, what can I do with it?"

"You can find the correlation between scores on the test and scores that serve as some criterion of success in school. The higher this correlation, the greater the **validity** of the test and the greater the improvement in your prediction of success in school from the score on the test."

"That's all very well, but what if a student happens to be having a bad day when he takes the test? A bleak day, a bad stomach, a family quarrel—any number of little things could result in a low score, and he is shunted off into a practical curriculum for those unlikely to benefit from instruction in academic subjects."

"The extent to which those day-to-day fluctuations can affect performance on the test can be determined by giving the test to a group of children one day and then to the same group some time later and finding the correlation between scores on the first and second administrations. The higher this correlation, the greater the **reliability** of the test and the greater the confidence that the score on a single administration is accurate."

"You've mentioned two correlations. One is an index of validity, and the other is an index of reliability. Since you are the world's only psychometrician, would you calculate those indices for me?"

"I'm kinda busy just now being a physiologist, a hypnotist, a lawyer, and a playwright, among other things, so let me just calculate one of them. I'll calculate validity, since a valid test must also be a reliable test. That is, if it measures what it says it measures, it must measure whatever it measures consistently. On the other hand, a reliable test need not necessarily be a valid test. Your buggy-license number divided by the distance between your eyes in millimeters would be a reliable index of your intelligence, but it would not be a valid index."

"This is useful. But it still doesn't tell me what intelligence is."

"Certainly it does. Intelligence is good performance in academic subjects in school. This is a **practical definition**."

"I like your practical definition as little as I like your operational definition. You are just shunting off the term from performance on the test to performance in school. Surely intelligence refers to a certain something within the individual rather than to the responses made by the individual. Surely it is some capacity of the individual that underlies performance in the test and in school. The validity correlation is merely a reflection of the underlying capacity the scores have in common."

"Yes, indeed," interrupts Thurstone. "It is something within the individual. It is, however, not a single capacity but a set of capacities. Binet's intelligence is simply a blanket term referring to a rough average of a number of quite distinct capacities. This is an **analytical definition**. I have stumbled on a means of finding what those capacities are."

11.2   Seven Intelligences—Thurstone

11.21   Factor Analysis

Pursuing this insight, Thurstone has constructed an intelligence test somewhat more sophisticated than Binet's. Like Binet, he began by administering a large number of items to a large number of children. However, whereas Binet used the responses to find the difficulty of the items, Thurstone used the responses to find the skills underlying the responses. He found the correlation between performance on each test item and performance on every other test item. If this correlation is high (that is, if those who did well on one item tended to do well on the other and those who did poorly on one item tended to do poorly on the other), then it is reasonable to assume that the same skill underlies performance on those two items. A close look at the content of the items would suggest what that skill is. This statistical technique of **factor analysis** ferrets out the small number of latent skills underlying the large number of manifest responses.

11.22 *Primary Mental Abilities*

Using factor analysis, Thurstone isolated a set of seven skills (**primary mental abilities**) under Binet's blanket of intelligence.[102] Whereas Binet selected items that became easier as children got older, Thurstone selected items that best tested each of the seven skills. His test consists, then, of seven sets of items, with each set composed of those items most representative of each skill.

Here is a list of the seven primary mental abilities and one illustrative item for each of them. Since these are just trial items within the test, they are easier than the actual items. But they may give you some intuitive feel for each skill and provide a personal profile with respect to this set of skills.

(1) VERBAL ABILITY

This is a test of your ability to understand what you read.
Read proverb A.

A. Sail when the wind blows.

Two and only two of the following sentences have nearly the same meaning as proverb A. Find these two sentences.

✔ Strike when the iron is hot.
___ One must howl with the wolves.
✔ Make hay while the sun shines.
___ Make not your sail too large for the ship.

The first and third statements have been checked, because they have nearly the same meaning as proverb A.

Now check the two sentences in the group below that have nearly the same meaning as proverb B.

B. Tall oaks from little acorns grow.

___ No grass grows on a beaten road.
___ Little streams from little fountains flow.
___ The exception proves the rule.
___ Great ends from little beginnings.

(2) VERBAL FLUENCY

In the blanks below, write as many different words as you can that begin with S and end with L. The words may be long or short. You may use the names of persons or places or foreign words. Errors in spelling will not be counted against you.

As examples, the first three lines have already been filled in for you. Write as many other words as you can.

1. _Sell_
2. _Saul_
3. _Spell_
4. _____
5. _____

(3) NUMERICAL ABILITY

In this test you are shown some arithmetical problems that have already been worked out. Four answers are given for each problem. One of these is always the right answer. You are asked merely to check the right answer. You may use the space on the page for figuring, but do not waste time working out the exact answer.

In the first problem below you can readily see that the first number is nearly 4 and the second number is nearly 7. Since 4×7 equals 28, look for the answer that is nearest 28. This is the third answer, and it is checked.

$$4.12395 \times 6.82187 \;=\;$$

      7.563327 _____
     14.012468 _____
     28.133051 ✔
     56.103378 _____

In the problems below use any tricks or shortcuts to find out which answer is correct, and check that answer. Do not waste time checking exact answers, because one of the given answers is the correct one.

$$\frac{53.29736}{5.01258} \;=\;$$

     6.5654 _____
   10.6327 _____
   91.7136 _____
 134.6973 _____

$$(197)^2 \;=\;$$

  11,569 _____
  23,417 _____
  38,809 _____
  62,187 _____

(4) SPATIAL ABILITIES

In this test you will be shown a series of pictures of hands. Some of these pictures represent right hands, and others represent left hands. Below each picture you will find two small squares.

If the picture represents a right hand, put a check mark in the right square; if it represents a left hand, put a check mark in the left square, as shown in the following samples, which are correctly marked.

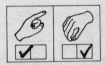

Now mark the samples below in the same way.

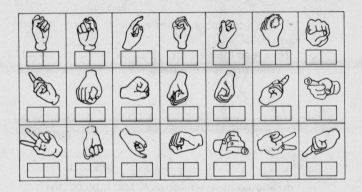

(5) PERCEPTUAL ABILITY

Here is a row of faces. One face is different from the others. The face that is different is marked.

Look closely to be sure that you see why the middle face is marked. The mouth is the part that is different.

Here is another row of faces. Look at them and mark the one that is different.

You should have marked the last face.

Here are more pictures for you to practice on. In each row mark the face that is different from the others.

(6) INDUCTIVE REASONING

Read the row of letters below.

ababab___

The next letter in this series would be *a*. Write the letter *a* in the blank at the right.

Now read the next row of letters, and decide what the next letter should be. Write that letter in the blank.

cadaeafa___

You should have written the letter *g*.

Now read the series of letters below, and fill in each blank with a letter.

cdcdcd___
aabbccdd___
abxcdxefxghx___

You should have written *c*, *e*, and *i*, respectively.

Now work the following problems for practice. Write the correct letter in each blank.

aaabbbcccdd___
axbyaxbyaxb___
abmcdmefmghm___
rsrtrurvrwrxr___
abcdabceabcfabc___

(7) MEMORY

In each row below is written a name. You are to learn the names so well that, when the last name is given, you can write the first name. On the following page the last names are listed in a different order. You will be asked to write the first names. If writing helps you to remember, you may copy the first and last names in the blanks below. Study silently until you are told to stop. Begin studying now. Do not wait for any signal.

First Name	Last Name	First Name	Last Name
Mary	Brown	_____	_____
John	Davis	_____	_____
Ruth	Preston	_____	_____
Fred	Smith	_____	_____

In the first row the correct first name has been written. Without looking at the names above, write the correct first names in the other blanks.

First Name	Last Name
Ruth	Preston
_____	Brown
_____	Smith
_____	Davis

11.3   120 Intelligences—Guilford

11.31   The Structure of Intellect

Computer programmers have an expression—GIGO (garbage in, garbage out)—to dramatize the fact that the quality of the printout of a computer is determined by the quality of the instruction they give it. This is a useful antidote to the awe in which such an instrument is held. Factor analysts could use an analogous expression—let us say, LILO (little in, little out)—to reduce the excessive awe in which this instrument has sometimes been held. The skills that emerge from factor analysis are dependent on the items that are put in. Guilford constructed a tremendous number and variety of items and, indeed, uncovered a tremendous number and variety of skills.[36] There is not just one way to be intelligent, as suggested by Binet, or seven ways, as suggested by Thurstone, but 120 ways.

Whereas Thurstone's seven skills were established empirically, Guilford's 120 skills were established empirically and rationally. In examining the skills that emerged from the factor analysis, Guilford observed that each of them could be conceptualized as involving a particular operation on a particular type of content to yield a particular product. By identifying five operations, four contents, and six products (see Figure 11-5), he was able, by analogy, to increase his empirically derived skills to $5 \times 4 \times 6$, or 120, rationally derived skills. He is currently working on test items for each of those skills.

11.32   Implications for Education

Binet's one way to be intelligent was a practical solution to a practical problem. Guilford's 120 ways to be intelligent is a theoretical statement about the structure of human intellect. It does, however, reflect back on the original practical problem. If there are 120 skills, there are 120 types of instruction. Our educational system should strive to develop all those skills. Guilford points to at least two major omissions. "Social" content and "divergent-production" operation

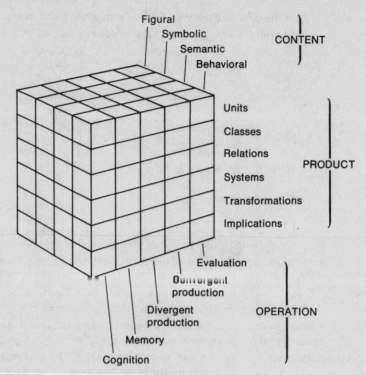

Figure 11-5. Guilford's Three Faces of Intellect. Each skill involves one of the operations performed on one of the types of content to yield one of the products and is represented by the cube where the three intersect.

are grossly neglected. We are taught to deal with our physical world much more than with our social world. The physical genius who is a social moron is a familiar stereotyped product of our overly physical education. We are taught logical thinking much more than creative thinking. We are trained to converge from a number of alternative answers to the one teacher-ordained correct answer. We are not trained to diverge from one question to a number of possible answers.

Anxiety seems to be the dominant fact—and is threatening to become the dominant cliché—of modern life. It shouts in the headlines, laughs nervously at cocktail parties, nags from advertisements, speaks suavely in the board room, whines from the stage, clatters from the Wall Street ticker, jokes with fake youthfulness on the golf course, and whispers in privacy each day before the shaving mirror and the dressing table.

Time, March 31, 1961

12 Pathological Approach

12.1 Function through Malfunction

12.11 The Client-Therapist Relationship

One approach to the understanding of the function of a system is through malfunction. You can discover how it works by observing how it sometimes does not work. This approach appears initially to be ridiculous. Why observe a malfunctioning system when you can study a functioning system? The logical answer is that a complete description of function should include a description of possible malfunctions. But the real answer is probably more psychological than logical. We tend to take functioning systems for granted and attend to them only when they are malfunctioning. We are motivated to understand them only in order to repair them. I owe the little I know about the internal-combustion engine to the tendency of the ones I have owned to break down. The mechanic, in explaining what went wrong and what expensive things he must do to right that wrong, invariably informs me of how the system should function. Malfunction can be explained only in terms of function.

The same motivation has provided considerable information about the function of the nervous system. Psychotherapists, confronted daily with clients who feel that their nervous systems are not functioning as well as they wish, are strongly motivated to understand how the nervous system should function. This therapist-client confrontation generates more motivation to understand than does the experimenter-subject confrontation, which has provided most of the information presented so far in this book. It may also, surprisingly, be more objective. The initiative in the therapist-client relationship is taken by the client, whereas the initiative in the experimenter-subject relationship is taken by the experimenter. The behavior of the client may, then, be less influenced by the biases of the therapist than the behavior of the subject will be by those of the experimenter. Despite rigorous controls to try to preserve objectivity, an experiment often tells more about the experimenter than about the subjects. The client presents his total personality—"warts and all"—to the therapist, whereas the subject presents only that limited aspect of himself dictated by the experimental design. Clients who seek out therapists are, admittedly, a biased sample of our species, but this built-in bias is being reduced by the recent humanistic trend toward applying the clinical approach to "normal" people in order to make well people better as well as "sick" people well.

12.12 Classification of Clients

12.121 Functional and Structural Disorders

Disorders of the nervous system may be either functional or structural. In structural disorders the malfunction can be attributed to organic damage to the nervous system; in functional disorders no such physical damage can be observed. This distinction may be clarified by considering the strange case of the Locomotive God.[61] An English professor in a Midwest college lamented that he had to spend his entire life in his home town because, in order to leave, he would have to cross railway tracks, of which he had an irrational fear. This fear was traced back to a day in his childhood when, in running away from his mother, he was almost hit by a train. His subsequent aberrant behavior was due to a functional disorder. Had the train not just scared him but struck him and damaged his brain, he would have had a structural disorder. Since this distinction is never applied to any other subsystem of the organism, it may be worth further consideration as a means of casting some light on the special status of the nervous system.

It has been argued that the use of the term "functional" is merely a confession of ignorance. Since there is a structure for every function, there is a corresponding malstructure for every malfunction. So-called functional disorders are simply those for which the physical damage has not yet been determined. All that need be decided is which, in a particular case, is the precipitating cause. The malfunction-malstructure relationship, like the function-structure relationship, is a chicken-egg problem. Structuralists point to the many aberrations caused by syphilis, and functionalists counter with psychosomatic diseases in which ulcers are caused by anxiety. In light of the intimate function-structure relationship, such effects are not at all surprising. Indeed, it is surprising that anyone is surprised. Although in particular cases malfunction or malstructure may be the precipitating cause, most disorders involve a complex interaction between both as malfunction causes malstructure, which causes further malfunction, which causes further malstructure, and so on.

Some people tend to think that a structural disorder is more "real" and more disturbing than a functional disorder. However, a hysteric who cannot use his hand even though there is no organic damage is just as incapacitated as a paralytic whose hand is indeed paralyzed. Indeed, a functional disorder may be even more disturbing. A doctor can tell a patient with tuberculosis precisely what is wrong, point out a dark patch on an X-ray picture, and explain exactly what must be done to cure him. A therapist cannot give the same reassurance to a client with neurosis. The client does not have neurosis in the same sense that the patient has tuberculosis. Just as he does not have experiences but is his experiences, he does not have a neurosis but is a neurotic. Since his nervous system is the physical basis of his personality, a disorder of his nervous system changes his personality. Joe with tuberculosis is still Joe, but Joe with neurosis is someone else. Furthermore, his symptoms interfere with his cure, because they disturb his relationship with his therapist. However, if the therapist can explain (or, rather, if the client can understand) the cause of the neurosis, he need not continue to explain the cure. In neurosis, unlike tuberculosis, understanding *is* the cure.

The important distinction between functional and structural disorders is not that one is more basic or more disturbing than the other but that they refer to different systems. A structural disorder is a malfunction of the nervous system, and a functional disorder is a malfunction of the organism-environment system. Since the nervous system is the only subsystem of the organism that "knows" the environment, it is the only system to which the term "functional" applies. The analogy with the internal-combustion engine might clarify this distinction. If a car skids on an icy road, it would be futile to look for some damage within the engine to explain this malfunction. It is a functional disorder. Unless the car skids into a tree, which damages the engine, this malfunction will not result in malstructure and thus further malfunction. However, unlike his car, the driver has a memory, and the event persisting in his nervous system as a memory may cause further malfunction. He may become excessively careful or nervous on icy roads and thus increase the probability of another accident, or he may refuse to drive again under any conditions. Since memory must have some structural basis, it could still be argued that a functional disorder is simply a structural disorder in which the physical damage has not yet been found. However, it is useful to distinguish between a system that is malfunctioning because it has been damaged and a system that is functioning as it should but with inappropriate content.

Another major distinction among disorders of the nervous system is based on the *severity* of the symptoms. The symptoms of the neurotic are mild, and the symptoms of the psychotic are severe. The **neurotic** is sufficiently in contact with reality to function in society, although his functioning is impaired by irrational fears, pointless worries, psychosomatic pains, and irritating mannerisms; the **psychotic** is so far out of contact with reality that he is not competent to function in society and has to be hospitalized.* These categories are not clearcut but merely reflect an arbitrary distinction along the abnormal-normal dimension. We used to talk more in terms of a dichotomy than of a dimension. There were the sane (like you and me) and the insane, who had to be locked up to protect the sane (like you and me) from them. One of Freud's great contributions was his demonstration that the most bizarre aberrations of the psychotic are simply exaggerations of symptoms evident in all of us, or, conversely, that we are all a little bit crazy. He replaced a dichotomy with a dimension, a smug minority with a sensitive majority, a little pride with much humanity, caretakers with caregivers.

Since few readers are psychotic but many are neurotic, let's glance at a few representative neuroses, which are defined by their symptoms. **Hysteria** is characterized by anesthesia, amnesia, and paralysis. It is apparently functional rather than structural, since none of these symptoms are due to organic damage. Glove anesthesia is insensitivity to touch in the area normally covered by a glove. It makes no anatomical sense, since the known distribution of sensory nerves requires that the arm also be insensitive. All the symptoms are selective. Functional blindness is the inability to see certain things, amnesia is the inability to remember certain things, and paralysis is the inability to do certain things. **Obsessive-compulsive neuroses** are characterized by—you guessed it —obsessions and compulsions. An obsession is a thought that cannot be purged, and a compulsion is an act that cannot be prevented. You get a glimpse of an obsession when you can't get a commercial jingle out of your head. You get a glimpse of a compulsion when you repeatedly check the alarm button on the clock the night before an important appointment.† **Phobic neuroses** are characterized by irrational fears. The important word is "irrational." You are not neurotic if you fear tigers when you are in their cage and they are hungry. You

*A more flippant distinction is that the neurotic builds castles in the air, whereas the psychotic lives in them. The psychiatrist collects the rent.

†You all know someone who is compulsively clean. You flick ashes into an ashtray, and it is immediately whisked away to be cleaned; you breathe and are criticized for making a film on the furniture; you get up for a glass of water and find your bed made when you get back. If you don't know someone who is compulsively clean, watch Felix Unger of *The Odd Couple*. Cleanliness may be next to godliness, but overcleanliness is close to insanity.

are neurotic if you fear kittens under the same circumstances or tigers when you are in a penthouse apartment in downtown Manhattan.

12.13 Classification of Therapists

Professionals who treat disorders of the nervous system (psychotherapists, psychiatrists, clinical psychologists, psychoanalysts, and so on), like professionals who treat disorders of the other subsystems of the organism (dermatologists, endocrinologists, gynecologists, left nostrilogists, and so on), are concerned with diagnosis and therapy. They find out what ails you and then decide what to do about what ails you. The causes and the cures of most disorders of the other subsystems are known, and the cure tends to follow the cause almost with the precision of a corollary. Scurvy is caused by a deficiency of vitamin C and is cured by a diet of vitamin C. However, the causes of the disorders of the nervous system have not yet been discovered, and, even if they were, the cures would not necessarily follow so automatically. If a neurosis is caused by a deficiency of, let us say, love, it does not follow that it is cured by a diet of love.

In the absence of known causes and concomitant cures, many causes are being hypothesized and many cures are being attempted. Thus, whereas professionals who treat disorders of the other subsystems tend to be classified in

terms of the system in which they specialize, professionals who treat disorders of the nervous system tend to be classified in terms of the cause they assume and the cure they attempt. The cause is implied in their theory, and the cure is effected by their therapy. Every theory in psychology tends to have a corresponding therapy. Indeed, since each therapist is his own unique instrument, there are, in a sense, as many therapies as there are therapists. The interaction between the theory and the therapy of the therapist is not unlike that between the theory and the hypotheses of the experimenter. The theory determines the therapy, as it does the hypotheses. When the therapy works, as when the hypothesis is confirmed, the theory is supported. The utility of the therapy is a reflection of the validity of the theory. Let me attempt simply to present the three major points of view within psychology. Humanism has been presented as a Third Force to counter the excesses of the first and second forces of Freudianism and behaviorism. Let's look at the theory of each of these forces in turn.

12.2   Freudianism

12.21   Stages of Development

Freud sees personality development as a set of stairs rather than a ramp. Your life energy, or libido, is satisfied in turn through various bodily orifices. The horizontal parts of the steps are characterized by the **erogenous zone** through which the libido is currently satisfied, and the vertical parts are characterized by the various little domestic dramas in which the energy is passed on from one orifice to the next. The oral stage, in which satisfaction is gained through the mouth, is superseded, through weaning, by the anal stage, in which satisfaction is gained through the anus. This stage is in turn superseded, through toilet training, by the phallic stage, in which satisfaction is gained through the genitals. Sexual energy has now arrived where it belongs, but not in the form it must take. The next transition, from the phallic stage to the genital stage, represents a change not in locale of the energy but in its focus. It involves a breathless domestic drama, much more complicated than the two preceding ones, followed by a breathing spell called the latency period. The drama here differs for boys and girls, whereas before the dramas were the same. Since I have never been a little girl, let me consider only the case for the little boy. The stage is set for Oedipus. Enter the heroine—the source of all goodness—the mother. Little Oedipus' sexual energy is thus directed at her. Enter the villain—the mother's lover and hence Oedipus' rival—the father. The **Oedipus complex** is this love of mother and consequent hate of father. The castration complex is a corollary fear that the father will castrate him.* To avoid the resultant anxiety, the desire for the mother is repressed. After the subsequent latency period, during which Oedipus identifies with father and decides to settle for a girl just *like* the girl who married dear old Dad, sex again rears its lovely head in the genital stage. The libido is, however, now directed toward a less frowned-upon partner, and Oedipus is concerned with Electra's satisfaction as well as his own.

I CAN'T COPE WITH ALL THESE BODILY ORIFICES!

Freud's theory of development makes sense within the framework of Darwin's theory of evolution. Nature loaded Jack and Jill with hunger and thirst so that they may survive as individuals, but she also loaded them with sex so that we may survive as a species. Since nature is more concerned with the survival of the species than with that of the individual, sex is probably an even more powerful drive than hunger or thirst. It is Dame Nature, not Sigmund Freud, who is obsessed with sex. Some would still argue against childhood sexuality on the ground that sex need not rear its lovely head until puberty, when it can perform its procreative function. However, nature does not require merely that Jack and Jill get together to procreate but that they stay together to care for the resultant child during that long period of infant dependency in our species. Nature very ingeniously uses the parents' own long period of infant dependency to build in

*This drama is going on, of course, entirely inside the head of the child. The father never says "You can't have her—she's mine" or "If you don't stop messing around with my wife, I'll cut it off." The child wishes to disarm his rival in the obvious manner and then projects this wish to the father. An eye for an eye, a tooth for a tooth.
Girls may substitute Electra complex for Oedipus complex and penis envy for castration complex and work out a similar drama for themselves.

this caring mechanism so that they will, in turn, care for their children during their period of infant dependency. Freud is more concerned with love than with sex.

If you are reluctant to accept the Freudian theory of development, your feelings may stem mainly from the fact that you don't remember having passed through those stages and that you are hesitant to ascribe sexual yearnings to the innocent 4-year-old cherubs you know. You don't remember the stages because, as the theory states, you repressed them. Resistance to the theory is evidence for it. Freudians need not, however, pull such a subtle move. They need only point out that you also don't remember your previous intellectual stages, although Piaget has demonstrated conclusively that they exist (as we will see in Section 13.33). Your resistance to infantile sexuality is caused by a superficial, sentimental view of infancy (who says infants are good?) and a narrow, distorted view of sex (who says sex is bad?). Convinced? I hope not! I'm certainly not convinced by my own argument. We cannot, however, dismiss the Freudian theory of development from our heads merely because it does not sit well in our stomachs.

In Section 3.232 we learned that, when Lorenz arranged to be the first large, moving object a gosling saw during a certain critical period, the gosling followed him rather than mother goose. Nature left a small gap in the blueprint for the development of the gosling to be filled in by the environment. However, in our species nature leaves huge gaps to be filled in during the development of each child, and there is therefore much danger of the plan going wrong. Freud documents how this long, complex process of development in our species can go wrong. He explains many aspects of adult personality in terms of failure to pass successfully through the various stages **(fixation)** or in terms of the return to a previous stage **(regression)**. Compulsive smokers and loquacious talkers are fixated at the oral stage. The oral character is very dependent, is inclined to peptic ulcers, and is an eternal optimist. The world is one great big nipple. The anal character is obstinate, stingy, and orderly. Male homosexuals are men who have repressed the desire for mother too much and whose repression is thus generalized to all women. Impotents are men who have repressed the desire for mother too little and whose anxiety associated with desire toward her is thus generalized to all women.

12.22   Ego, Id, and Superego

Even those of us who have successfully passed through Freud's stages of development are not immune from functional disorders. There is a continual battle throughout our lives between forces within us. This battle may perhaps best be presented in terms of drama. To my suggestion that Darwin provided a frame for psychology (Section 2.13), I add here a further suggestion that Freud provides a frame within that frame. He applies the Darwinian principles to the nervous system of our species. Darwin provides our theater, and Freud provides our stage. On this stage Freud introduces the three major characters of his cerebral cast: the lusty, mischievous Id, the wise, realistic Ego, and the nagging, moralistic Superego. Around these characters he writes some magnificent scripts—morality plays in which Ego triumphs over the wild Id and the fastidious Superego, tragedies in which Ego is routed by Id or imprisoned by Superego, comedies in which impish Id sneaks its wishes in disguise past the staid censor of the Superego or fools the too-literal Ego with jokes. Since these scripts contain many of the great themes in literature, perhaps Oedipus, Hamlet, Frankenstein, and Dr. Jekyll and Mr. Hyde strike responsive chords in us because they reflect dramas that occur within our own nervous systems. Freud wrote the original script. His critics within psychoanalysis merely tamper with it. For example, Adler preferred the themes of Horatio Alger and Jung those of Herman Hesse; Reich cast Id as hero, and Sullivan preferred Superego in that role. Freud's critics outside psychoanalysis either refuse to attend the play or stomp out during a scene that offends their sensitivities (although, by couching their criticisms in Freudian terms and anti-Freudian arguments, they betray the fact that they have at least read the reviews). Sober scientists, shuddering with horror at his unscientific language, fail to fully appreciate that his dramatic terminology is merely a heuristic device. Freud was a trained neurologist who knew as much about the structure of the nervous system as anyone else of his time. But who would attend—or attend to—a play about Axon and Dendrite meeting at Synapse?

Freud's theory can be translated into a language that is more prosaic but more palatable to modern tastes. Your nervous system is a subsystem of you as a person, and you as a person are, in turn, a subsystem of a social group. Within this hierarchy of systems within systems, your nervous system has three major functions: it constructs a subjective map of your environment (ego), it mediates between your environment and your other subsystems (id), and it introjects the principles of your social group (superego). The id, ego, and superego are thus the biological, psychological, and sociological aspects of you, and the stage on which they meet is your nervous system. Freud describes how the ego evolves out of the id and how the superego, in turn, evolves out of the ego. This evolution has a valuable down-to-earthing effect. Psychology is firmly anchored in biology, and sociology is, in turn, firmly anchored in psychology. The various scripts are the descriptions of the struggles of the ego to obtain and maintain an accurate subjective map of your environment despite the incessant demand of the id, which chants "I want," and the nagging sermons of the superego, which preaches "Thou shalt not." Since the ego tries to maximize truth and the id tries to maximize pleasure, they come into conflict when truth and pleasure are incompatible. Berelson and Steiner, in summarizing the scientific findings about human behavior, describe man as "a creature who adapts reality to his own ends, who transforms reality into a congenial form, who makes his own reality."[7] In the conflict between pleasure and truth, it seems that pleasure usually wins. Since the ego is concerned with laws and the superego is concerned with rules, the two come into conflict when laws and rules are incompatible. Rules are created by man to prescribe his conduct, and laws are created by man to describe his environment (see Section 16.222). Studies of conformity suggest that, in the conflict between rules and laws, rules usually win. Thus recent research tends to confirm Freud's view that any accuracy in your subjective map of the environment is a very limited, hard-earned, and precarious accomplishment. Your rationality is a mere tip of a mainly irrational iceberg.

Functional disorders of the nervous system are due to the fact that its various functions are incompatible in some situations. The potentiality for functional disorders will always remain unless we can build a world in which truth is invariably pleasant and rules are invariably rational. The more accurate your subjective map of the objective world, the more mentally healthy you are. This does not necessarily mean that, if you are mentally healthy, you lack imagination. You can take a woman and a fish from the objective world and make a mermaid in your mind, but you recognize her as your own creation. Since none of us has a perfectly accurate map, we are all, to varying degrees, mentally ill. The neurotic who distorts his subjective map to satisfy his wishes and to conform to rules is slightly ill, and the psychotic whose subjective map is only slightly linked to the objective world is very ill. The person whose ego has lost the battle with the id is mentally ill, and so also—it is becoming increasingly evident—is the "good, law-abiding citizen" whose ego has lost the battle with the superego.

12.23 Defense Mechanisms

This continuous conflict within you creates anxiety. Since anxiety is the worst of all possible states, you develop various strategies, called **defense mechanisms**, to avoid it. You may conveniently forget the thought that arouses anxiety by pushing it down into the unconscious mind. This is **repression**. Since thoughts associated with the original anxiety-arousing thought may also cause anxiety, they, too, may be repressed. Since every thought is somehow associated with every other thought, huge complexes of thoughts may be repressed, resulting possibly in multiple personalities (Section 20.22). You may remember the thought but disguise it in various ways. You can justify it as having a more noble motive **(rationalization)**; you can attribute it to others **(projection)**; you can pretend to the opposite thought **(reaction formation)**. Let's illustrate each mechanism with the thought "I hate X." (You may substitute for X anyone you like.)

Repression	"X? Who's he?"
Rationalization	"Sure, I hate X, but it's nothing personal."
Projection	"X hates me."
Reaction formation	"I love X."

All of us use such defense mechanisms.* Some of us, however, use them to excess, which leads to neuroses. The various mechanisms could be classified into two broad strategies for dealing with anxiety: blocking and dodging. Excessive use of blocking strategies leads to hysteria. Anesthesia is blocking at the

stimulus level, amnesia is blocking at the central level, and paralysis is blocking at the response level. Excessive use of dodging strategies leads to obsessive-compulsive neuroses. Obsession is dodging by thinking of something else, and compulsion is dodging by doing something else. If the anxiety is neither blocked nor dodged, the subject is hit with it. Failure of these two strategies leads to phobic neuroses. The internal anxiety is translated into an external fear.

12.3 Behaviorism

Both the advantages and the disadvantages of behavioristic theory and therapy derive from the fact that it is based on rigorous experiments with animals in the

*My favorite is rationalization. I heartily recommend it to you. It is the key to a happy life. Whenever I am tempted to go to a movie when I should really be preparing a lecture, I go. The best way to deal with temptation is to succumb to it. I go, however, with a clear conscience, because I tell myself that the movie will help me in my work: it is a psychological movie—it has people in it.

laboratory. Let's look at three such experiments and consider their implications for the causes of functional disorders of the nervous system.

12.31 Miller and His Rats

Miller put rats in a black box and gave them a shock.[72] He repeated this procedure 40 times. The rats subsequently did not like black boxes. They had come to fear black boxes, just as Albert came to fear rats (Section 4.122), through classical conditioning. In the second stage of the experiment, Miller provided a lever

that opened a door permitting the rats to escape from the black box. The rats were divided into two groups. Group 1 was shocked as soon as they were put into the black box, and group 2 was shocked a few seconds after being put into the black box. Both groups learned very quickly to press the lever to open the door to get out. The rats in group 2 were so quick that they got out before the shock was turned on. They learned, just as Thorndike's cats learned (Section 4.212), through instrumental conditioning. Although they all learned the same response, they learned different operations. Rats in group 1 learned to *escape* the shock, whereas rats in group 2 learned to *avoid* the shock. In the third stage of the experiment, the shock was disconnected. Whereas the response of pressing the lever to get out was gradually extinguished in the rats in the escape group, it was not extinguished in the rats in the avoidance group. The rats that learned to escape the shock stopped escaping when the shock was no longer there, but the rats that learned to avoid the shock continued avoiding, even though the shock was no longer there. This makes sense. The rats in the escape group knew that the shock was disconnected, but the rats in the avoidance group did not know and were not going to stay around to find out. Someone entering the laboratory during this third stage of the experiment would have considered the behavior of the rats in the avoidance group very irrational. They were working frantically to avoid a catastrophe that would never happen. However, to those who had observed the first two stages, the behavior would be perfectly rational. Someone entering the life of a neurotic during a later stage in his life experiment may consider aspects of his behavior very irrational. Could it be, as in the case of the rat, that this apparently irrational behavior is simply once-rational behavior persisting when it is no longer appropriate? An irrational fear of elevators makes sense when it is traced back to the day when the patient was stuck in one overnight between the 50th and 51st floors of the Empire State Building.

12.32   Brady and His Monkeys

A second experiment may throw some further light on the role of avoidance learning in neuroses. Brady put monkeys, two by two and side by side, into a strait-jacket-like apparatus and gave them a shock.[12] He repeated it many times, at regular intervals, with a warning signal before each shock. The shock to both monkeys could have been avoided if one of the monkeys (the executive monkey) had pulled a lever between the warning signal and the shock. The executive monkeys developed ulcers, and the nonexecutive monkeys did not. The fact that they both got shocked equally often demonstrates that ulcers are caused not by shock but by responsibility. The facts that the nonexecutive monkey had a nonfunctional lever to pull (so that it would not feel unloved and unwanted) and that the ulcers developed during rest rather than work periods demonstrate that ulcers are caused not by overwork but by overworry. Avoidance learning, then, appears to affect mental health only in cases in which it is possible, by one's own action, to avoid the pain. This rings true of man as well as monkey. We tend not to get upset about things we feel we can do nothing about. We worry more about the fact that the child for whom we are responsible does not brush after eating than about the fact that millions of children do not eat before brushing.

The interpretation of neurotic behavior in terms of avoidance learning is tantalizing but not completely satisfying. It has a ring of truth but is not the whole truth. Extrapolations from both Miller's and Brady's studies point toward a concept that may be more soul-satisfying—the concept of conflict. The fear of elevators, used as a human analogue to Miller's experiment, is not very tragic. A subject so inflicted could simply find an apartment on the ground floor, get a job selling shirts in a store basement, and lead an elevatorless and fearless life. The case is more severe, however, when the subject has learned to fear not elevators but women. A subject so inflicted could avoid women and lead a womenless and fearless life. Unfortunately, the womenless and fearless life tends also to be a miserable life. Whereas nature has not equipped him with a tendency to approach elevators, she has loaded him with a compulsion to approach women. Thus his biology pushes him toward women and his psychology pulls him away from women. He can't live without them, and he can't live with them. He is in conflict. An extrapolation of Brady's study from monkey to man also points in the same direction. Assessment studies of human subjects reveal that it is not the aggressive, independent person who develops ulcers (as Grandmother would predict) but the meek, dependent person. Perhaps the ulcers are the result of the discrepancy between his true meek nature and the false aggressive role he must play in our competitive society. He, too, is in conflict.

12.33   Masserman and His Cats

Experiments by Masserman suggest that **approach-avoidance conflict** may indeed cause neuroses.[67] He designed a Rube Goldberg apparatus such that, when a switch is pressed, a light flashes, a bell rings, and a pellet of cat food drops into a box. A cat is trained to press the switch and, over a period of months, gets used to working this way for its supper. One sad day, however, it presses the switch, the light flashes, the bell rings, the pellet of cat food drops into the box—and a blast of hot air hits the cat on the nose. The cat now has an approach tendency toward the box, since it is the source of pellets of food, and an avoidance tendency away from the box, since it is the source of blasts of air. The cat is in conflict. After a number of nasty blasts of air at irregular intervals, Masserman's cats refused to press the switch or approach the box. They became fearful of the sound of the bell and other harmless sounds and of the sight of the light and other harmless lights. They developed asthma and became sexually impotent. They paced compulsively up and down their cages and reacted to frustration with aggression. In short, they became neurotic.

Approach-avoidance conflict is only one species of conflict. The others are presented here as a service to those in search of conflict. **Avoidance-avoidance conflict** occurs when one must choose between two unpleasant alternatives. Examples range from the classic cases of choosing between the rock Scylla and the whirlpool Charybdis or the frying pan and the fire to the modern ones of choosing between abortion and a bastard or polluted water and polluted air. **Approach-approach conflict** occurs when one must choose between two pleasant alternatives. A psychologist once put a piece of sausage on either side of a dog to see if it would starve like the proverbial ass between two equally delectable bales of hay. The dog ate one piece and then the other and waited, tail wagging, for more conflict. If you are determined to have conflict, this would seem to be the type to have. It is tragic, however, in the cases in which the choosing of one pleasant alternative eliminates the other. A woman who has been proposed to by Burt Reynolds and Sean Connery (assuming her taste was for such as these) is not necessarily to be envied.

After driving his cats crazy, Masserman tried to cure them. He sent some to comfortable suburban homes for a rest cure. Many of their symptoms disappeared but unfortunately reappeared when they returned to the laboratory. He put some in a cage with a normal cat. Their symptoms tended to disappear as they watched the normal cat get food without blasts of air, but in some cases the normal cat became neurotic rather than the neurotic cat normal. He pushed some cats gradually closer and closer to the food box. The inhibitions against eating disappeared, along with many of the other symptoms, but there was a danger of panic if the process was not gradual enough. He gave some cats alcohol and drugs. Their symptoms often disappeared, but they sometimes became alcoholics and drug addicts. The obvious criticism—that what works for cats does not necessarily work for humans—is stultified somewhat by the fact that analogues of each of these techniques have been used on humans, and the same positive and negative aspects of each technique have been noted. Soldiers suffering from combat fatigue seem to recover when sent to the hospital for a rest cure, but they tend to fall apart again when returned to the front line. Delinquent kids paired with good, normal, boy-next-door kids often become good but sometimes turn the good kid into a delinquent. Children who are afraid of water may be cured if someone wades in with them gradually from the shallow end, but they will panic when thrown into the deep end. Neurotics can be cured by alcohol and drugs, but liquid or powdered happiness may become a means of temporarily avoiding anxiety.

12.4   Humanism

Since humanistic theory has developed as a reaction against Freudian and behavioristic theory, it can best be described in terms of reactions. As the diverse strands of the humanistic position become interwoven into some coherent pattern, it will become possible to describe it in positive rather than in negative terms.

12.41   Pessimism and Optimism

Freudianism and behaviorism are based on a pessimistic view of man. According to the Freudians, you are a mere battleground for the continuous conflicts between impersonal forces within you; according to the behaviorists, you are a mere switchboard for the wiring up of stimuli and responses. Humanism is based on an optimistic view of man. You are not only intrinsically good but you are intrinsically great. You have the potentiality to be fully human, just as the acorn has the potentiality to be fully an oak tree and the kitten to be fully a cat. We need not explain why there are Einsteins and Picassos but rather why we are not all Einsteins and Picassos. Because we are more complex than the acorn and the kitten, we are more likely to encounter obstacles that will prevent us from realizing our full potential. Functional disorders are simply cases of stunted growth. The pessimism of Freudianism and behaviorism spills over to man's relationship to society. You must introject the principles of society and pursue the ends of society, say the Freudians; you must adjust to society, however sick, in order to survive in it, say the behaviorists. Humanists do not see any basic conflict between the ends of the individual and the ends of society. An economic view based on scarcity may have created the impression that man is competitive, but the economic view based on plenty, which is currently evolving, will permit the basic cooperativeness of man to emerge. Our two basic problems, according to Maslow—that of the Good Person and that of the Good Society—are interrelated.[66] The creation of the Good Person aids in the creation of the Good Society, and the Good Society is that which encourages the creation of the Good Person. The Good Person embodies the values of the good, the true, and the beautiful, and the Good Society (in which doing well is doing good) reinforces those values.

12.42   Determinism and Voluntarism

Freudianism and behaviorism are based on determinism. Your behavior today is determined, according to the Freudians, by traumatic experiences in some long-gone yesterday; your behavior today is determined, according to the behaviorists, by your conditioning in all your yesterdays. One practical implication of the theoretical position of determinism is that you are not responsible for your behavior. "We're depraved 'cause we're deprived" chant the street gangsters in *West Side Story*. This may partially account for the popularity of Freudian and behavior therapists. They are modern priests absolving the parishioners who lie on their confessional couches. Humanism is based on voluntarism. The client is master, not victim, of his fate. He has made his bed, but, if he does not want to lie in it, he can unmake it and remake another. You are responsible for your functional disorders, and you will be responsible for removing them. Determinism is popular among those who don't want to take the blame for a bad life, and voluntarism is popular among those who want to take the credit for a good life. Clients tend to present themselves to therapists because they see their lives as bad and thus tend to be determinists. Humanistic therapists insist that the clients become voluntarists and accept both the blame and the credit for their own lives.

12.43   The Therapist's View and the Client's View

Freudianism and behaviorism focus on the world view of the therapist. The therapist has a theoretical structure into which the client is fitted. Freudians see him as a sick patient who has to be cured; behaviorists see him as a maladjusted case who has to be readjusted. Diagnosis is the process of fitting the client into a category, and therapy is the process of getting him back out again. Freudians and behaviorists tend to be sane-chauvinists. That is, they are prejudiced about what sane behavior is, and they judge any behavior that deviates from their standards as insane. Humanism focuses on the world view of the client. The humanist attempts to see the world as his client sees it, because he recognizes that the client's behavior can be understood only in terms of his experience. The client reacts to the world as he sees it, not to the world as it is and certainly not to the world as the therapist sees it. Behavior that appears bizarre makes sense in terms of an unusual view of the world. The client is neither sick nor maladjusted but just different. Madness is an altered (and not necessarily worse) state of consciousness.

Train up a child in the way he should go: and when he is old he will not depart from it.

Proverbs 22:6

When I was a child, I spake as a child, I understood as a child, I thought as a child: But when I became a man, I put away childish things.

I Corinthians 13:11

13 Ontogenetic Approach

13.1 The Ontogenetic Dimension

Developmental psychologists take the ontogenetic approach to the understanding of the nervous system. That is, they describe the development of organisms from birth to death. Although this chapter reflects the prevailing emphasis on the short span between infancy and adolescence in our species, keep in mind that this is only a small sample of our long life journey from womb to tomb.

The path to maturity involves a series of stages alternating with relatively abrupt transitions rather than a gradual unfolding of our potentialities. Each stage is superseded, in a predetermined order, by the next stage. We sit before we stand, we stand before we walk, and we walk before we run. The nature and order of the stages of motor development are clear, because motor development can be directly observed from behavior. The nature and order of the stages of cognitive development are not so clear, because they must be inferred from behavior. As we will see, however, Piaget has demonstrated that cognitive development follows the same orderly, step-by-step pattern as motor development.

13.2 Motor Development

13.21 California Infant Scale

Bayley constructed the **California Infant Scale of Motor Development** by observing the motor abilities of 60 children at frequent intervals from birth to 36 months of age and calculating the mean age at which the various motor skills are attained.[6] The scale consists of a list of 76 skills with the age in months at which they are, on the average, acquired (for example, sits alone, 6.2; stands up; 10.6; walks alone, 13.0).

13.211 *Raw, Deviation, and Percentile Scores*

Such catalogs of skills are the staple fare of Spock-style books, which are surveyed by anxious parents to determine whether their Johnny is keeping up with the Jones' Johnny. From this scale of means, Mrs. Smith can tell whether Johnny is ahead of, on, or behind schedule. For example, if her 15-month-old Johnny is not walking yet, she can tell that he is behind schedule. More formally, she can subtract the mean age from Johnny's age, and, noting that the result (the **deviation score)** is positive, she concludes that he is behind schedule. But how far behind schedule? By a series of statistical manipulations, this deviation score can be transformed into a **percentile score**, which indicates the percentage of children who can walk by 15 months. Let's say, then, that Johnny's **raw score** of 15 months is transformed into a deviation score of 2 months, which is in turn transformed into a percentile score of 79. Since only 79% of all children are walking by 15 months, it is not yet time to panic. However, if Johnny is still not walking at 20 months and it is determined, in the same way, that 99.7% of all children are walking by 20 months, Mrs. Smith would be advised to consider the possibility that some pathology is preventing normal development.

13.212 Longitudinal and Cross-Sectional Methods

The California Infant Scale was devised by studying the same children throughout the period of development in which the experimenters were interested. This is the **longitudinal method**. Sometimes this technique is not practical and an experimenter must resort to the **cross-sectional method** in which different children of different ages are studied in the same experimental situation. For example, a bright young man named Gardiner studied the development of deductive reasoning by administering the same test of deductive reasoning to a representative class at each grade level from 4 to 12.[26] This strategy is based on the dubious assumption that the grade-12 group is equivalent to the grade-4 group when they reach grade 12. A better strategy, since it does not require this assumption, would be to test the grade-4 group every year until they reached grade 12. Since this was his doctoral thesis, since he was already pretty old, since he wanted to finish school before starting his retirement, since the children would not promise to stay around for 8 years for the sake of science, since the children may, God forbid, have remembered something from one year to the next, since . . . well, Gardiner chose the more practical cross-sectional method over the more valid longitudinal method.

13.22 Maturation and Learning

The description of motor development involves us once again in the nature-nurture issue. Does this aspect of behavior develop as the natural unfolding of the intrinsic potentiality of the organism, or does it develop through the interaction of the organism with its environment? Is it caused by maturation or by learning? As you would expect, the answer is, as before, both. Two important concepts emerge from the complex interaction between maturation and learning.

Two identical twins, *T* and *C*, were trained in stair climbing just before the stair-climbing stage in motor development.[28] *T* was given six weeks' training, and then *C* was given two weeks' training. After the eight weeks, both were tested and both performed equally well. Thus two weeks' training at the correct time is as valuable as six weeks' training at the wrong time. What is the correct time? The correct time is the time at which the child is "ready" to climb stairs **(readiness)**. It is futile to provide training for a task until the maturation necessary for the performance of that task has taken place. Maturation is not only a necessary condition for motor development but is almost a sufficient condition. Instruction plays a relatively minor role. Hopi Indian children are strapped onto cradleboards on the first day of life and remain there almost continuously (they must, of course, be taken off once or twice a day to be cleaned) for the first three months and for progressively less and less time as they grow older. Two Hopi Indian villages have succumbed to the strange ways of the white man and now leave their children lying around loose. A study comparing the motor development of cradleboarded and noncradleboarded Hopi Indian children found no difference.[20] The children who spent most of their early months hanging around on their mother's backs and from branches of trees and who were unable to move anything but their head developed just as well as those with complete freedom of movement. Thus motor development is a matter of maturation relatively unaffected by experience. If, however, the children were left hanging around in very strong cradleboards until they were 20 years old, they would probably not develop normally. This brings us to another concept.

13.222 Critical Period

You will remember that, when Lorenz arranged for himself to be the first large, moving object young geese saw on emerging from the egg, the geese adopted him as their mother (Section 3.232). Spalding performed the same experiment, but the geese did not follow him; rather, they ran away from him.[96] This was not because he was less motherly-looking than Lorenz or because he was not large enough or did not move fast enough; it was because the geese saw him when they were four days old. There appears to be a **critical period** for imprinting, during which it must take place or will never take place. Those responsible for the schedule of instruction must gear it to the already established schedule of maturation. Instruction must not take place too early, before the organism is ready for it, or too late, after the critical period has passed.

13.3   Cognitive Development—Piaget

13.31   Jean Piaget

The Piagetian revolution is not so familiar as the Darwinian revolution or the Freudian revolution.* However, it is probably just as important. Whereas Darwin replaced the animal-human dichotomy with a continuum and Freud replaced the normal-abnormal dichotomy with a continuum, Piaget replaced the child-adult dichotomy with a continuum. Note that these three who made a revolution did so by destroying, not creating, dichotomies.

Piaget was a precocious child who, unlike many such early starters, continued to outpace his peers and his times and is still precocious today in his seventies. He published his first scientific paper at age 10, refused an important position as curator of a museum at 14, and completed his doctorate at 22. He was trained in biology and interested in epistemology (the study of the process of knowing), so for half a century he has studied developmental psychology, which he sees as the link between the apparently unrelated subjects of biology and epistemology.

This lifetime of work remained relatively unknown until recently—partly because of the difficulty of translating from Piaget French into layman French and from French into English, but mainly because the spirit of the times has taken half a century to catch up with him.[24]† Piaget has painted, in bold, broad strokes, the outline of the development of our species from infant to adult, and hundreds of disciples are now filling in the details.

13.32   The Clinical Method

13.321   Talking to Children

Piaget uses the clinical method. That is, as Freud did, he tries to understand his subjects by talking to them. Unlike Freud, however, he does not try to under-

---

*Neither is it so easy to pronounce. But perhaps this is just another way of saying that it is not so familiar. Yet I have always been impressed by the fact that most great thinkers seem to have carefully selected names that sound good with the "-ian" suffix. Check out your own name to see how *your* revolution will sound. Gardinerian? I'll never make it, although perhaps someone with a penchant for alliteration will grant me a Guess.

†Partly because of these difficulties in translation and partly because his work is spread out through so many sources (Flavell lists 25 books and more than 150 articles in his 1963 bibliography), I refer you, against my general principles, to a middleman, Flavell, rather than to the master himself.

stand his subjects as children by talking to them as adults; he has no faith in retrospective accounts of childhood by adults. It is not so much that they have forgotten how it was because it was so very long ago; it is not even the more subtle effect of selective recall, in which holes in a burlap past are patched with velvet. Rather, it is that one of the effects of qualitative changes from stage to stage is that it is no longer possible to see the world as one saw it when in a previous stage. If development is a series of steps rather than a gradual slope, the steps below cannot be seen clearly by looking back from the steps above. Perhaps we are as unaware of our previous selves as the butterfly is of his career as a caterpillar.

So Piaget talks to children to find out how children think. He doesn't, of course, ask them directly. "Hey, kid, are you developing through alternating assimilations and accommodations?" Kids don't know how they think. I doubt if you know how you think. I'm not even sure—God forbid—that I know how I think. But kids think even though they don't know how they think, just as hens lay eggs even though they don't know how they lay eggs. In a sense, children are the foremost authorities on the thinking of children, and each child is the world's foremost authority on his own thinking. In another sense, however, Piaget is a greater authority on the thinking of Petit Guy than Petit Guy is himself. Petit Guy is the expert on the laws that apply only to Petit Guy, and Piaget is the expert on the laws that apply to all children. Children are best at thinking as children, and Piaget is best at thinking about children thinking as children. Since Piaget cannot observe their thinking directly, he has to observe the correlated process of talking and make inferences about thinking. Since some children cannot talk yet he sometimes has to observe the correlated process of behaving and make inferences about thinking. Sometimes he finds it convenient to observe both talking and behaving. That is, he asks a child to do something and talk about what he is doing. By squatting down beside children and really listening to what they are saying and by carefully watching what they are doing, Piaget glimpses the surprising world of the child. The children tell him their secrets in words and show him their secrets in actions.

13.322 Scientific Limitations?

Piaget has never taken a course in psychology. It shows. Even if he were to take a course in experimental psychology today, he would probably flunk. He breaks all the hallowed rules of the hallowed halls. Let me illustrate by showing how he breaks one rule from each of the traditional sections of a research report and then giving Piaget's rationale (or rationalization?) for breaking each of these rules.

Introduction.

Piaget makes no attempt to review the relevant literature except for occasional references to his own previous work.

but

He ties his own work together beautifully and then ties this work to other disciplines. Every aspect of development, from thumb sucking in the newborn infant to problem solving in the adolescent, is included within the same coherent framework and is anchored solidly to biology on one side and to epistemology on the other. A man can afford to be an island when he is a continent.

Method.

Piaget does not specify dependent and independent variables or control extraneous variables. He seems to think that all variables should be independent (or rather interdependent) and certainly that no variable should be controlled. He conducts demonstrations rather than experiments.

but

The clinical method is more appropriate than the experimental method. In the clinical method the behavior of the child determines the procedure of the psychologist, whereas in the experimental method the procedure of the psychologist tends to determine the behavior of the child. The experiment often reveals more about the thinking of the experimenter than about the thinking of the subject.

Results.

Piaget seldom uses statistics or specifies the number of subjects in his sample or the method by which they were selected.

but

Sampling and statistical techniques are required only in studying superficial variables. No one questioned the generalization of heart transplants merely because the first patient was only one individual and a South African. Piaget is dealing with such basic cognitive processes in species *Homo sapiens* that what is true of his daughter Jacqueline can reasonably be said to be true of all children.

Conclusions.

Since he is using the clinical rather than the experimental method, Piaget can provide only mere descriptions, not explanations, of phenomena.

but

There is nothing "mere" about description. $E = MC^2$ is a

descriptive proposition. Descriptive studies of development had fallen into disrepute because, in unimaginative heads, they had produced only variations of the proposition "Kids get better as they get older." Piaget has made descriptive studies of development respectable again.

13.33 The Theory

13.331 Function, Structure, and Content

Developmental psychology was described as the link between biology and epistemology. Developmental psychology is concerned with the structure of the brain, whereas biology is concerned with its function and epistemology is concerned with its content. Let's look in turn at function, structure, and content in order to see how structure links function to content.

The function of the brain is to adapt the organism to its environment. So far, Piaget is a good Darwinian. But then he becomes more specific. Adaptation involves the complementary processes of **assimilation** and **accommodation**. The brain assimilates information from the environment and then changes in order to accommodate that information. The process of growth is like the progress of a worm as it stretches forward and then pulls itself up, stretches forward and then pulls itself up, and so on. The process of intellectual growth is much like the process of physical growth, since the latter involves the assimilation of food and the changing of the body to accommodate that food. The assimilation of information differs from the assimilation of energy, however, in that the former requires qualitative changes in the structure of the mind, whereas the latter requires only quantitative changes in the structure of the body. That is, mental growth in our species is more like the physical growth of the tadpole into the frog or the caterpillar into the butterfly than like physical growth in our species.

As the structure changes qualitatively, the child is said to move into a new stage. There are three broad stages: sensorimotor (roughly from 0 to 2 years), concrete operations (2 to 11 years), and formal operations (11 to 15 years). Of course, there are many substages within each stage, the transition from one stage to another is not abrupt, and the stages should not be tied too rigidly to ages. It is impossible to describe in a sentence the changes that take place in this sequence of stages, but here are a few attempts. The child deals directly with reality (sensorimotor stage), then with propositions about reality (concrete operations stage), and then with propositions about propositions (formal operations stage). The child becomes emancipated from the tyranny of his environment as his behavior becomes less and less determined by the stimuli impinging on him. The child escapes from the present by learning to deal with the potential as well as with the actual. The child moves from egocentricity, in which reality is defined in terms of his own actions, to objectivity, in which reality exists independently of his actions. It is these structure changes that link the function of the brain to its content. The content is the product of this process of alternating assimilations and accommodations to these evolving structures within the brain. Your "content" could be considered as your subjective map of the objective world.

This model of development may reconcile certain apparent mysteries. For example, development appears to be both continuous and discontinuous. Piaget suggests that function is continuous, whereas structure is discontinuous. Individual members of our species are both similar and different. Piaget suggests that they are similar in function and in structure (they must all use the same means to go through the same stages in the same order) but different in content (they all assimilate different information from the environment). Thus **nomothetic laws** (those that apply to all individuals) can be applied to structure, and **idiographic laws** (those that apply to a specific individual) can be applied to content. Piaget's theory can be summarized as in Figure 13-1.

Biology	Developmental Psychology	Epistemology
function	structure	content
adaptation assimilation accommodation	stage sensorimotor concrete operations formal operations	
continuity	discontinuity	
	nomothetic	idiographic

Figure 13-1. A Summary of Piaget's Theory

13.332   Stages of Development

Let's take a closer look at the three broad stages of intellectual development, the sensorimotor, concrete operations, and formal operations stages. You, who are in the third stage, perceive the world as composed of objects, which continue to exist even when you are no longer looking at them and which preserve their height, area, and volume even when they are moved from one place to another. You believe that the Statue of Liberty is still there, even though you are back in Rattlesnake Gulch, Missouri, and that it would still be 150 feet high, even if it were shipped back to France. It is difficult to see how the world could be perceived otherwise. Yet children do, and you, as a child, did. Experiments conducted by Piaget over half a century have permitted us to see the world through the eyes of a child. When he presented his daughter Jacqueline with a bottle, she made appropriate reaching movements and gurgling noises as long as she could see it, but she lost interest completely when he put it behind his back (sensorimotor stage). Out of sight, out of mind. When she began to reach for it when it was behind his back, she had attained object constancy (concrete operations stage). When he poured water from a tall thin glass to a short fat glass and asked Jacqueline if there was then more or less water, she would say "less" if she was concentrating on the vertical dimension and "more" if she was concentrating on the horizontal dimension. When she recognized that the volume was necessarily the same, she had attained conservation of volume (formal operations stage).* These principles are learned by insight rather than by trial and error (Section 5.313). Kagan has suggested that the smile is the infant's way of saying "Eureka." The stagelike nature of our development seems thus to be a reflection of the insight-like nature of our learning.

13.333 Practical Implications

Piaget has provided us, at long last, with a general theory of development on which a total practice of instruction can be based. In the dark days before Piaget there were educators—all relevance but no rigor—teaching day by day as well as they could with whatever mélange of methods they had chanced to pick up, and there were psychologists—all rigor but no relevance—performing isolated experiments and tossing off teaching tips as afterthought implications of their results. Rigor times relevance is a constant, and Piaget has increased that constant.

The major dichotomy among educators has always been between those who advocate inside-out education and those who advocate outside-in education. The inside-outers see development as the natural unfolding of the intrinsic potentialities of the organism. Extremists imply that we should just sit back in awe as we witness this wondrous process. The outside-inners see development as the handing down of the accumulated wisdom of previous generations to each new generation. Extremists imply that the organism is a passive receptacle into which information is poured. Piaget provides a precise description of the interaction between inside-out and outside-in development, which correspond roughly to accommodation and assimilation. The outside-inners are correct in

---

*These stages apply, of course, not only to Jacqueline (probably the world's most studied subject) or only to Swiss children, but to all children. If there is an infant lying around your house, try these simple experiments yourself and get a surprising glimpse into the world as the child sees it.

the sense that instructors must focus on assimilation, since they can do nothing about accommodation directly. The outside-inners are correct in the sense that accommodation is the primary process, since assimilation must be geared to accommodation. There are critical periods that are optimal for the assimilation of particular information; the same information presented too soon or too late cannot be accommodated. Now that Piaget has painted the broad picture of the inside-out unfolding of our potentialities, we can dovetail our outside-in instruction to it. Rather than attempt to maximize—that is, cram in as much as possible as soon as possible—we can aspire to optimize the outside-in information.

Inside-outers tend to emphasize intrinsic (internal) motivation, and outside-inners tend to emphasize extrinsic (external) motivation. Piaget, like all biologists, recognizes that our species, of all species, is the most intrinsically motivated. It is only the psychologists who have taken their cue from physics rather than from biology who feel the need to invent outside forces to push and pull us to get us into motion. The child manipulates and explores to get stimulation for his nervous system, just as he eats and drinks to get nourishment for his digestive system. We do not need the elaborate apparatus of extrinsic motivators in the traditional educational system. We need only capitalize on the child's intrinsic interest by laying out a smorgasbord of appropriate resources. Just as naive organisms select a balanced diet from a cafeteria of food, so will they select a balanced diet from a cafeteria of resources. Intelligence and indus-

try in the traditional educational system would be replaced by interest in a Piaget-based system.

Inside-outers tend to emphasize biological maturation, and outside-inners tend to emphasize cultural acquisition. The 3 Rs are cultural acquisitions. Furth has argued brilliantly from Piaget's theory that less emphasis should be placed on them. Communication over the visual channel (writing and reading) should be delayed until communication over the auditory channel (speaking and listening) is firmly established. The former is mainly culturally determined, whereas the latter is mainly biologically determined. Reading and writing are recent, superimposed, superficial, artificial, cultural acquisitions. By trying to teach reading and writing too soon, using extrinsic motivation, we encourage false accommodation to verbal formulas. The child accommodates to words rather than to objects, and the groundwork is laid for an adult life spent in a disembodied, detached world of words. When the child finds his auditory channel inadequate to communicate what he wants to communicate, then he will be ready to read and to write. You may have to wait until he is 9 years old before he is finally ready. But it is easier to teach a 9-year-old who is ready to learn than it is to reteach a 9-year-old who has been turned off by being taught too soon.

All progress is based upon a universal innate desire on the part of every organism to live beyond its income.

Samuel Butler
The Way of All Flesh

A mollusk is a cheap edition [of man] with a suppression of the costlier illustrations, designed for dingy circulation, for shelving in an oyster-bank or among the seaweed.

Ralph Waldo Emerson
Power and Laws of Thought

Creatures extremely low in the intellectual scale may have conception. All that is required is that they should recognize the same experience again. A polyp would be a conceptual thinker if a feeling of "Hello! thingumbob again!" ever flitted through its mind.

William James
The Principles of Psychology

14 Phylogenetic Approach

14.1   The Phylogenetic Dimension

Psychologists are often criticized for spending so much time working with animals. They tend to defend themselves in terms of practical advantages. You need not make appointments with animals, or establish rapport with them, or pay them for their services. You can cage animals, shock them, and interbreed them. There is a better answer. I study the behavior of rats because I am interested in the behavior of rats. Every phenomenon is worthy of scientific scrutiny, including the behavior of rats. Animal behavior is worth studying to gain an understanding of animal behavior. There is an even better answer. I study the behavior of rats because I am interested in the behavior of humans. Since rat and man both developed according to the same principles, as expounded in the theory of evolution, some insight into man can be gained by the study of the rat. Just as we get some insight into an organism by tracing the development of that organism (ontogenetic approach), we can get some insight into a species by tracing the development of that species (phylogenetic approach).

The first nine months of ontogenetic development was once considered as a high-speed rerun of phylogenetic development. Ontogeny recapitulates phylogeny. Embryologists and paleontologists worked for half a century within this hypothesis, but the case for the **theory of recapitulation** was finally dismissed for lack of evidence.

There may, however, be certain formal similarities between ontogenetic and phylogenetic development. Both processes are characterized by continuous discontinuity, as Piaget demonstrated for ontogenetic development and Darwin demonstrated for phylogenetic development. Ontogenetic development is continuous with respect to function (alternating assimilations and accommodations take place as the growing person adapts to his environment) but is discontinuous with respect to structure (qualitatively different structures emerge in order to accommodate what is assimilated). Phylogenetic development is continuous with respect to function (organisms evolve through adaptation to the environment) but is discontinuous with respect to structure (different organisms evolve to fit different environments). Piaget had to convince us of the discontinuity, since he had to fight the prejudice that a child is a miniature adult; Darwin had to convince us of the continuity, since he had to fight the prejudice that man is unique.

14.2 Evolution of Individual Behavior

14.21 Evolution of Structure

Since behavior is the output of the nervous system, it is determined by the structure of the nervous system. If you are equipped with the nervous system of a caterpillar, then you are condemned to behave like a caterpillar. You will never write sonnets. Fortunately, you will never aspire to writing sonnets. Both the capacity and the aspiration are beyond the scope of your limited nervous system. Innovations in the structure of the nervous system permit corresponding innovations in behavior. Let's glance at the structure of the nervous system at selected points on the phylogenetic scale and consider the corresponding function that such structure permits.

14.211 Amoeba—Irritability

The simplest form of life, the amoeba, consists of only one cell. There is not much you can do with your life if you are only one cell, and frankly (fortunately, amoebae can't read), the amoeba leads a very dull life. However, it exhibits the characteristic property of living as opposed to nonliving systems: it is irritable. This does not mean that it is hard to get along with (I haven't met a bad-tempered one yet) but rather that it responds to stimuli. The tendency to move toward or away from a particular stimulus is called a **tropism**. Such tropisms are normally adaptive, but, with changes in the environment, they may become maladaptive. The positive phototropism (tendency to move toward light) of the moth is adaptive, since light is good for moths. When man introduced light produced by an open flame into the environment of the moth, this mechanism, which had been designed for its survival, resulted in its death. The direction and

I SHALL NOW DO MY 8,930,620th IMPRESSION OF A FRIED EGG!

BORED AMOEBAS

the strength of the response are completely determined by the stimulus. The organism is wholly at the mercy of its environment.

14.212 Worm—Encephalization

As we make a huge leap up the phylogenetic scale from the amoeba to the worm, we find that a number of innovations have resulted in a vastly more complicated nervous system. The single cell of the amoeba is responsible for the reception of all stimuli and the production of all responses. As the number of cells increases, specialization begins. Some cells become responsible for the reception of stimuli and some for the production of responses. Within the former, some cells become responsible for the reception of light and some for the reception of sound. This process of progressive specialization is called **differentiation**. With differentiation comes **centralization**. Cells with the same function tend to clump together. Cells that work together stay together. With centralization comes **encephalization**. Cells responsible for the reception of stimuli gravitate toward the head end of the organism. This makes sense, since it is the head end that first comes into contact with the stimulation as the organism moves. With the improvement in neural design comes an improvement in behavioral capacity. The worm can learn, as we discovered in Section 3.12. Since learning involves the linking of a stimulus to a response, the input neurons of the nervous system must be potentially linkable to more than one output neuron. This linking is possible in the nervous system of the worm but not in that of the amoeba. Although the worm is free to make response *A* or response *B*, it is still at the mercy of the environment, since its nervous system consists of direct links between sensory and motor neurons.

It is only with the development of association neurons, which mediate between sensory and motor neurons, that the organism escapes the tyranny of the environment. It can then choose not only whether to make response *A* or response *B* but whether to respond or not to respond. Thus it is no coincidence that, in the octopus, we find the beginning of association cells and also the beginning of the capacity not to respond. The spontaneous response of the octopus to the stimulus "crab" is the response "grab."* Young has been able to teach octopuses to inhibit this response for a few seconds.[113] The spontaneous response of the octopus on seeing a crab is to go straight to it. Young put a glass screen between the octopus and the crab and found that the octopus was capable of

learning to go around the screen to get at the crab. This detour behavior is very significant. In turning away from the crab, the behavior of the octopus is directed not by the stimulus of the crab but by an image of the crab. We see here the beginning of mental life. The octopus can make a sketchy subjective map of the objective world and operate within the map as well as within the world. This emancipation from the environment is possible only if there is a part of the nervous system (neither sensory nor motor) in which images can be stored. The capacity not to respond, or, more accurately, to delay responding, is a sophisticated accomplishment of living systems. The length of delay possible is a useful index of phylogenetic development.

*Or, more accurately, grab, grab, grab, grab, grab, grab, grab, grab.

In our final leap from octopus to man, it is not clear precisely what the innovations are; there appears superficially to be simply an extension of the improvements already noted. The number of cells has increased, and, with this, specialization, centralization, and encephalization have been extended. The ratio of association to sensorimotor cells has increased, permitting an increase in the length of the delayed response and the complexity of the subjective map of the objective world. Compared with the octopus, then, we are sensitive to a wider range of stimuli, we have a larger repertoire of responses, and we have a greater capacity to inhibit those responses.

Some theorists have argued that there is no qualitative change in structure but, at a certain level of complexity, there is a qualitative change in function. Consciousness emerges. Sperry refers to the association areas as the "uncommitted cortex" because they are not linked to either sensory or motor functions, and Koestler refers to consciousness as the "unsolicited gift." The uncommitted cortex yields the unsolicited gift. We could perhaps argue that the octopus is conscious, since he has an image of a crab. We would certainly be willing to attribute consciousness to our sleeping dog as he tosses and growls, apparently in the throes of a doggish dream. Unfortunately, there is no way to interview animals to discover the exact point on the evolutionary scale at which this phenomenon emerges.* Neither is there any way to determine when "self" becomes an element within the subjective map, so that consciousness evolves into self-consciousness, or any way to determine at what level of self-consciousness an organism aspires to self-understanding. Maybe it is this search for self-understanding (in which we are engaged in this book) that distinguishes us from our furrier friends farther down the phylogenetic scale.

Adler argues that there is indeed an innovation peculiar to the nervous system of our species—an innovation that permits the means, if not yet the end, of self-understanding.[1] It enables us to bundle a set of percepts of individual crabs into a general concept of crab. We thus have a conceptual, as well as a perceptual, map of the objective world. This conceptual map is a much more efficient storage and retrieval system than the perceptual map. A word is worth a thousand pictures. It is easier to retrieve a concept from thousands of concepts than a percept from millions of percepts. We needn't rummage through the millions of mind pictures our eyes have taken in our lifetime to find the one we

*By wandering about Dublin Zoo looking into the eyes of animals, I once got a feeling for emerging consciousness as one ascends the phylogenetic scale. I had no feeling of empathy with the crocodile; I felt a glimmer with the lion; but I experienced such a feeling of fellowship with an orangutan called Adam that I found myself asking his permission to take his photograph. No wonder our feeling of uneasiness in zoos is strongest around the monkey house!

want. Also, we can label those concepts and trade labels with other people so that each of us is not limited to that small repertoire of concepts it is possible to build directly out of percepts in our short lifetimes. We can use the recently acquired trick of recording those labels so that our accumulation of concepts can survive us and enable our children to stand on our shoulders and thus see farther than we can. By means of this accumulated knowledge of the world, we have changed the world. Our environment created us, but now we create our environment. We have escaped the tyranny of our environment. We are finally free.

14.22 Evolution of Function

We have seen that the evolving complexity of the nervous system permits a concomitant versatility of behavior. The nervous system so evolved, according to the theory of evolution, because the resultant behavior contributed to the survival of the species. Let's look at some examples of animal behavior to see how they contribute to survival.

14.221   Instinct

If a model of the head of a bird with a red dot on the beak is shown to baby herring gulls, they will open their mouths. If a model of a gaping open mouth is shown to adult herring gulls, they will drop worms into it.* A baby herring gull that has the response of opening the mouth wired to the stimulus of a head with a red dot on the beak will therefore eat and survive and procreate other baby herring gulls with this behavior built in.

Many species besides man have to go through some courtship procedure before mating. The male has to perform some elaborate ritual before he can get on with it. The peacock makes a pompous display of his feathers to the peahen; the male bowerbird constructs an intricate pattern of leaves and flowers for the female to inspect; the male in some species of insects performs a dance in front of the female. An inadequate male will not be able to perform this ritual satisfactorily and will be rejected as a suitor by the female. Thus his defective genes will not be transmitted to the next generation. How could such a complex behavior pattern evolve? Perhaps the sex drive produces a state of restlessness that compels the organism to go through its repertoire of behaviors. Those males who performed the more pleasing responses out of the entire repertoire of possible responses were selected by the females. This process, repeated generation after generation, gradually shaped the appropriate courtship behavior.

*Moral: Keep your mouth shut when you are around herring gulls.

Such behaviors acquired over the lifetime of a species are, however, stereotyped. Once created, they cannot be destroyed, even though they are no longer functional. A certain type of wasp drags its prey to the mouth of its nest, goes inside to check if everything is okay, comes out, and drags the prey inside. A waspologist amused himself by moving the prey away from the door every time the wasp went inside. Time after time the wasp would drag its prey to the door and then go inside to check if everything was okay, even though it had just checked a moment before. Behaviors acquired over the lifetime of a single organism may be more adaptive to changing circumstances. Let's say an animal is thirsty. The state of thirst makes it restless. It goes through its repertoire of behaviors. One response, going to the waterhole, leads to a satisfying state of affairs. Thereby the probability that this response will be repeated is increased. Thus Thorndike's trial-and-error learning contributes to the survival of that organism. If the waterhole dries up, the response will no longer be followed by a satisfying state of affairs, and the probability of the response will decrease. Thus extinction as well as conditioning contributes to the survival of the organism.

14.223 Learning to Learn

In Section 5.313 we considered Köhler's studies of insightful learning. Birch replicated Köhler's studies using apes that he had raised in cages, and he found they could not perform the tasks.[9] He argued that the insight learning of Köhler's apes depended on previous learning. Köhler's apes had been raised in the jungle, where they had a great deal of experience with sticks. Harlow performed an experiment to test formally the role of such early experience in later problem solving.[38] He taught a monkey to discriminate between two objects—say, a cup and a bottle. The objects are mounted on blocks, and the blocks are placed over two holes. A raisin is placed consistently in the hole below the cup. A barrier is raised. The monkey pushes aside one object and gets a raisin if he chooses correctly and nothing if he chooses incorrectly. Harlow counted the number of trials until the monkey reached a certain criterion, such as six correct choices in a row. The monkey was then taught to discriminate between two other objects—say, a toy truck and an ashtray. Continuing with a number of unrelated discriminations, Harlow found that the monkey took progressively fewer and fewer trials to reach the criterion, until finally it learned in only one trial. That is, it would look under object *A* in trial 1 and, if it found a raisin, would continue to choose object *A* every time; if it did not find a raisin, it switched to object *B* in trial 2 and continued to choose object *B* every time. The monkey had changed, then, from a trial-and-error learner for the first discrimination into an insightful learner for the last discrimination. It had learned to learn. Thus Harlow suggests that trial and error and insight are two different phases of one continuous process rather than two different types of learning. The reason, then, why insightful learning increases at the expense of trial-and-error learning as one ascends the phylogenetic scale is that there is an increasing capacity to learn to learn.

This finding suggests a means of comparing intelligence from species to species. Is a giraffe smarter than an ape? Such questions are notoriously difficult to test. If we used Köhler's test with the bananas suspended overhead, the test would not be fair to the giraffe if they were out of its reach, because it is not physically capable of grasping a stick; similarly, the test would not be fair to the ape if the bananas were within the giraffe's reach, because the giraffe could get them merely because it had long legs and a long neck. Even if the giraffe *could* reach the banana, it wouldn't because giraffes don't like bananas. What do we pay giraffes to work for us? Leaves from banana trees? How many leaves from a banana tree are as much of an incentive to a giraffe as one banana is to an ape? Such single tasks are of little value in establishing a phylogenetic intelligence test. A psychologist once sheepishly admitted that he got lost while cleaning out a covered maze he had built to test sheep and took longer to find his way to the goal box than his stupidest sheep. We do no better than our friends farther down the scale when we are confronted with such a mechanical task. Where we do gain on them, however, is in our ability to benefit from experience. On the second trial in his maze, the psychologist would do better than his sheep. If an experiment were conducted in which fish, cats, dogs, and monkeys were taught in mazes appropriately adjusted for their size and means of locomotion, they would all perform equally well at first, but, on subsequent trials, the higher animals would do progressively better (see Figure 14-1). The fish in this situation cannot benefit at all from experience; the monkey can get ahead by working hard during the day and going to school in the evening.

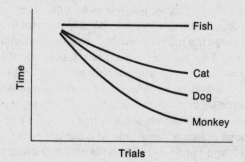

Figure 14-1. *Learning to Learn*

Vygotsky, a brilliant Russian psychologist, suggested that intelligence is the ability to benefit from experience and that intelligence tests should be designed with this idea in mind.

14.3   Evolution of Social Behavior

14.31   Beginning of Social Behavior

14.311   Amoeba—Tropism

If a group of amoebae is scattered randomly on a surface, strongly lit except for one patch of shadow, they will soon all be huddled together under the shadow. This looks superficially like the beginning of social behavior. They huddle together, however, not because they love one another but because they share a negative phototropism. We have to go farther up the phylogenetic scale to find behavior that can be considered truly social.

14.312   Ant—Collectivism

Ant colonies have many things in common with human societies. There is aggression against members of outgroups. Ants visiting by accident from neighboring colonies are attacked and killed. There is a division of labor. Worker ants build the anthill, sentinel ants defend it, and stud ants populate it. The society is based, however, on instincts built into each ant rather than on contracts between the ants. The antisocial behavior of attacking strangers is based purely on smell. A local ant rolled in the juice of squashed foreign ants is killed, and a foreign ant rolled in the juice of squashed local ants is welcomed with open antennae. The role of a particular ant in the colony is completely determined by its genes. A worker ant can never aspire to be a stud ant. There can be no class struggle in an anthill. Thus we have not yet found the beginning of truly social behavior.

14.313   Chimpanzee—Cooperation

A colony of chimpanzees has much more in common with a group of humans. When one chimp leaves the colony, it is lonely and depressed; when it returns, it is recognized and welcomed back. Chimps cooperate by working together to pull a box of bananas into the cage when one cannot pull it in alone. They also groom one another. There is a hierarchy of dominance in which each chimp is submissive to those above and dominant over those below. However, when a female is in heat, some males may permit her to step temporarily over them in the hierarchy in return for her favors. (Prostitution may indeed be the world's oldest profession.) Certainly here at the level of the chimpanzee we see true social behavior. Indeed, Yerkes has gone as far as to say "One chimpanzee is no chimpanzee." Morris has suggested that the shape of the ape, which leaves one awkward part of the back unscratchable and results in the need for an I'll-scratch-your-back-if-you'll-scratch-mine contract, heralds the dawn of social behavior.

14.314   Man—Culture

Whereas we recognize the essential continuity from other animals to man, we also sense some qualitative differences which appear to involve social behavior. How does the social behavior of man differ from that of the chimpanzee? The following experiment may provide a clue. A couple raised an ape named Gua with their son, Donald.[52] They treated both as alike as they possibly could in order to see how human an ape can become when reared in a human environment. Gua, not surprisingly, developed much more quickly in motor skills. He climbed curtains before Donald had even struggled to his feet. Gua, somewhat surprisingly, also developed more quickly in intellectual skills, but, at a certain point, Donald overtook him and raced ahead. That certain point was the point at which Donald had learned to speak. Gua never quite got the knack of it. It is this capacity to speak that will permit Donald to pass on what he learns in his lifetime to his children. Thus acquired characteristics can be passed on—not through the genes, as Lamarck suggested, but through communication. Since Donald Jr. can thus benefit from the accumulated experience of all past generations, he is not limited to what he can acquire through direct experience in his own short lifetime. The knowledge piled up by man in this fashion has enabled him to transform his environment. Some evolutionary theorists argue that the further evolution of man is no longer determined by the principles expounded in the theory of evolution. Mother Nature, like all good mothers, has planned her own obsolescence. Man is no longer adapting to the environment but is adapting the environment to himself. The destiny of man is now in his own hands.

14.32   Beginning of Antisocial Behavior—Lorenz

Let's look at one argument suggesting that man's own hands is a rather precarious perch for his destiny. Millions of words have been said and millions of notes have been sung about the problem of war and the prospect of peace. The grim picture of man, atom bomb in hand and aggression in heart (or, more accurately, in hypothalamus), devising his own destruction, is constantly before us—so constantly, indeed, that we are tiring of the same hoary platitudes about the cause of war and the same whimsical slogans for an end to war. We are becoming dangerously insensitive to talk of missile gaps and credibility gaps, of confrontation and escalation, of underagent and overkill. It is refreshing, then, to see something new. It is even more refreshing to see something not only new but probably also true. Lorenz' book *On Aggression* is based on a lifetime of reason and research rather than on a moment of emotion and prejudice.[63] As in the case of individual pathology, he considers first diagnosis and then therapy in this most severe of social pathologies.

14.321   Diagnosis—Function and Malfunction

It is well known that Freud explained human behavior in terms of sex. It is not so well known that, after his experiences in World War I, he added aggression as a basic human motive. Sex was the expression of the life instinct, and aggression was the expression of the death instinct. These two motives war for control of the organism until eventually aggression wins. The aim of life is death. Lorenz argues that this Freudian slogan is contrary to all that is known of living systems. Like all good Darwinians, he believes that the aim of life is not death but more life. He prefers to consider aggression not as an antisurvival mechanism but a survival mechanism that has somehow gone wrong. He sees it as analogous to the positive phototropism of the moth, which is designed to nurture its life but, because of environmental changes, leads to its death.

We are concerned here with intraspecies aggression rather than with interspecies aggression, with fighting between cobra and cobra rather than between cobra and mongoose. It is intraspecies aggression that threatens the extinction of a species. When dingoes were introduced into Australia, they eliminated not their prey, the rabbits, but their rivals for the prey, the marsupials. More predators reduce the prey, which reduces the predators, which increases the prey, which increases the predators, and so on throughout this cycle to maintain a seesaw balance.

The most obvious function of aggression is to ensure that the strongest males of the species win the females and thus pass on their strength to the next generation. Two bucks in a herd of deer will fight, and the winner trots off with the doe to get on with the business of propagating the species, while the loser skulks off to sulk and worry about his mortality. Thus the species gets progressively stronger in exactly the same way that the necks of the giraffes got progressively longer (Section 2.12). A less obvious function of aggression is to ensure the equal distribution of a species over the available territory. The survival value of this function is obvious when we consider that it is better for plumbers to be spread out over the country than concentrated in one city. If the means of sustinence of a species is such that the individuals are more likely to survive if they spread out, one member will stake out a territory for himself and defend it from the other members.* Note that he does not defend it against members of other species, just as the plumber does not mind if a butcher moves in next door.

The function of intraspecies aggression is not to kill the rival but to humiliate him. A survival mechanism that results in death is not very efficient. In the case of species with the capacity to kill, it is necessary to build in an inhibitory mechanism to prevent killing. Thus a wolf getting the worst of a fight can throw in the towel by presenting its vulnerable jugular vein to its rival, who will stop fighting and permit the loser to slink away. In the case of species without the capacity to kill, no such mechanism is needed. Thus a dove, which does not normally have the capacity to kill another dove, will peck one to death when it is caught in a trap. Man is in this respect more dove than wolf. One man is seldom able to kill another man with his bare hands. However, man has developed weapons that give him an unplanned-by-nature capacity to kill. He is a dove who has suddenly grown the teeth of a wolf. Nature could not anticipate such a

*A weak defender can almost invariably defeat a strong trespasser. The extra strength gained from fighting on home territory is seldom taken into account by those who precipitate and analyze *our* intraspecies fighting. "But," said a young American friend about to be drafted, "they're fighting in their home jungle, and I was brought up in Manhattan!"

development and has not provided the necessary inhibitory mechanism. Cultural evolution has outrun natural evolution. Weapons not only provide a means of aggression but increase the amount of aggression. They render man relatively safe from his natural enemies among other species and thus channel his aggression more and more against other members of his own species. The resultant fighting among neighboring tribes creates a respect for the aggressive members, who are thus more likely to procreate and pass on their aggressiveness to the next generation. We are the unfortunate inheritors of millions of years of accumulated aggression.

14.322   Therapy—Individual and Social

What can we do about it? Lorenz has a number of suggestions. Man must become more humble. Darwin told him that he was an animal like all animals. Man has recovered from this blow to his ego but has consoled himself with the notion that he is that perfect animal toward which nature has been aspiring for billions of years. Lorenz takes away even this solace to man's wounded pride by telling him that he is "... the long-sought missing link between animals and really humane beings." Man must swallow this pill too.* He must recognize himself as a part of nature and not apart from nature. In this way he will recognize his aggressive instincts and thus take the first step toward controlling them.

For the second step of devising an effective means of control, Lorenz has two suggestions. Our aggression can be channeled toward constructive ends, or it can be curbed by ritual. International sports contests, like the Olympic Games and the Space Race, may be serving as constructive alternatives to war. Another alternative might entail the placing of a scapegoat in every home—perhaps one like Al Capp's kigmy, which loved to be kicked. Another possible outlet is sex. Gorer[33] has observed that the two broad characteristics that distinguish tribes with no record of aggression are a lack of a clear-cut distinction between the sexes and a healthy and hearty sex life. He suggests that perhaps the mod generation, with its long-haired, flamboyantly dressed men and its short-haired, pant-suited women and its admonition to make love, not war, has stumbled unconsciously on a solution. The battle of the sexes replaces the war of the nations.

Natural means of attack have been countered by natural means of defense. The lethal teeth of the wolf have been thwarted by the inhibition against using

*The bitter pill is made more palatable by humor. Man takes himself too seriously but does not take humor seriously enough. It is a valuable device for letting the air out of inflated egos. Mark Twain said "Man is the only animal which blushes. Or needs to." Konrad Lorenz suggested that man is the only animal which laughs. Or needs to.

them to kill. Cultural means of attack must likewise be countered by cultural means of defense. The lethal guns of man must be thwarted by a prohibition against using them to kill.* One species of fish that does not attack the vulnerable flank of defeated opponents has thus earned the name of the heavyweight champ Jack Dempsey, who refused to take advantage of opponents helpless on the ropes. Jack Dempsey the fish was prevented by built-in inhibitions, but Jack Dempsey the man refrained because of learned prohibitions.

*There is such a prohibition, but, unfortunately, it applies only to our *immediate* neighbors.

We are not hypocrites in our sleep.

William Hazlitt
On Dreams

The conscious mind allows itself to be trained like a parrot but the unconscious does not—which is why St. Augustine thanked God for not making him responsible for his dreams.

Carl Gustav Jung
Psychology and Alchemy

Dreaming is better than parties.

Tiny Tim
Beautiful Thoughts

15

Approach through Altered States

15.1 Altered States of Consciousness

Psychology lost consciousness in the 1920s and did not come to until the 1950s. It lost consciousness because behaviorists had argued convincingly that there was no means of making private experience public, and thus consciousness was inaccessible to scientific scrutiny. It came to because objective indices of subjective states were discovered, and thus consciousness came within the range of the scientific searchlight.

Now that consciousness is a respectable topic, psychologists have another approach to add to their arsenal: they can gain understanding of "normal" consciousness, paradoxically, by altering it. For instance, sensory-deprivation experiments, by dramatically altering the consciousness of the subjects, have suggested the need for some minimal level of stimulation for the normal functioning of the nervous system.

Taboo topics have toppled as psychologists have explored techniques for altering states of consciousness. Subjects have attained altered states by chanting mantras and gazing at mandalas, by exposing themselves to enriched and impoverished environments, by meditating and by being hypnotized, by taking drugs and by not taking food, by having electrodes implanted in their brains and by watching feedback from their brains, by going to sleep and by staying awake too long. The study of consciousness has become not only respectable but fashionable. One symptom of the tremendous current interest in changing one's mind is the recent formation of the Association for the Psychophysiological Study of Sleep and the Biofeedback Research Society. The sleep watchers and the biofeedbackers and the as-yet-unorganized meditators and sensory-deprivers and drug peddlers and other mind-changing agents have provided us with more solid information about consciousness in the last two decades than we had accumulated in the previous two million years. They have produced a revolution in our thought about thought. One result of this revolution is a subtle shift from traditional spatial metaphors of mind to temporal metaphors. That is, we tend to talk now of states of consciousness rather than of levels of consciousness. The relative accessibility of different contents of consciousness changes as we move from state to state through time. Freud's image of mind as an iceberg with most of consciousness under the surface is being replaced by the image of mind as a ball bobbing about on the surface of the water exposing different parts at different times. Another result is the less critical tone used to refer to altered states. We no longer tend to talk glibly of any state other than "normal" as "abnormal" or "subnormal," and (as I noticed while typing this) we tend to put "normal" in embarrassed quotation marks. Another result is that we are beginning to recognize many other states of consciousness besides those of being alive or dead or, on a shorter time scale, awake or asleep.

Perhaps the various altered states of consciousness have much in common and, in some cases, may be identical. It will be fascinating to follow the more and more precise descriptions of these presently vague states and the relationships between them. In the meantime, by way of illustration, let's look at one strategy for altering our consciousness and the associated state. This is a strategy we all employ at least once a day (and, while in school, often several times a day): the simple strategy of falling asleep.

15.2   The D-State, for Instance

Most of us get a tantalizing glimpse of ourselves in an altered state of consciousness when we wake up and catch the tail end of a dream. The state in which dreams occur (let us call it the D-state) had been somewhat neglected by psychologists until relatively recently. This was partly due to the fact that there were no objective indices of this subjective state. Other factors contributing to the neglect are obvious. First, experimenters tend to work from 9:00 to 5:00, and subjects tend to sleep from 12:00 to 8:00. Psychologists understandably focus first on that subset of "what is" entitled "what is convenient." Second, psychology was considered the study of behavior, and man asleep seems extremely limited in behavior. However, as psychologists have, recently and reluctantly, expanded their focus from a 16-hour to a 24-hour day, they have found that man asleep can cast some unexpected light on man awake.

15.21   Research on Dreaming

15.211   Observational Study

The time is 1895, and the place is Vienna. More precisely, the time is 3:00 P.M. on Wednesday, July 24, 1895, and the place is the northeast corner of the terrace of the Bellevue Restaurant in Vienna. A young man sits there engrossed in thought. You may perhaps not recognize him immediately, for his hair has not yet become grayed and his frame has not yet become stooped by a troubled and tempestuous life. As you come closer, however, you recognize the unmistakable dark, penetrating eyes of Sigmund Freud. The exact time and place are emphasized because this is one of the few cases in the history of science in which the birth of an idea can be so pinpointed. Freud took his biographer, Ernest Jones, to this spot, and they chuckled over the possibility of erecting a marble tablet proclaiming "Here the secret of dreams was revealed to Doctor Sigmund Freud on July 24, 1895." What is that secret? The function of a dream is the fulfillment of a wish. Although we know the exact point in time and space when this idea first kindled in a human mind, we cannot trace upstream the flow of thoughts that led to it. We can guess, however, at some of the elements from which this insight emerged. We know that Freud had just developed at that time his method of free association (in which the patient is encouraged to say everything that enters his mind) and had often observed that his neurotic patients interspersed accounts of their dreams in their rambling monologues while lying on the now-familiar couch. We know that Freud had previously worked with psychotics and had observed a strong element of wish fulfillment in their hallucinations. We know that Freud was at that time conducting the world's first self-analysis and had observed a tendency to wish fulfillment in his own dreams. We know, in summary, that the insight was based on observation of the spontaneous responses of people in their everyday lives.

Freud subsequently elaborated this germ of an idea and incorporated it into his theory of personality. We have already considered the process of repression (Section 12.211), whereby the wishes of the id, which are unacceptable to the superego, are pushed down into the unconscious. When one is asleep, however, the superego is off guard, and such wishes of the id can be expressed. Yet they cannot be expressed blatantly, because the superego has posted a censor between the conscious and the unconscious mind. Thus these wishes are expressed in symbolic form to fool the censor. We satisfy our Oedipal yearnings neither by performing the dastardly deed nor even by dreaming of it, but by dreaming of shooting a cow or driving into a tunnel. Dream interpretation, then, involves tearing away the mask of this manifest content to reveal the true latent content beneath.

Freud's methods and theories have, with some justification, been criticized as lacking scientific rigor. Yet, in his work on dreams, we catch a first glimpse of man looking at this phenomenon with the scientific spirit. We see an observer looking the facts straight in the eye and letting them fall as they may, regardless of whether they present a flattering picture of man. Freud's theory is certainly a great advance over such ideas as: dreams are the actual experiences of the soul as it wanders around while the body is asleep, or dreams are visitations from the gods, or dreams are premonitions of the future, or dreams are the result of eating salami sandwiches late in the evening.

15.212 Experimental Study

Freud's observations and all other observations on dreaming were based not on dreaming directly but on what dreamers say they dream. Hall, a major researcher in this area, maintained that this situation is inevitable. However, Aserinsky, a graduate student who was precocious in the art of finding something while looking for something else, discovered, while observing the sleep patterns of infants, that rapid eye movements (REMs) accompany dreaming. Such an objective correlate of a subjective process provides a means of circumventing Hall's problem. You can tell from out here what is going on in there. You can at least tell whether the subject is dreaming, even if you can't tell what he is dreaming about. Kleitman, who has conducted a series of studies using this index, points out, however, that you can study the process of dreaming without knowing what is being dreamed about, just as you can study the process of thinking without knowing what is being thought about. A T.V. repairman needn't know anything about the content of T.V. programs.

One of the experiments reported by Kleitman suggests that Freud's train of thought was on the right track.[55] A group of subjects invited to sleep in a laboratory were awakened on several successive nights every time REMs began (that is, presumably, every time they started to dream). During the next few nights, when they were permitted to rest in peace, they dreamed significantly more than they had before they had been deprived of dreaming. When you are deprived of eating, you subsequently eat more; when you are deprived of dreaming, you subsequently dream more. You have a need to eat; you have a need to dream. Whether this need is to have unconscious wishes fulfilled, as Freud suggested, we do not know. Some supplementary subjective observations by Kleitman point in this direction. His dream-deprived subjects were irritable and anxious, which suggests that dreaming assists in maintaining mental stability.* Charles Fisher, a psychiatrist at Mount Sinai Hospital in New York City, has suggested: "The dream is the normal psychosis, and dreaming permits each and every one of us to be quietly and safely insane every night of our lives."

15.213 Assessment Study

Freud's theories have been criticized on the ground that his sample was not representative. He observed mainly neurotic, middle-class Viennese women. What is true of neurotic, middle-class Viennese women is not necessarily true of all people. The function of the dream may be the fulfillment of a wish in the repressed society Freud happened to study, but it may not necessarily hold true in a South Seas island society that is less hung up on sex. Kleitman's experiments have been criticized on the ground that he studied only the form of dreaming, without the content. His objective measure can tell only whether or not the subject is dreaming; it tells nothing of what the subject is dreaming about. The rich, varied content of dreams is squeezed into a poor on-off form. Exciting epics with Technicolor, quadriphonic sound, wide-angle screen, and a cast of thousands and dull soap operas on a black-and-white 14-inch screen are both reduced to the same message: the show is on.

Hall conducted a study of dreaming that avoided both these limitations.[37] He collected 10,000 dreams from a wide variety of normal subjects. Each subject

*Sophisticates in experimental design will recognize that a control group was awakened an equal number of times when they were not dreaming. Thus the not-unlikely possibility that the experimental group was irritable and anxious through deprivation of sleep could be checked. The control group showed neither the increase in dreaming nor the neurotic symptoms. Later studies have failed to confirm the adverse effects of both dream deprivation and sensory deprivation (reported in Section 2.252). Could it be that the ubiquitous college sophomore used in such studies has changed in the interval? Perhaps today's students are more into their own experience (as suggested by the great current interest in meditation, drugs, sensory awareness, and so on) and thus have less need for stimulation from the environment.

was requested to indicate for each dream (1) the dream setting, (2) the cast of characters, (3) the plot, (4) the emotions involved, and (5) whether or not it was in color.

Let's glance briefly, by way of illustration, at some typical results. (1) *Setting.* The favorite setting is the home, and the favorite room in the home is the living room. The most frequent settings are commonplace, yet they do not reflect the

time spent in each during waking hours. "In our dreams, we tend to show an aversion toward work, study, and commercial transactions and an affinity for recreation, riding, and residences." It seems, then, that night dreams, unlike daydreams, do not focus on far-away places with strange-sounding names. (2) *Cast.* The cast consists of strangers or close relatives and friends rather than public figures. "We may generalize our findings by saying that, while children are dreaming about their parents, their parents are dreaming about them, and while husbands are dreaming about their wives, their wives are dreaming about them." (3) *Plot.* The most frequent action is moving, although not, as is the stereotype, falling or floating. "In short, dreamers go places more than they do things; they play more than they work; their activities are more passive than active." (4) *Emotion.* Hostility is twice as common as friendliness. Apprehension is the most frequent dream emotion. (5) *Color.* Some people always dream in black and white, some people always dream in Technicolor, and some people dream sometimes in black and white and sometimes in color. No personality differences among those people and no significant differences between the contents of the black and white and Technicolor dreams have been found. "Color in dreams is merely an embellishment, signifying nothing in itself."

15.22   A Detour into Methodology

The juxtaposition of observational, experimental, and assessment studies of dreaming permits a comparison of these research strategies. Observational studies differ from the more familiar experimental studies in terms of rigor and relevance (Section 15.221); assessment studies differ from experimental studies in terms of cause and correlation (Section 15.222).

15.221   Rigor and Relevance

Psychological research seems to be constrained by the iron-clad law that rigor times relevance is a constant. That is, as rigor goes up, relevance must go down and, as relevance goes up, rigor must go down. Experimental studies are high in rigor but low in relevance, whereas observational studies are high in relevance but low in rigor. When a phenomenon is taken into the laboratory, the various extraneous variables can be carefully controlled and a precise statement can be made about what causes what. There is, however, a certain so-whatism about the results, for they are very remote from everyday life. We have already commented on such a case (Section 6.123). The learning of nonsense syllables in the laboratory is remote from the learning of nursery rhymes in the schoolroom. A phenomenon may not only be made irrelevant by being brought into the laboratory, but may even be distorted. What is observed may be changed by the act of observing it. Psychologists have long been aware that every experiment is, in a sense, an experiment in social psychology because of the presence of the experimenter. Similarly, school inspectors have always been aware that the class session is influenced by their presence.* Physicists have recently stumbled over the same problem, as embodied in the uncertainty principle. The location and direction of subatomic particles cannot be simultaneously observed, because the act of observing requires light, which interferes with the movement of the particles.

*What some of them don't know, however, is that some teachers tell the pupils that the inspector is coming to see how smart they are rather than how competent the teacher is. Furthermore, they tell the pupils that, in order to impress the inspector, when they know the answer to the question, they should raise their right hand, and when they don't know the answer, they should raise their left hand. This technique works very well until a particularly difficult question triggers a forest of left hands.

The logic of the experiment is impeccable. If all extraneous variables are controlled, the independent variable may reasonably be said to be the cause of the dependent variable. From an experiment we can conclude a specific causal relationship between two variables. From an assessment study we can conclude only that there is a correlation between two variables. This correlation could result from a number of possible causal relationships between the variables.

An assessment study first demonstrated a correlation between smoking and cancer. It is reasonable (but not necessary) to infer, then, that smoking causes cancer. But it could be that cancer causes smoking. Cancer could be a pathological state of the cells that predisposes a person to crave for tobacco. We have already observed cases in which the direction of the causal relationship that would appear to underlie a particular correlation has been challenged. Studies of early sensory deprivation (Section 11.113) suggest that we are smart because we are rich rather than rich because we are smart. Studies of cognitive dissonance (Section 2.253) suggest that we read Ford Mustang ads because we own a Mustang rather than own the Mustang because we read Mustang ads.

An assessment study demonstrated a correlation between the annual consumption of liquor and the average salary of professors. It is unlikely that there is a direct causal relationship underlying this correlation. It is more probable that a third variable causes both to vary together. As financial conditions improve, the sale of luxury items and the salaries of professors both increase. An assessment study demonstrated an inverse correlation between the price of cotton in the South and the number of lynchings. It is probable that this correlation stems from a causal chain within which these two variables are links.* Low prices cause frustration, which causes aggression, which causes lynchings. Thus a correlation between any two variables *A* and *B* may be attributed to one or more of the causal relationships diagramed in Figure 15-1.

15.23   Back to Dreaming

15.231   *Dreaming as Drama*

Possibly the best way to describe the current conception of the D-state is in terms of a play in which the dreamer is the playwright, producer, director, choreographer, stage manager, costume designer, leading actor, critic, and sole member of the audience. The dream is the poor man's drama.

*The observed correlation between the power blackout in parts of the Northeast in the fall of 1965 and the increase in birthrate nine months later probably reflects this type of causal relationship. I leave it to you to figure out the missing links.

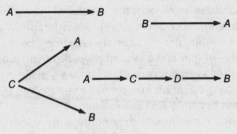

Figure 15-1. Possible Causal Relationships Underlying the Correlation between Variables A and B

Though the presentation of the play is determined by psychological factors, the theater seems to be provided by physiological factors. The theater was probably around for some time before the Johnny-come-lately neocortex invaded the empty stage to present its four or five nightly dramas. That is, dreaming appears to be an overlay function of sleeping, just as speaking is an overlay function of breathing.

Many of the phenomena of the D-state can be described in terms of the dreamer as spectator. The relaxation observed just prior to the dream indicates that the spectator is settling down to watch the performance just before the curtain rises. The REMs during the dream represent the spectator following the action of the play. Inattention to external stimuli stems from the spectator's being engrossed in the show. Sleep talking, sleepwalking, and that tantalizing sleep smiling result from a failure to maintain the as-if emotions appropriate to the watching of a play. The real emotion that wakes us from a nightmare, like the real emotion generated were an actor to have a real heart attack on stage, is a failure to maintain that peculiar as-if emotion. The idiosyncratic symbols are due to the dreamer's being the playwright as well as the only member of the audience. Under such circumstances, because of the great overlap of experience between him-as-playwright and him-as-spectator, he can afford to be subjective and concise.

Other phenomena can be described in terms of the dreamer as playwright. The fact that creative people tend to have creative dreams is no more surprising than the fact that creative people tend to write creative plays. The many "explanations" of the function of the dream may perhaps be explained by the statement that there are as many functions of dreams as there are dreamers, just as there are as many functions of plays as there are playwrights. Dreams, like plays, may indeed be designed for catharsis (release), for reform, for enlightenment, for problem solving, for entertainment, or for any combination or permutation of these reasons. The varied contents of dreams can also be explained in terms of the varied styles of the dreamers. Your dreams may be bizarre if you are an unheralded member of the Theater of the Absurd. If you often dream that you are dreaming, then perhaps you are a latent Pirandello, who was famous for his plays within plays. Your dreams may be pornographic—scene after primal scene—if that is the kind of playwright you are. Thus interminable debates as to whether a symbol reveals or conceals meaning or whether a dream is a creation or a compensation may perhaps be resolved by the obvious observation that the dream depends on the dreamer.

Some phenomena may perhaps be understood in terms of the dreamer as critic. He catches the Late Late Show and reviews it in the morning. It is a form of projective test in which he both creates and interprets the stimulus. Through the mechanism of the self-fulfilling prophecy, the interpretation of the dream, rather than the dream itself, may come true. Thus there may indeed be some basis for the claim that the dream has predictive power.

15.232   D-State and W-State

We tend to think of the D-state as being intermediate between the sleeping state (S-state) and the waking state (W-state) along some single dimension of depth of consciousness. It seems, however, that the D-state is qualitatively different from both the S-state and the W-state, although it has some characteristics of each. The nervous system is functioning under a different set of constraints in the D-state than in the W-state. In the W-state the nervous system is dealing with both input and stored information; in the D-state it is dealing only with stored information. That is, whereas in the W-state the nervous system is interacting with the environment, in the D-state it is engrossed in its own affairs. Since, in the W-state, the nervous system is dealing with the objective world, it must operate according to the reality principle; however, in the D-state, the nervous system is dealing with the subjective world, and it may operate according to the pleasure principle. Alternately and simplistically, the nervous system in the W-state tries to maximize truth and the nervous system in the D-state tries to maximize comfort. Perhaps creativity and psychopathology could usefully be discussed in terms of the presence or absence of compatability between truth and comfort within the nervous system.

We also tend to think of the D-state as determined by the W-state. That is, the content of our dreams is a residue of the previous day in the W-state. Dreams are determined by unresolved conflicts or unsolved problems or unfulfilled wishes or overfilled stomachs. It could be argued, however, that the W-state is determined by the D-state. Your interpretation of a dream could trigger a decision. Or, the mood of a dream may linger after the content has gone and may set the mood for the day.* Robert Louis Stevenson saw his waking self as a mere scribe for recording the stories spun out for him in dreams, and Carl Gustav Jung allowed his waking life to follow the insights of his dream life.

It may be more productive, however, to think of the two states as the functioning of the nervous system in two alternate modes of apprehending the objective world. You have two subjective maps of the objective world: the perceptual map and the conceptual map. In the D-state you are operating within the perceptual map, and in the W-state you are operating within the conceptual map. Your symbolization is perceptual in the D-state and conceptual in the W-state. That is, in the D-state a policeman is a symbol for authority, but in the W-state "authority" is the symbol for authority. We have tended to be overentranced with the new toy of the conceptual map and have neglected the basic tool of the perceptual map. We in our W-state have become alienated from ourselves in our D-state. You can't get any more alienated than that. The fact that we are all dramatists in our dreams suggests that we are all artists. Those recognized as artists are simply those who are more in tune with themselves in the D-state.

*This could be the basis of the wrong-side-of-the-bed phenomenon. I solve this problem myself by putting the wrong side against a wall or, if that doesn't work, by going back to bed and starting again.

Every man takes the limits of his own field of vision for the limits of the world.

Arthur Schopenhauer
Studies in Pessimism. Psychological Observations.

The painter should not paint what he sees, but what will be seen.

Paul Valéry
Mauvaises Pensées et Autres

There is an inevitable divergence, attributable to the imperfections of the human mind, between the world as it is and the world as men perceive it.

James William Fulbright
Speech in the Senate (March 27, 1964)

16

Normative Approach

16.1 Descriptive and Prescriptive Disciplines

Psychology has been predominantly a descriptive rather than a prescriptive discipline. That is, it has been concerned with actual man rather than potential man, with what man is rather than with what man could be, with being rather than becoming. Only recently have humanistic psychologists shown an interest

POTENTIAL MAN

ACTUAL MAN

in potential man. The logic of the normative approach is to compare actual man with potential man—how we do operate our nervous systems with how we ought to operate them. We establish certain criteria for the effective operation of the nervous system and examine the extent to which those criteria are satisfied.

The consideration of these criteria is the province of the prescriptive disciplines. The major prescriptive disciplines are the branches of philosophy—ethics, logic, and aesthetics—concerned, respectively, with the criteria for the good, the true, and the beautiful. Or, in the more modern language of de Ropp's *Master Game*,[21] ethics, logic, and aesthetics are concerned, respectively, with principles for the effective playing of the Religion Game, the Science Game, and the Art Game. Presumably in the noblest game of all, the Master Game, the criteria all come together. The good is the true is the beautiful.

Although ethics and aesthetics have aspired to absolute criteria (for instance, the Golden Rule in ethics and the Golden Mean in aesthetics), their criteria nevertheless seem riddled with relativism. That is, what is good and what is beautiful in one culture are bad and ugly in another culture. Even subcultures within our own culture have different criteria for what is good and what is beautiful. There is, however, some hope of absolute criteria in logic. Let's focus on logic, then, in the hope of discovering principles that apply to all members of our species.

16.2   Subjective Map of Objective World

One useful criterion of truth is the extent to which your subjective map is an accurate representation of the objective world. Let us consider first the accuracy of your perceptual map (**veridicality**) and then the accuracy of your conceptual map (**rationality**).

16.21   Veridicality

Perception deals with cases in which the world-as-seen is the same as the world-as-is, and misperception deals with cases in which the world-as-seen differs from the world-as-is. Although the former is more important, the latter is more studied. This may stem partly from a tendency for psychologists to take veridical perception for granted and partly from the fact that nonveridical perception is more dramatic. Misperception is certainly more relevant to real-life concerns: beauticians and designers, artists and con artists, jurors and conjurors all have vested interests in misperception. Let's look first at misperception due to the stimulus (Section 16.211) and then at misperception due to the subject (Section 16.212). This classification is of course arbitrary, since perception always involves an intimate interaction between perceiver and perceived. In the former cases, however, the effect is universal and thus apparently primarily caused by the stimulus; in the latter cases the effect varies from subject to subject and thus is apparently primarily caused by the subject.

16.211   *Misperception due to Stimulus*

You will recall (Section 10.211) that the original method of psychology was introspection, and the original goal was the analysis of the mind into its elements. You saw how a group of psychologists called behaviorists reacted against the method. Let's look now at how a group of psychologists called Gestaltists reacted against the goal. The **Gestalt psychologists** argued that, in many cases, an experience cannot be analyzed into elements, since there is more in the perception than the sum of the sensations. The whole is greater than the sum of the parts. Wertheimer, the founder of the group, performed the following experiment to demonstrate this principle. He placed two lights side by side and flashed them one after the other at differing time intervals. If the time interval was long, the subject reported two lights flashing one after the other. If the time interval was short, the subject reported two lights flashing simultaneously. If the time interval was just right, the subject reported a light moving from the position of the first light to the position of the second light. This is the **phi phenomenon.** It illustrates the Gestalt principle, since the perception (a moving light) contains more than the sum of the sensations (two stationary lights).

The phi phenomenon is an **illusion of movement:** there is a perception of motion without any corresponding objective motion. (This illusion of movement is created by a series of arrows flashing at optimal intervals around the marquee outside a cinema. It is also created by a series of stills flashed at optimal intervals inside the cinema.) Other familiar illusions of movement are the impression that your train is moving when another train passes it in the station, the impression that the bridge on which you are standing is moving when you watch the water rushing by it, and the impression that the moon is moving as clouds move in front of it.

Less familiar illusions of movement are those created with concentric or parallel straight lines by Op artists. Since these figures are very disturbing, they have been used in restaurants to augment the familiar uncomfortable chairs and thus increase the turnover.

A second type of misperception is the discrepancy between an objective length, area, or direction and the perceived length, area, or direction. Figure

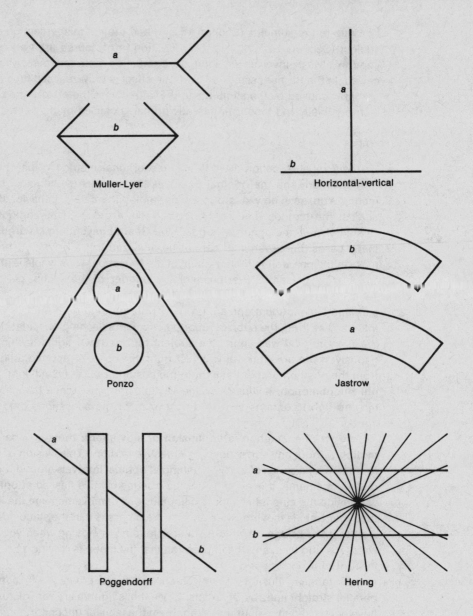

Figure 16-1. Six Examples of Geometric Illusions. In the top four diagrams, a and b are equal, although a appears larger in each case. In the bottom two diagrams, a and b are straight, although they appear to be out of line in the Poggendorff illusion and curved in the Hering illusion.

16-1 provides a sample of such **geometric illusions,*** and Figure 16-2 provides a sample of theories to explain those illusions, using the **Muller-Lyer illusion** as an example.

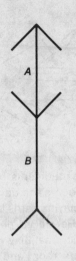

The **eye-movement theory** states that the impression of length is obtained by moving the eye along a line from one end to the other. B seems longer, since the outward arrows cause your eye to move farther.

The **perspective theory** states that the apparent length is affected by the perspective read into the figure. B seems farther away and thus objectively longer.

The **confusion theory** states that you confuse the part of the figure to be judged with the figure as a whole. B seems longer because the absolute length of the figure to which it belongs is longer than that to which A belongs.

The **good-figure theory** states that, when a figure embodies some characteristic, you tend to see that characteristic expressed as fully as possible. B seems longer because A is compressed to permit closure of the diamond embodied in the figure of which it is a part.

Figure 16-2. Theories of Geometric Illusions

Which of these theories is correct? Take your pick. Your guess is as good as mine—or anyone's. None of the theories handle the facts adequately. The Newton of geometric illusions has not yet arrived. It may be you. It is interesting to note the inverse correlation between the adequacy of a theory and the number of alternative theories. The duplicity theory handles the facts within its domain beautifully. The facts fit into it with a satisfying click that makes you feel good inside. It has no rivals. The Young-Helmholtz theory handles the facts of its domain reasonably well, but you are left with a slightly bitter taste at the contortions necessary to handle the contrast effects and the embarrassing fact of the psychological primacy of yellow. It has a few rivals. The eye-movement theory does not handle the facts of its domain at all well. It has many rivals.

A gentleman named Ames caused psychologists some embarrassment by unearthing phenomena that they cannot yet explain. Ames was not a

*The vertical-horizontal illusion is used by dress designers when they recommend vertical stripes to short fat girls and horizontal stripes to long skinny girls. The other illusions could also be used. Why not, for instance, make dresses for short and long girls using the Muller-Lyer illusion?

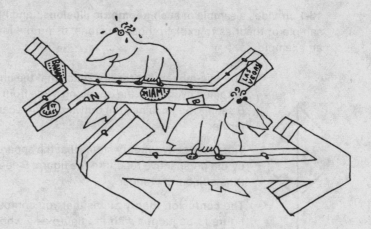

psychologist but an engineer. He did not conduct experiments but arranged demonstrations. He blew up lighted balloons in dark rooms and gave an illusion of an approaching ball. He superimposed far on near playing cards by cutting off edges and gave the illusion that they were nearer. He placed people behind windows in a **distorted room** and created the impression that they were huge or tiny. He rotated a lighted **trapezoid window** in a dark room and created the impression of an oscillating rectangle.

Such illusions have so far best been explained in terms of past experience. Since all the myriad windows we have ever seen have been rectangular, we induce that the trapezoid window is rectangular. We refuse, then, to violate this assumption by permitting the narrow end to be closer than the broad end. Such a situation is, of course, impossible with rectangular windows. Thus, whenever the narrow end comes to the front, it is pushed back again, and the oscillating effect is created. This explanation has been supported by the finding that the Zulu, who live in a circular culture without any experience of windows or rectangles of any kind, do not experience the illusion.

It would be interesting to check whether the moon illusion is universal, since it is an inevitable part of the past experience of all cultures. The **moon illusion** refers to the fact that the moon looks larger at the horizon than it does overhead. If you try looking at the moon through your legs (not necessarily right now), you will see that the illusion is reduced. This suggests that past experience plays a role. You have little experience at looking at the moon through your legs. Try looking at the moon through your portable reduction screen (that is, look through your hand curled in such a way as to eliminate the background), and you will find that the illusion is lost. This suggests that context plays a role. Perhaps we see the moon at the horizon as far away because of all the intervening terrain and adjust to preserve size constancy.

16.212 Misperception due to Subject

Sherif put subjects all alone in a dark room with a single, stationary point of light.[90] They invariably reported that the light moved. The reports, however, varied considerably. Some said it moved to the left, some said it moved up, some said it moved a few feet, and some said it moved a few inches. This illusion of movement, the **autokinetic effect,** is reduced by providing a framework around the dot. The variance in reported directions and distances may be reduced by having the subjects judge the movement of the dot as a group. They rapidly come to a consensus. The group judgment also serves as a framework. Unstructured situations like this permit subjects to read into them what they wish. This is the logic of the various projective tests, in which a subject's response to an inkblot, an ambiguous picture, or a noncommittal incomplete sentence provides information about the subject.

Perception has for some time been recognized as an intimate interaction between the perceived and the perceiver, but until the 1940s the emphasis was on the characteristics of the perceived. At that time a movement toward an emphasis on characteristics of the perceiver was initiated. It came to be called the New Look, by analogy with a simultaneous development in the world of fashion. In one of the more dramatic studies in this tradition, starving men presented with ambiguous figures for brief intervals tended to perceive them as depicting food.* In a less dramatic but more typical study, poor boys and rich boys were asked to adjust a circle until it was the same size as a quarter.[13] On the average, the poor boys made the circle significantly larger than did the rich boys, suggesting that a quarter was more important to them.

The effect of group pressure on perception was demonstrated in a classic experiment performed by Asch.[3] When the subject arrived in the experimental room, seven other people—ostensibly also subjects but actually stooges following Asch's instructions—were already assembled. The task was to say which of the three lines at the left in Figure 16-3 was equal to the line on the right. The stooges were instructed to say line 2, although line 1 was obviously the correct answer. What did the subject do when his turn came and he had to decide between the evidence of his senses and the consensus of his peers? He tended to yield to the group pressure. Only about 25% of those tested remained independent on all trials. Independence can be increased by increasing the discrepancy between the correct answer and the group answer, by having the subject commit himself to the correct answer in advance, or by arranging for one of the stooges to agree with him. According to Gleitman, "One deviate is a nut, but two deviates are a minority group."

Figure 16-3. Stimulus in Asch Experiment

16.22 Rationality

16.221 Laws of Thought—Boole

In 1854 Boole published his book *Laws of Thought,* in which he presented logic as the study of—you guessed it—the laws of thought.[11] He considered his three famous fundamental laws (if a proposition is true, then it is true; any proposition

*A psychologist performed the same experiment, using blank slides, just before lunch at a psychological convention. The delegates saw food. A wag called this a study in immaculate perception.

must be either true or false; no proposition can be both true and false) to be descriptions of the way the mind worked. Thus he saw logic as a descriptive discipline. His position has been implicitly assumed, though seldom explicitly advocated, in most research on reasoning. The vast majority of studies have focused on error; that is, valid reasoning occurs simply because "that's the way the mind works," and all that needs to be explained is error. Theoretical treatments of reasoning have tended to degenerate into a catalog of sources of such error.

16.222 The Logical Syntax of Language—*Carnap*

In 1934 Carnap published his book *The Logical Syntax of Language,* in which he presented logic as the study of the rules of deduction rather than of the laws of thought.[15] This distinction between rules and laws is important. Indeed, we could perhaps characterize prescriptive disciplines as the study of rules and descriptive disciplines as the study of laws. (The differentiation has been clouded somewhat by the legal profession's use of the word *law* to refer to what are actually rules.) A traditional distinction has been that rules are made by man, whereas laws are made by God. However, they are both man-made. Laws are made by man to describe his environment, and rules are made by man to prescribe his conduct. And, since they are both created by man, they can both be violated by man—but with different consequences. You can violate the drug laws (that is, rules) by taking LSD and risk a prison term or a fine. You can also defy the law of gravity by trying to fly from the roof of your house, but here you risk injury or death. Our prisons are set up for those who violate the rules, whereas our hospitals are set up for those who violate the laws. Our mental hospitals occupy an ambiguous middle ground. The rules of man are somewhat more arbitrary and whimsical than the laws of nature. Nature is merciless in the prosecution of those who violate her laws, but she is always fair.

Carnap's position has had little effect on empirical research on reasoning but is potentially very fruitful. It suggests how the previously isolated studies of deductive reasoning can be fitted congenially within the framework of psycholinguistics. The argument is as follows. A language can be considered as sets of units arranged in a hierarchy—phonemes, morphemes, sentences, discourses—and sets of rules for combining units at each level to yield meaningful units at the next level in the hierarchy. The study of the rules for combining phonemes to yield morphemes is vocabulary, the study of the rules for combining morphemes to yield sentences is grammar, and the study of the rules for combining sentences to yield discourses is—as defined by Carnap—logic.

16.223   Logic and Psychology—*Piaget*

The most significant work on the relationship between the descriptive discipline of psychology and the prescriptive discipline of logic—that of Piaget and his co-workers—owes its inspiration to neither Boole nor Carnap. Piaget is his own logician. In 1957 Piaget published his book *Logic and Psychology,* in which he presented logic as a theoretical tool in the description of the mental structures that govern reasoning.[79] We have seen (Section 13.332) how he traces the comedy of errors through infancy, childhood, and adolescence. Each error is explained in terms of a mental structure that does not yet accurately reflect relationships within the objective world. Piaget finally leaves the mature thinker with a propositional structure that would appear to make him immune from error. The apparent discrepancy between the existence of this structure and the demonstration of error in the ubiquitous college sophomore participating in studies of reasoning can be resolved by the following suggestion as to the relationship between logic and psychology.

16.224   *Synthesis of Views—Gardiner*

This suggested relationship is a synthesis of elements from Boole, Carnap, *and* Piaget.[26] Let's imagine an empty universe, and into that universe let's introduce the proposition. In the beginning, there was the proposition. At the risk of appearing too familiar at such early acquaintance, let us call it simply p. Let's borrow Boole's laws of thought to define our proposition as anything that must be either true or false and cannot be both true and false (or, in shorthand, p is true or p is false, or, in shorterhand, p or $\bar{p}$). Our proposition looks lonely all alone in its empty universe, so let's introduce another proposition and call it q. If our two propositions get together (as inevitably they must), they will generate four possible states of affairs: *either p* is true and q is true, *or p* is true and q is false, *or p* is false and q is true, *or p* is false and q is false. Or, in shorthand:

$$p \cdot q \quad \text{or} \quad p \cdot \bar{q} \quad \text{or} \quad \bar{p} \cdot q \quad \text{or} \quad \bar{p} \cdot \bar{q}.$$

This set of possibilities illustrates Piaget's propositional structure that underlies mature thinking. Now let's introduce words that state a relationship between two propositions, eliminate a subset of the alternatives within the propositional structure, and determine the status (true, false, or undetermined) of one proposition on the assertion or denial of the other (see Figure 16-4). English has words for the elimination of every possible subset of alternatives within the propositional structure. (It is an interesting empirical question whether all languages have such means; any language that doesn't would not be able to generate logic and mathematics as easily as could a language that does.) We'll borrow from Carnap the notion that the task of logic is the enumeration of rules to combine sentences to form discourses and that the task of psychology is the investigation of the extent to which those rules are understood by particular individuals, and we'll propose that those rules are essentially the meanings of the words listed in Figure 16-4. For each of those words (or logical operators, to be more precise) there are two rules: one about the assertion of one of the propositions and one about its denial. Look at Figure 16-5. Try the 12 test items for each of the rules, and check the answers at the end of the chapter to find out how many of the rules you know. You may find that, although you have Piaget's propositional structure as an implicit premise, you can still make errors in logic because you do not know the meanings of the logical operators.

Status[1]	Name of Relation	Logical Operator	Alternatives Eliminated	
FU	contrariness	not both p and q	$p \cdot \bar{q}$	
TU	superimplication	if p, then q	$p \cdot \bar{q}$	
UF	subimplication	if q, then p	$\bar{p} \cdot q$	
UT	subcontrariness	either p or q or both	$\bar{p} \cdot \bar{q}$	
FT	contradiction	either p or q	$p \cdot q$	and $\bar{p} \cdot \bar{q}$
TF	equivalence	p if and only if q	$p \cdot \bar{q}$	and $\bar{p} \cdot q$
TT	independence	—		
FF	independence	—		
UU	independence	—		

[1]If any proposition p is true, any other proposition q may be true, false, or undetermined. If any proposition p is false, any other proposition q may be true, false, or undetermined. By pairing each of the first three conditions with each of the second three conditions, we get nine possible relationships between any two propositions. These nine possible relationships are listed above. The relationships are described by means of abbreviations, with the first letter referring to the status of q when p is true and the second letter referring to the status of q when p is false. Thus FU means "If p is true, then q is false, and, if p is false, then q is undetermined." Note that relationships 7, 8, and 9 are essentially the same, since the status of q is unaffected by the truth and falsity of p. Since logic is concerned only with those cases in which the status of one proposition affects the status of another, those relationships are not considered here.

Figure 16.4 The Logical Operators

In summary, Boole's laws of thought and Piaget's propositional structure are necessary conditions for correct deductive reasoning, but they are not sufficient conditions, since you must also know Carnap's rules of deduction.

1. Suppose you know that:
Not both *p* and *q*.
p.
Then would this be true?
q
YES NO MAYBE

2. Suppose you know that:
There is not both a marble in box 1
and a marble in box 2.
There is not a marble in box 1.
Then would this be true?
There is a marble in box 2.
YES NO MAYBE

3. Suppose you know that:
If Pat goes to church,
then she sees Mary.
Pat went to church today.
Then would this be true?
Pat saw Mary today.
YES NO MAYBE

4. Suppose you know that:
If pencils are made of wood,
then rulers are made of rubber.
Pencils are not made of wood.
Then would this be true?
Rulers are made of rubber.
YES NO MAYBE

5. Suppose you know that:
If worms do the twist,
then dogs play the trumpet.
Dogs play the trumpet.
Then would this be true?
Worms do the twist.
YES NO MAYBE

6. Suppose you know that:
If a zillig is a zog,
then a mugwump is a mig.
A mugwump is not a mig.
Then would this be true?
A zillig is a zog.
YES NO MAYBE

7. Suppose you know that:
Either *p* or *q* or both.
p.
Then would this be true?
q.
YES NO MAYBE

8. Suppose you know that:
Either there is a marble in box 1,
or there is a marble in box 2 or both.
There is not a marble in box 1.
Then would this be true?
There is a marble in box 2.
YES NO MAYBE

9. Suppose you know that:
Either the pencil belongs to Dick,
or it belongs to Jane.
The pencil belongs to Dick.
Then would this be true?
The pencil belongs to Jane.
YES NO MAYBE

10. Suppose you know that:
Either birds have two legs,
or animals have four eyes.
Birds do not have two legs.
Then would this be true?
Animals have four eyes.
YES NO MAYBE

11. Suppose you know that:
Cats play catcher
if and only if dogs play pitcher.
Cats play catcher.
Then would this be true?
Dogs play pitcher.
YES NO MAYBE

12. Suppose you know that:
Effels squip
if and only if anvics ruman.
Effels do not squip.
Then would this be true?
Anvics ruman.
YES NO MAYBE

Figure 16-5. Test of Understanding of Logical Operators

16.23 Veridicality and Rationality

Veridical perception and rational conception are assumed in other sciences but constitute a problem in psychology. The optimism of science has been dampened a little recently by the Heisenberg Principle (the position and direction of a subatomic particle cannot both be recorded simultaneously), which suggests a limitation to observation, and by Godel's Theorem (it is impossible to prove that a set of propositions are all consistent), which suggests a limitation to reason. But, despite these setbacks, scientists persist in their faith that the universe is understandable and that the human brain has the capacity to understand it. It is a healthy attitude. Though it sounds inappropriate to science, we must keep the faith. It is a shock to me to find that some people consider the universe incomprehensible. It is a further shock to find that some people consider the universe potentially understandable but not by them. Perhaps the basic trust that things make sense, and that one can make sense of things oneself, is established at an early age. Yet some children—probably because they must cope with irrational parents—never develop this faith. A major concern of educators should be the re-establishment of this trust, without which instruction is futile.

But what if the skeptics are right? What if there is no order to the universe or no means by which we could discover this order? One worries sometimes. In Section 9.122 we looked into the eye of the frog and found that he perceives not what is but that subset of what is that is useful for him to perceive. Who are we to assume that what we perceive is what really is rather than just an expurgated version that is relevant to our survival? The fact that our highly evolved modality of vision picks up only a sliver of the potential range of electromagnetic energy adds fuel to our doubts. Could it be that, besides the cultural blinkers our language imposes on us (as some anthropologists have suggested), we wear even more limiting biological blinkers imposed on us by the structure of our nervous system? If you're looking for something to worry about, ponder this problem for a while.

Answers to Problems

1. no   2. maybe   3. yes   4. maybe   5. maybe   6. no   7. maybe   8. yes
9. no   10. yes   11. yes   12. no

Analogies prove nothing, that is quite true. But they can make one feel more at home.

Sigmund Freud
New Introductory Lectures on Psychology

Though analogy is often misleading, it is the least misleading thing we have.

Samuel Butler
Notebooks. Music, Pictures, and Books

17 Analogical Approach

17.1 Of Mechanisms and Organisms

One approach to the understanding of the nervous system is to study another system and draw analogies from it to the nervous system. This oblique strategy of learning about one system by observing another is particularly appropriate to psychology. Since the nervous system is the most complex of all systems, it is advisable to look to simpler systems for insights that may help unravel its complexity. Analogies usually serve to make the unfamiliar familiar. In psychology they also serve to make the familiar unfamiliar. Psychologists are so close to their subject matter—indeed, they *are* their subject matter—that they cannot see it clearly. Thus, studying an analogous system permits us to stand back and get a good look at ourselves.

17.2 Analogizing

17.21 A New Model of Man

17.211 Of Computers and Humans

The man-made mechanism that, to date, most closely approximates his nervous system is the computer. Structural similarities between computers and nervous systems suggest possible functional similarities. The binary on/off basis of the computer is reflected in the all-or-none law of neural transmission. Analog and digital computers correspond to the perceptual and conceptual maps of the nervous system. Input and output of the computer are equivalent to stimulus and response of the nervous system. Both the computer and the nervous system are information systems processing input and stored and feedback information. This analogy has been used to develop a new model of man.

17.212 Of Plans and Images

Three brilliant young men spent a year together at the Institute for Advanced Study in the Behavioral Sciences with nothing to do but read and write and think and talk. Under these ideal conditions something was bound to happen. It did. They wrote a book entitled *Plans and the Structure of Behavior,* which exploded in the field of psychology and shook it at its foundations.[71] In that book Miller, Galanter, and Pribram argue as follows. The optimists within psychology have tried to explain your behavior using the model of the empty box. They explain what comes out entirely in terms of what goes in (input information). The pessimists within psychology have insisted that it is necessary to insert into that box another box, representing everything you know about the world. They explain what comes out in terms of what goes in (input information) plus everything that has gone in before (stored information). The pessimists are not pessimistic enough, for it is necessary to insert yet another box, representing instructions about what to do with this input and stored information. Miller, Galanter, and Pribram explain what comes out in terms of what goes in (input information) plus everything that has gone in before (stored information) plus information about discrepancies between input and stored information (feedback information).

This argument was based on the analogy between the nervous system and the computer. A computer has input and output corresponding to what comes in and what goes out (as in the optimists' model), a memory unit corresponding to everything you know about the world (as in the pessimists' model), and a program corresponding to the instructions for processing the input and stored information (as in the Miller, Galanter, and Pribram model). For memory unit read **image,** for program read **plan,** and a new model of man—the TOTE unit—is born (see Figure 17-1). TOTE refers to the sequence that underlies behavior. You test (T) your present state (as represented in input information) against a desired state (as represented by stored information in the image), perform an operation (O) according to a plan to reduce any discrepancy between them, test again (T), and so on through alternating tests and operations until the discrepancy is removed, at which time exit (E)—the plan is discontinued. Behavior is viewed, then, not as a series of responses to stimuli (reflex arc) but rather as a series of operations to remove a discrepancy between the present state and a desired state (feedback loop). The reflex arc is dead. Long live the feedback loop!

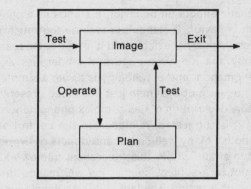

Figure 17-1. The TOTE Unit

The analogy breaks down when we consider that we can switch from one plan to another. The programmer must do this for the computer by taking out one program and inserting another. Who programs the programmer? The sequence of plans is orchestrated by inner speech. That is, we talk to ourselves. This is not so unlikely as it may at first appear. Vygotsky has pointed out that children give a running commentary on their own actions. This overt commentary, forced underground in adults by social pressure, may persist in covert form to direct our behavior.

17.22   Old Topics within the New Model

17.221   Hypnosis

Miller, Galanter, and Pribram proceeded to reinterpret many traditional topics in terms of this new model. Let me illustrate with the traditional taboo topic of hypnosis. Although hypnosis has many profound effects on behavior, psychologists, the students of behavior, have neglected it. One standard explanation for this neglect is historical accident. Psychology has neglected hypnosis for the same reason medicine has neglected it. Doctors began to use hypnosis as an anesthetic but discarded it because more efficient anesthetics were later discovered. Freud began to use hypnosis to facilitate recall of early experiences during psychoanalysis, but he discarded it because he discovered the free-association method soon after. A second standard reason is conservatism. Hypnosis has acquired a bad name through association with stage magicians and international spies. It is much too controversial and powerful to be touched by a conventional and respected scientist. These two factors probably contribute to the neglect. However, although hypnosis has no exclusive practical application and although it has been used for entertainment, it exists. Because of its many dramatic effects on behavior, it stands as a challenge to those who would explain behavior. It stands perhaps as too much of a challenge. It may be that psychologists have neglected it for the same reason they have neglected human dignity and moral courage and tenderness and poignancy: it is a complex phenomenon, and psychology is as yet a simple science.

The new model of man just described presents a glimmer of hope for a satisfactory description of this complex phenomenon. A subject in a hypnotic trance has, it is suggested, relinquished the control of his plans to the voice of the hypnotist. Many well-documented facts of hypnosis may be described, without undue strain, within this theoretical framework. The fact that it is difficult to hypnotize a subject against his will means that he refuses to relinquish his planning function. The fact that the subject tends not to do things he would not normally do means that the impression that the hypnotist's voice is his own inner voice must be maintained. The fact that the hypnotist uses sleep suggestion means that he is capitalizing on the subject's lifetime of experience in suspending his planning function. When the subject suspends his own planning function, he is susceptible to the insistent plans of the hypnotist, since planlessness is death.

11.222 Problem Solving

The new model of man may also serve as a framework for the many chaotic facts about problem solving. Everyday problems range from the sublime (What's it all about, Alfie?) to the ridiculous (Which of my two ties will I wear today?), from the trivial (as sometimes appear in the "Dear Abby" column) to the important (as sometimes appear on the United Nations agenda). All these diverse problems can be fitted within our new model so that we can discuss problem solving in general.

A problem is defined as a discrepancy between the present state (as represented in input information) and the desired state (as represented in stored information), and problem solving is defined as the set of operations required to get from the present state to the desired state. The problem-solver follows the TOTE sequence. In his alternating tests (thought) and operations (action), we see how this feedback-loop model, unlike the reflex-arc model, orchestrates thought and action.

Three dimensions along which problems differ with respect to the test phase are feasibility, clarity, and completeness. Let's glance at each in turn.

Feasibility.   One of the major differences between the problems you face in school and the problems you face out of school is that the school problems always have a solution. The answer is always in the back of the book or, at least, in the back of the teacher's mind. Science shares this optimistic, onward-and-upward, every-problem-has-a-solution attitude. Millions of dollars and thousands of man-hours are poured into cancer research to answer the question "What is the cure?" even though the question "Does a cure exist?" has not been answered. However, in considering our out-of-school problems, it may be useful to ask: "Does a solution exist?" Perhaps our training in school and in science sets us scurrying too readily after myths like the Golden Past and the Perfect Woman.* On the other hand, many great discoveries and inventions have been made by people who refused to accept the prevailing attitude that something was impossible. Once you know that something is feasible, you are well on your way to doing it (just as, when you know that your passport is in that trunk in the attic, you are certain to find it). I don't think the fact that the Soviet Union developed the atom bomb soon after the United States did and the United States launched a satellite soon after the Soviet Union did can be explained entirely by spying. Similarly, the four-minute mile and the seven-foot high jump were psychological rather than physical barriers; as soon as the first athletes broke these barriers, a spate of others did too.

Clarity. Sometimes the present state and the desired state in a problem are not clear. The housewife who has just awakened from the American Dream and is vaguely discontented would find it difficult to define her desired state. Her problem is not so much that she cannot attain what she wants as that she doesn't *know* what she wants. But even if you know what you want, you may not be able to recognize it when you find it. Once I was asked to pick up a girl I didn't know at a dormitory and bring her to a party. I found myself leering at girl after girl as they came downstairs, because I had no means of recognizing the one I was to meet. We also have to know where we are before we can determine where we want to go. We've all had the experience of getting lost on the way to a party, phoning the hostess for directions, and realizing, when she asks the obvious question, that we don't *know* where we're phoning from. The process of writing Given (present state) and Required (desired state) before Proof (means of getting from present state to desired state) in a geometry problem is no mere academic ritual. It sets out clearly where we are, where we're going, and how we're going to get from here to there. It serves as a good model for the solution of all problems.

Completeness. You may discover, on laying out what is given and required, that the information is incomplete. This information is in itself valuable. You know where you are, where you want to go, and that you can get there from here; but you have no transportation. Some essential element is missing. It may be empirical information. In this case your problem reduces to finding the in-

*I found her after searching for 20 years, but she didn't want *me*—she was searching for the Perfect Man.

formation from the appropriate sources. It may be a logical element. In this case your "solution" would be to determine that the problem is insoluble as presented. Great breakthroughs in science are often not so much a solution to a problem as the demonstration that there is no solution possible.

Three dimensions along which problems differ with respect to the operate phase are appropriateness, efficiency, and elegance. Let's glance at each in turn.

Appropriateness. We tend to build up a repertoire of plans appropriate to most of our everyday problems. This can be useful, since it means that we need not devise a new plan for each new problem. The advantage can become a disadvantage, however, in cases in which the established plan is not appropriate. Gleitman has defined a difficult problem as one in which the obvious plan is the wrong plan. Overmotivated people tend to persist with the obvious plan. Thus they tend to do well with simple problems but badly with difficult problems. Undercreative people also tend to persist with the obvious plan. Creative people have the flexibility to generate many plans and the persistence to test them all.

Efficiency. Two plans may be equally appropriate, in that they both result in a solution; yet one may be more efficient than the other. A systematic plan may be efficient when there are only a few alternatives to explore but not when there are many. Thus, to find all the new words that can be made from the letters in the word *time,* it would be efficient to go systematically through all the one-letter words, all the two-letter words, all the three-letter words, and then all the possible four-letter words. This systematic plan would not be efficient in finding all the new words in the word *temptation.* Here it is perhaps better to resort to heuristic plans in which the more likely alternatives are explored. Thus you would look for words beginning with *te* and *ta* but not with *tm* and *tp.* Also, on noticing that *temptation* contains *time,* you would write down all the words you had already found in *time.*

Whether heuristic or systematic plans are more efficient depends mainly on the number of possible alternatives under consideration. When considering all the possible English words in seven letters, as we do in Scrabble, we resort to heuristic plans, since there is a huge jump in the number of possible alternatives between four and seven letters. A few alternatives, however, can each be evaluated in turn.

Elegance. Two plans may be equally appropriate and efficient, but one may be more elegant than the other. Elegance is a very subtle quality that, subjectively speaking, makes you feel warm inside. Wertheimer once watched a high school teacher present a mechanical means of finding the area of a parallelogram by multiplying the base by the altitude. However, the students were puzzled when the altitude missed the base; their mechanical method could not transfer to this new situation. Wertheimer recommended an insightful solution in which the students cut the triangle off one end and affixed it to the other, thus yielding a rectangle whose area is easy to find and a solution that generalizes to all parallelograms. I encountered a similar situation when I discovered that some eighth-grade students I was teaching had been taught the mechanical plan of "shifting the number to the other side and changing the sign" in solving equations. But when the number was a multiplier or a divisor, their plan no longer worked and they got confused. It took some time to substitute the understanding that, since an equation is a balance, we must do exactly the same to each side in order to maintain that balance.

17.3 Simulating

17.31 Simulating Subfunctions

Mechanisms may be used to simulate organisms as well as to provide a source of analogies. Let's look at an attempt to construct a physical model of the visual system. What is the nature of the link between the receptors for light in the retina and the projection area for light in the occipital lobe of the cortex? Rosenblatt combined his interests in psychology and electrical engineering by building an electronic model to simulate this psychological process.[83] His first assumption was that the neurons from the retina to the occipital lobe were connected randomly. This assumption was built into his model by connecting each of the cells in a 24 × 24 panel (representing the retina) randomly with wires (representing the neurons) to each of the cells in another 24 × 24 panel (representing the occipital lobe).* His second assumption was that a particular stimulus becomes associated with a particular perception only through experience. The experience of punishment of a wrong response to a stimulus has the effect of decreasing the probability that those neurons that fired on this response will fire the next time this stimulus is presented. The experience of reward of a correct response to a stimulus has the effect of increasing the probability that those neurons that fired on this response will fire the next time this stimulus is presented. This assumption was built into his model by increasing the resistance of the wires firing for a wrong response and decreasing the resistance of the wires firing for a correct response. By ingenious mechanical means, he presented the letter E or F in various positions and orientations and recorded the machine's "answer" as to which letter was presented. He "punished" and "rewarded" it for wrong and correct answers by

*This, incidentally, was a difficult task for the technicians who did the wiring. It is usually done with great care, and the task of wiring randomly disturbed them.

increasing and decreasing, respectively, the resistance in the wires that fire. The machine "learned" to make this discrimination correctly every time after a number of trials. The shape of its learning curve was similar to that already seen for humans (Section 4.113). The fact that the product of this physical system is similar to the product of a biological system lends credence to the position that the structure of the physical system is similar to the structure of the biological system. The closeness of fit of the learning curve of the machine and the learning curve of man is an indication of the validity of the assumptions about man built into the machine.

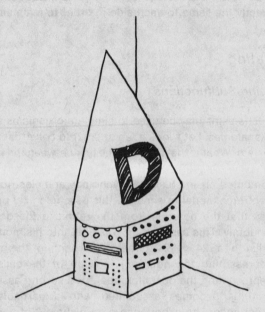

17.32   Simulating Self

If you can gain some understanding of a subfunction of your nervous system by simulating it, then you ought to be able to gain some understanding of yourself by simulating yourself—that is, by designing a mechanism that can do everything you can do. Just as the ultimate test of your understanding of the internal-combustion engine is that you can build one and make it work, the ultimate test of your understanding of yourself is that you can build yourself and make it work. It is a bootstrap operation, however, because, in order to simulate yourself, you would have to understand yourself. This thought experiment may be of value, though, because the attempt to design yourself may help you understand yourself.

You may first be tempted to try the traditional method of simulation by reproduction. Although this technique is fun, it is neither efficient (it takes so long—for incubation and growth, that is) nor effective. The replica never seems to come out exactly right; the child may not only be of the wrong sex but often contrives stubbornly to be of the wrong opinions. Humans have been seeking immortality by replicating themselves in this way for millions of years and have never completely succeeded.

Inspired by talk of transplants, you may try to reconstruct yourself from your various elements. Since one heart is very much like another heart and one lung is very much like another lung, these organs would not present a problem. You would run into trouble with the brain, however, because your brain is like no other brain. Your uniqueness lies in your nervous system. In a brain transplant it is the donor, not the recipient, who survives.

It is not necessary, however, to use biological materials. Your project is to simulate your function rather than to replicate your structure. That is, you want to build a mechanism that acts like you rather than looks like you. But since the task of replication is relatively easy (as a trip through Madame Tussaud's Wax Museum or Disneyland will attest), you may as well replicate your structure too. Indeed, it may be essential. Structure and function are so intimately interrelated that perhaps no other structure could perform precisely the same function. Besides, the criterion of your success would be that your friends respond to your robot as they would to you. This would require that it look like you as well as act like you.

17.322   *Ends*

This exercise of simulating ourselves raises some ethical issues. The goal of psychology—to understand ourselves—sounds harmless, but the fact that self-understanding implies self-simulation makes the enterprise ominous. Psychology has been so undisturbing and so undisturbed for so long because it has been so unsuccessful. As we get nearer and nearer our goal of self-understanding, and thus self-simulation, we will probably be confronted by mounting apprehension in ourselves and intervention by others. Your replica would be the ultimate in automation. Thus far we have been able to rationalize automation: anyone who *could* be replaced by a machine *should* be replaced by a machine; let the machines do the mechanical things and free us for the human things. As the machines become more and more humanlike, however, the domain of essentially "human things" shrinks and shrinks.

This exercise of simulating ourselves leads also, strangely enough, to humanistic concerns. As our machines become more and more "human," we are forced into a deeper and deeper consideration of what *is* essentially human. Critics set up criteria of what is human, simulators counterexample with a mechanism that meets those criteria, and the critics are forced to make their specifications more and more detailed. There is as much discussion of "self" in the simulation literature as there is in the humanistic literature, as attempts are made to design mechanisms that are self-initiating, self-reproducing, self-conscious, or self-understanding.

One by-product of the consideration of what is essentially human is a greater appreciation of ourselves. I remember, after hearing Rosenblatt describe the incredible technical difficulties he had faced in building a machine that could learn to distinguish the letters *E* and *F*, feeling a surge of pride in my taken-for-granted brain, which had made continuous mind movies all day every day for almost 30 years. All the awesome computer can do is arithmetic—though admittedly very quickly. It can do only what it is told, and it must be told in a very simple language. There is no way it can ever be any more intelligent than the programmer who instructs it. It is a dunce compared with that magnificent mobile movie studio cum movie theater of your mind.

Brain. An apparatus with which we think that we think.
Ambrose Bierce
The Devil's Dictionary

The brain is viewed as an appendage of the genital glands.
Carl Gustav Jung
Time, February 14, 1955
(on Freud's theory of sexuality)

18 Physiological Approach

18.1 Structure and Function

Have you ever heard the shaggy-dog story of the gluck maker? Briefly, a man enlisting in the navy describes his occupation as that of a gluck maker. Unwilling to display their ignorance, his superiors consent to permit him to make a gluck machine. After several months and several thousands of dollars, the gluck machine is finally ready. It is trundled out onto the deck, all huge and shiny and bristling with levers, dials, and flashing lights. It is lifted up by a crane and dropped over the side. As it sinks into the water, it goes "gluck, gluck, gluck." Any little humor in this story stems from the discrepancy between a complex structure and a simple function. There is a similar humor in the use of the most complex structure in the universe—the human brain—as a sort of telephone switchboard for linking incoming stimuli to outgoing responses. Nature is too stingy for this situation to be likely. The structure of a system is only as complex as it need be to perform its function.

The telephone switchboard analogy was inspired by the behaviorists' argument that, since the nervous system is so complex, it is more fruitful to focus only on what can be observed going in and coming out. Many psychologists argue that the need for the peripheralism of the behaviorist and the part-peripheralism of the postbehaviorist has passed. Their approach was appropriate only for a time, when the description of the brain as a "cerebral jungle" or a "great raveled knot" was justified. The jungle is now being cleared. The knot is now being unraveled. Modern techniques are revealing the secrets of this most mysterious system. It is now possible to explain the function of the nervous system in terms of the structure of the nervous system. Let's look at the facts on which this explanation would be based. Let's look at the brain behind the scenes. First, however, we'll glance at two techniques for discovering the function of a structure.

18.11 Ablation

18.111 The Perfect Design—Teitelbaum

The logic of an **ablation** study is simple. A structure is removed, and a function is observed. If there is a malfunction, then it can reasonably be inferred that this structure has something to do with this function. You use the same logic every time you take out a fuse, observe the lights that go out, and infer that that fuse controls those lights. The logic can be strengthened by observing the function before removing the structure to make sure that there is not already a malfunction and by conducting an autopsy after observing the function to make sure

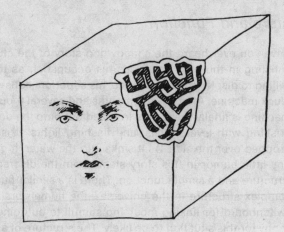

that the whole structure and nothing but the structure has been removed. The ideal ablation study, then, involves the following steps:

1. pretest function
2. remove structure
3. post-test function
4. conduct autopsy

You already know of an ablation study. Teitelbaum, you will remember, had reason to believe that the structure called the hypothalamus is associated with the function of eating (Section 2.232). He removed parts of the rat's hypothalamus and observed the animal's eating behavior. The rat's failure to stop eating until a certain body weight was reached led Teitelbaum to conclude that the function of that part of the hypothalamus is to switch off eating behavior.

18.112   An Approximation—Phineas Gage

Since human subjects are notoriously reluctant to have parts of their brain removed and to die to have autopsies performed, this perfect design can only be approximated. Some people oblige by having accidents, which offer some insight into the function of certain structures. One such person was Phineas Gage, a foreman on a construction gang who was tamping down a stick of dynamite with a crowbar when the dynamite went off and shot the crowbar through his frontal lobe. Since the function of the frontal lobe was something of a mystery, psychologists suddenly became interested in Phineas Gage.[34] An obvious first function to test was intelligence, since the relative size of the frontal lobe increases as one ascends the phylogenetic scale. An intelligence test was administered to Phineas Gage, and his intelligence was found to be average. A first limitation of these natural experiments is revealed here. Accidents cannot be anticipated, and thus pretests cannot be conducted. Phineas Gage could have been a genius reduced to mediocrity by the accident. It is more likely, however (considering how the accident occurred), that the injury did not produce any deficiency in intelligence. It was difficult to see exactly what deficiency it did produce. Apart from having a hole in his head, Phineas Gage seemed perfectly normal. But subtle changes were noted in his personality. Phineas Gage swore. Most of us swear, but Phineas Gage swore in front of ladies, which was frowned on in those far-off days. Phineas Gage pinched nurses. Many people pinch nurses, but Phineas Gage pinched nurses and didn't feel bad about it afterward. He seemed, then, to lack concern about the consequences of his actions. When he was discharged from the hospital, he was unconcerned about holding a steady job and providing for his family. These deficiencies suggest that the frontal lobe is vaguely associated with the function of anticipating and planning for the future. Phineas Gage wandered from place to place and put himself and his crowbar on public display to earn a living until he died, under suspicious circumstances that required an autopsy. This point illustrates a second limitation of such natural experiments. Autopsies are usually not performed, and thus the exact structural damage is rarely determined. A third limitation is that an accident is usually a very clumsy experiment. In the case of Phineas Gage, parts of the frontal lobe had not been destroyed and other parts of the brain had been destroyed. Thus intelligence cannot be unequivocally dissociated from the frontal lobe; neither can planning be unequivocally associated with it. Even if a pretest had been performed, the exact structure removed, and an autopsy conducted, a fourth limitation would remain. It is impossible to conduct control studies to verify if the malfunction is due to the removal of the structure or to the breaking of a chain of structures of which it is merely a single link. It is necessary to study the whole system of structures as well as each single structure.

18.12   Stimulation

Many of these difficulties can be circumvented by the alternative technique of **stimulation.** We have already seen (Section 9.11) the normal means of stimulating cortical neurons. Physical energy impinges on the appropriate sensory receptor, where it is transformed into nerve impulses, which travel to the appropriate projection area of the cortex. The same effect can be obtained by applying a mild electric shock directly to the cortical neurons. If you stimulate a certain structure and observe a certain function functioning, then it is reasonable to infer that this structure is associated with this function. If you stimulate the occipital lobe and observe that the subject reports visual sensations, then the function of the occipital lobe is presumably to receive visual stimuli. If you stimulate the frontal lobe just in front of the central fissure and observe that the subject's arm rises (without his intention and to his surprise), then the function of that part of the frontal lobe is presumably to initiate responses.

18.2 Structure of the Nervous System

18.21 The Neuron

18.211 All-or-None Law

The basic unit of the nervous system, as of all living systems, is the cell. More specifically, it is that specialized cell called the **neuron.** The nervous system consists of 10 billion neurons, give or take a billion. The neuron is a cell like all cells except that it is sensitive to environmental stimulation. When stimulated by the appropriate form of energy, it fires. That is, an impulse passes along it. The neuron fires in an all-or-none fashion, like a pistol. Either it fires or it does not fire, and, when it fires, it fires at full strength. Just as the pistol fires when the

trigger is pulled hard enough and does not fire when the trigger is not pulled hard enough, the neuron fires when the stimulus is strong enough and does not fire when the stimulus is not strong enough. The point at which the stimulus is just strong enough to fire the neuron is called the threshold. Just as the bullet does not move faster if the trigger is pulled harder and as the victim is not killed deader, the impulse does not move faster if the stimulus is stronger.

18.212   *Refractory Period*

If all stimuli above the threshold produce impulses of the same speed, how can we differentiate between a strong and a weak stimulus? The strong stimulus produces an impulse that is not faster but oftener. Strength of stimulus is thus translated into frequency of impulse. The mechanism underlying this transformation is as follows: After the neuron has fired, there is a refractory period during which the threshold is higher than normal. There is first an **absolute refractory period,** during which the threshold is infinite, and then a **relative refractory period,** during which the threshold is lower than infinite but higher than normal (see Figure 18-1). During the absolute refractory period, the neuron cannot be fired by any stimulus; during the relative refractory period, the neuron can be fired but only by stimuli stronger than those that would normally just fire it. The relative refractory period permits the translation of stimulus strength into impulse frequency. During the relative refractory period, the threshold becomes

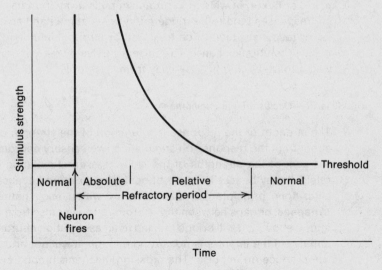

Figure 18-1. Relative and Absolute Refractory Periods

progressively lower. Thus the stronger the stimulus, the sooner the neuron can be fired again and the more impulses will be fired per second. The absolute refractory period determines the upper limit. If it is, for instance, 1/1,000 of a second, then the upper limit is 1,000 impulses per second. The calculation of the upper limit for neurons in the auditory nerve illustrates the destruction of a beautiful psychological theory by an ugly physiological fact. Once upon a time it was thought that the frequency of sound waves was translated directly into frequency of nerve impulses. The human ear can pick up frequencies of up to 20,000 cycles per second, but the neurons in the auditory nerve were found capable of firing only up to about 1,000 impulses per second. So much for that theory.

18.22   The Reflex Arc

18.221   Sensory, Association, and Motor Neurons

The 10 billion or so neurons in the nervous system may be divided into three groups. There are **sensory neurons,** responsible for receiving stimuli; **motor neurons,** responsible for initiating responses; and **association neurons,** responsible for linking sensory with motor neurons. A **reflex arc** is a direct circuit of sensory, association, and motor neurons linked so that stimulation of the sensory neurons triggers an immediate response from the motor neurons. Reflexes may be **extensor,** in which the organism reaches out to its environment, or **flexor,** in which the organism pulls away from its environment. Extensor responses tend to be triggered by weak stimuli and small objects, whereas flexor responses tend to be triggered by strong stimuli and large objects. This makes evolutionary sense. Organisms survive by reaching out to small objects, which they eat, and pulling away from large objects, which eat them.

18.222   The Synapse—Occlusion and Facilitation

The strength of the response is a function of the strength of the stimulus. The strength of the response on stimulating two sensory neurons is not necessarily the sum of the strengths of the responses on stimulating each neuron separately. It may be less because of **occlusion** or more because of **facilitation.** An all-or-none principle operates not only within each neuron but also at the **synapses,** or gaps between the neurons. If the impulse from a sensory neuron is strong enough, it will bridge the gap to an association neuron and produce a full impulse; if the impulse is not strong enough, it will not bridge the gap and thus will produce no impulse. The crossing mechanism apparently involves the secretion of a chemical called **acetylcholine,** which fills the gap. Nerve gases used during World War II inhibited the secretion of this chemical, preventing impulses from crossing synapses and causing immediate paralysis and eventual death. Psychedelic drugs used today may facilitate the secretion of this chemical, permitting impulses to cross synapses normally not crossed and causing novel perceptions and associations. Occlusion is the result of an association neuron firing to the two sensory neurons but also to either alone. Facilitation is the result of an association neuron firing to the two sensory neurons but not to either alone (Figure 18-2).

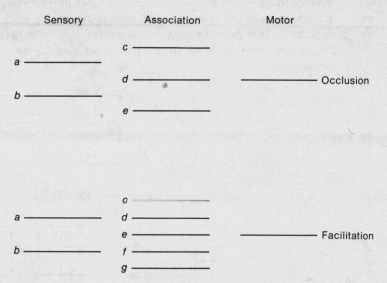

Figure 18-2. Occlusion and Facilitation. In the top diagram, sensory neuron a fires association neurons c and d, and sensory neuron b fires association neurons d and e. Since either a or b fires d, the response to both a and b together is less than the sum of the responses to both separately. In the bottom diagram, sensory neuron a fires association neurons c and d, and sensory neuron b fires association neurons f and g. Since neither a nor b fires e separately but do so together, the response to both a and b together is greater than the sum of the responses to both a and b separately.

18.23   The Nervous System

The structure of the nervous system from top to bottom complicates this simple model of the nervous system from outside to inside. The human nervous system represents the current climax of the processes of differentiation, centralization, and encephalization described in Section 14.212. Association neurons have developed very specialized functions, have clumped into structures responsible for each of those functions, and have gravitated toward the head end of the organism. The simple reflex arcs at the spinal cord for immediate responses are supplemented by complex chains through the brain for delayed responses. The chains through the brain are further divided into those through the lower brain for involuntary responses and those through the upper brain for voluntary responses.* A schematic diagram is presented in Figure 18.3. Control within the nervous system tends to be hierarchical. That is, structures in the cortex tend to control those in the brainstem, and structures in the brainstem in turn tend to control those in the spinal cord. Control within the nervous system tends to be inhibitory. That is, structures in the cortex tend to inhibit responses of the brainstem, and structures in the brainstem tend to inhibit responses of the spinal cord.†

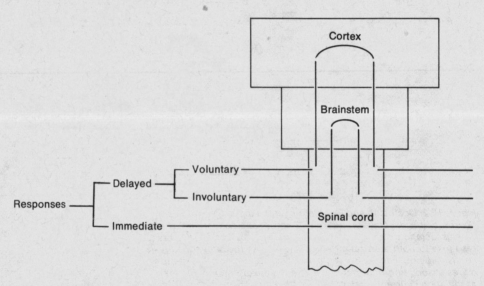

Figure 18-3. The Vertical Organization of the Nervous System

*The voluntary-involuntary distinction is somewhat vague. You get a feel for it, however, when you recognize that the command "Stop bleeding," grunted by the mobster boss to the cringing gunman in many a gangster movie, is less reasonable than the command "Stop talking." Bleeding is one of the functions of the lower brain, and talking is one of the functions of the upper brain.

†Spinal reflexes are stronger when the control of the brain is removed. The pioneer work on reflexes was done by Cabanis on the decapitated bodies of the victims of the guillotine during the French Revolution. I read elsewhere that Kuhne worked on the severed heads of the victims, making optograms of their last perception from the retinas. I don't know if Cabanis and Kuhne worked together. The picture of them waiting around for their respective parts is rather grim.

18.3   Function of the Nervous System

18.31   Cortical Structures

18.311   Projection and Association Areas

The areas of the cortex that are directly linked to sensory and motor neurons are called **projection areas.** The function of **sensory projection areas** is to receive stimuli through the sensory neurons from the receptors, and the function of **motor projection areas** is to initiate responses through the motor neurons to the muscles and the glands. The location of the various projection areas is indicated in Figure 18-4. Some facts about the motor projection area are worth noting. The size of the area in the cortex associated with each muscle group in the body is related to the subtlety of function, rather than the size of structure, of that muscle group. Thus the back, although large, is represented by a small area, and the hand, although small, is represented by a large area. The cortex is divided into two hemispheres, side by side, with the motor projection area of the left hemisphere controlling the right side of the body, and vice versa.* Thus injury to the motor area in the left hemisphere results in paralysis on the right side of the body. The left hemisphere is usually dominant over the right hemisphere. When two parts must work together, the most efficient arrangement is to have one part

*We have, essentially, then, two brains. This fact does not, however, guarantee our survival as a species. The dinosaur also had two brains—fore and aft, rather than side by side—but he is no longer with us, as documented in the following poem by BLT, a columnist for the *Chicago Tribune.*

> Behold the mighty dinosaur
> Famous in prehistoric lore
> Not only for his power and strength
> But for his intellectual length.
> You will observe by these remains
> The creature had two sets of brains—
> One in his head (the usual place)
> The other at his spinal base.
> Thus he could reason a priori
> As well as a posteriori.
> No problem bothered him a bit.
> He made both head and tail of it.
> If something slipt his forward mind
> 'Twas rescued by the one behind.
> And if in error he was caught
> He had a saving afterthought.
> Thus he could think without congestion
> Upon both sides of every question.
> Oh, gaze upon this model beast,
> Defunct ten million years at least.

dominant over the other.* Thus most people are right-eyed, right-handed, and right-footed. In an age of agitation for equal opportunities for minority groups, a word should be said for the left-handers forced to live in a right-handed world, where desks, golf clubs, checkbooks, and even written language are designed for the majority. Some left-handed individuals, like Leonardo da Vinci and Babe Ruth, have done well in motor activities nevertheless.

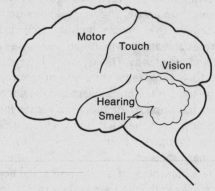

Figure 18-4. Location of the Various Projection Areas in the Cortex

18.312   Localization versus Mass Action

The areas of the cortex that are not projection areas are **association areas.** It is reasonable to link the remaining structures with the remaining functions. Association areas, then, are presumed to be responsible for the various complex processes (like perceiving, reasoning, remembering, planning, and so on) that intervene between the stimulus and the response. Whereas the various projection areas have been linked to the various sensory modalities, the various association areas have not been so linked to the various complex mental functions. Where there is doubt, there is inevitably debate. Some psychologists argue that each function is precisely localized in a particular structure **(localization),** and some argue that, for certain functions, the association areas of the cortex act as a whole **(mass action).** As a corollary to the latter position, it is argued that one part of the cortex can take over the function of another if it is destroyed **(equipotentiality).** Let's look at some evidence for mass action, some evidence for localization, and then a possible reconciliation of the two positions.

*People with no clear-cut cerebral dominance tend to be clumsy. One disadvantage of this arrangement is that, when you are lost with no visual cues, you tend to walk in circles when you are trying to walk in a straight line. You eventually stumble on a set of footprints that just seem to go on and on and on.

I honestly believe that I am left-handed because nanna forced me to stutter when I was a child.

The laws of mass action and equipotentiality were formulated by Lashley on the basis of a series of experiments.[60] He trained rats to run a maze, removed parts of their association areas, and retested them on the maze. Removal of the association-area structure did result in a deficiency in the maze-running function, thus linking, as expected, this structure with this function. He found, however, that the extent of the deficiency was related not to the location of the ablation, but to the extent of the ablation. The more association area removed, the greater the deficiency, regardless of where it was removed from. Goldstein and Scheerer performed an analogous experiment with human subjects and obtained analogous results.[32] The brain damage was caused by accidents rather than effected by surgery, and the deficiencies were in abstract reasoning rather than maze running. It was difficult for patients with parts of their association areas removed to disentangle themselves from concrete reality. They could not pretend to drink water from an imaginary glass. They could not interpret aphorisms like "A rolling stone gathers no moss" in anything but literal terms. They could not repeat a lie like "Snow is black." Extensions and distortions of reality, as in the metaphor and the lie, are uniquely human accomplishments. Lower organisms, with their responses more directly linked to stimuli, must tell it like it is. Patients with the intervening association area removed must return to this unwitting honesty. The more association area removed, the more true to their concrete environment they must become and the greater the deficiency in abstract reasoning.

Some deficiencies in higher mental functions have, on the other hand, been identified with very precisely localized areas of the association cortex. Ablations in particular areas result predictably in the inability to recognize familiar objects **(agnosia),** the inability to use language **(aphasia),** and the inability to make purposeful movements **(apraxia).** The location of those ablations suggests that the association area is divided into (1) specific association areas for organization of information from each sensory modality, located near the projection area for that modality, and (2) a general association area for organization of information from all modalities.

Gleitman makes an analogy that suggests a possible reconciliation between these two apparently irreconcilable positions. Imagine a regiment of soldiers all trained in rifle firing and some trained also in machine-gun firing. Reduction in the rifle firing capacity would be related to the number of soldiers killed, whereas reduction in machine-gun firing would be related to the particular soldiers killed (Figure 18-5). Similarly, if a set of cells had a general as well as a specific function, the mass-action principle would apply to its general function and the localization principle to its specific function. Lashley obtained some evidence for this position when he demonstrated a decrease in maze-running ability as a result of removing the occipital lobes of blind rats. It appears, then, that the occipital lobe has the general maze-running function and the specific visual reception function.

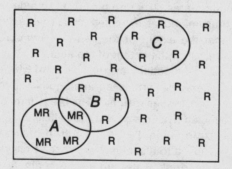

Figure 18-5. Reconciliation of Mass Action and Localization. The killing of the soldiers in each of sets A, B, and C would have the same effect on rifle firing, as mass action predicts, but would have a different effect (A would destroy it, B would reduce it, C would not affect it) on machine-gun firing, as localization would predict.

18.32 Finding the Function of a Given Structure

The sensory and motor projection areas of the cortex have been clearly identified with the functions of receiving stimuli and initiating responses, respectively. It seems reasonable to link the remaining structures—the association areas—with the remaining functions—the higher mental processes that intervene between the stimulus and the response. In this section we will consider the attempt to determine the function of one of those structures, the frontal lobe; in the next section we will consider the attempt to identify the structure associated with one of those functions, remembering.

18.321 The Mystery of the Frontal Lobe

The function of the frontal lobe is a mystery. Since the frontal lobe increases in relative size as one ascends the phylogenetic scale, it would appear to have something to do with intelligence. However, you will remember that the unfortunate Phineas Gage, who had a crowbar shot through his frontal lobe, got an average score on an intelligence test after the accident (Section 18.112). The effect seemed to be not so much a decrement in intelligence as an inability to inhibit inappropriate responses.

18.322 Not Responding

This finding suggests that the function of the frontal lobe is that of not responding. Experiment after experiment suggests that the deficit in patients with frontal-lobe damage is that they lack the capacity to not respond. The reason we have had so much difficulty in determining this function is that it is hard to differentiate between responding and not not responding. After the fact, however, the explanation seems obvious. As we ascend the phylogenetic scale, the ratio of association to projection areas of the cortex increases. It is these association areas, which are linked to neither sensory input nor motor output, that free us from the tyranny of our environment by permitting us the luxury of not responding. Our "uncommitted cortex" is located primarily in the frontal lobe. The repertoire of possible responses also increases as we ascend the phylogenetic scale and, with it, the need to inhibit responses. Since the organism is spontaneously active, what needs to be explained is not why it responds but why it makes only one response at a time out of its vast repertoire of responses and why it sometimes chooses not to respond at all. The explanation is beginning to emerge. The frontal lobe inhibits inappropriate responses. Remove it and we become, like our friends farther down the phylogenetic scale, at the mercy of our environment. But why does the frontal lobe say "no" to the environment? Perhaps it has plans of its own. We have already discussed Miller, Galanter, and Pribram's distinction between plans and images (Section 17.222). They speculate that plans are associated with the frontal lobe and images with the rest of the cortex.

18.33   Finding the Structure for a Given Function

18.331   The Mystery of the Missing Memory Trace

I tell you something new today, and you remind me of it tomorrow. Obviously something happened way down among your neurons when I gave you that information. What happened? Where did it happen? How did it happen? Since you have preserved this information over time, there must be a certain "something" that is stored "somewhere." But what and where is it? Many psychologists have assigned themselves to this baffling case of the missing memory trace.

18.332   Not Anywhere because Everywhere?

A spate of recent evidence suggests why the missing memory trace has created such a mystery: we could not find it anywhere because it is everywhere. The ubiquitous is paradoxically elusive. Early chemists spent much time looking for "phlogiston," the inferred ingredient of combustible materials that was consumed when they burned. The search was abandoned when it was realized that combustibility is an intrinsic property of some materials. We early psychologists have spent much time looking for "memory," the inferred component of the nervous system in which information is stored. Perhaps we have reached the stage at which this search can be abandoned, since the capacity to retain information is an intrinsic property of the nervous system. Memory is not an element of the nervous system but a property of it. We don't have memories—we *are* our memories.

We have already considered two theories of memory—McConnell's theory that information is stored chemically (Section 3.12) and Hebb's theory that information is stored neurologically (Section 5.32). The two theories are not necessarily incompatible. Memory involves three subfunctions of information processing: assimilating, retaining, and retrieving—that is, getting information into the store, holding it there, and getting it back out again. The process whereby we make deposits and withdrawals in our memory bank need not be the same process whereby they are stored there. Perhaps assimilating involves the activation of neural circuits, as Hebb suggests, and retrieving involves the reactivation of the same neural circuits. However, the retaining of the information in the interval may involve the coding of the neural circuit into the RNA molecule. Thus the memory areas are processing centers rather than storage depots. Location is irrelevant, because the same pattern serves as a key to the chemical code regardless of its location. The debate about whether memory involves a change in the relationship between neurons or a change within each neuron may perhaps be resolved (as are so many debates in science) by the recognition that both positions are partially true.

Man can will nothing unless he has first understood that he must count on no one but himself; that he is alone, abandoned on earth in the midst of his infinite responsibilities, without help, with no other aim than the one he sets himself, with no other destiny than the one he forces for himself on this earth.

Jean Paul Sartre
Le Étre et le Néant

He was welded into a single personality which was dominated by a single desire. For some moments he could not flee, no more than a little finger can commit a revolution from a hand.... There was a consciousness always of the presence of his comrades about him. He felt the subtle battle brotherhood more potent even than the cause for which they were fighting. It was a mysterious fraternity born of the smoke and danger of death.... He suddenly lost concern for himself, and forgot to look at a menacing fate. He became not a man but a member.

Stephen Crane
The Red Badge of Courage

19 Sociological Approach

19.1 Systems within Systems within Systems

19.11 Levels of Analysis

I have defined psychology as the study of the nervous system. Since the nervous system is part of a hierarchy of systems within systems within systems, some insight into its function can be gained by studying the systems above and below it within this hierarchy. A group is a system of which a person is an element, a person is a system of which the nervous system is an element, a nervous system is a system of which a neural structure is an element, a neural structure is a system of which a neuron is an element, and so on. In the last chapter we focused on the level below the nervous system (physiological approach); in this chapter we'll focus on the level above the nervous system (sociological approach). Of course, the same phenomenon can be considered at each different level. Propositions can refer to a system within the hierarchy or to a relationship between systems within the hierarchy. The following propositions, for example, could be made in a discussion of LSD:

"LSD facilitates the secretion of acetylcholine, which increases the probability that an impulse will cross a synapse."	physiology
"Because there is a greater probability of impulses crossing synapses, there is more likelihood of new combinations of ideas and thus greater creativity."	physiological psychology
"A student under the influence of LSD is reported to have jumped out of a third-story window assuming that he could fly."	psychology

"After many trips, acidheads tend to refuse to partici-   social
pate in any group activity."   psychology

"Legislation against LSD isolates the subculture of   sociology
users and puts a high tariff on acid, so that the users
fall prey to the subculture of pushers."

19.12   Reductionism

There is a tendency within this hierarchy toward reductionism. That is, it is
assumed that any proposition at one level can be reduced to an equivalent
proposition at the next lower level and that this lower-level proposition will be
more meaningful. It is further assumed that a system can be *described* only at its
own level of analysis and that it can be *explained* only in terms of the system
below, and that an explanation is more valid than a description. Thus sociology
is reduced to psychology, and psychology is reduced to physiology. But taking a
specific proposition and reducing it from the sociological level to the psychological level and then to the physiological level suggests a flaw in the reductionist
doctrine. "Nixon defeated McGovern in the 1972 presidential election" is a
proposition at the sociological level. It could be reduced to propositions about
the decisions of the delegates as they voted for one of the two candidates. Such
propositions at the psychological level could in turn be reduced to propositions
about impulses passing over synapses at the physiological level. However, it is
obviously inappropriate to discuss the outcome of an election in terms of impulses crossing synapses.

Each phenomenon should be considered at all *appropriate* levels of analysis.
There is as little need for the psychologist to wait for the physiologist to complete his analysis as there is for the physiologist to wait for the psychologist to
complete his. The work of the physiologist is no more "fundamental"; the two
approaches complement each other. The psychologist describes the phenomena that the physiologist must explain, and the physiologist describes
the limitations of this description. The important thing is to be aware of the level
of analysis at which we are working and to know when we switch from one level
of analysis to another. Many debates in science result from scientists talking
past one another at different levels of analysis.

19.13   Social Psychology and Psychological Sociology

The focus of this book is on you as a system. In the last chapter, however, we
moved in for a close-up, focusing on subsystems of which you are composed. In
this chapter we will move out for a long shot, focusing on supersystems of which

you are an element. In the last chapter you were looked at under the micro-scope; in this chapter you will be looked at through the telescope.

If psychology is the study of the individual and sociology is the study of the group, then social psychology, the study of the relationship between the individual and the group, tends to be more psychological than social. Most social-psychological studies focus on social influences on the individual. Social perception, social learning, and social motivation are simply subtopics of perception, learning, and motivation, in which the emphasis is on the impact of the social rather than the physical environment on the individual. Only a few studies in social psychology—or, better, psychological sociology—emphasize the social over the psychological by putting the focus on the group, with the individual as an element of the group. We will consider social psychology in Section 19.2 and psychological sociology in Section 19.3.

19.2   The Individual and the Group

19.21   Social Needs

The need-reduction theory (Section 2.2) explains behavior purely in terms of physiological needs, like hunger and thirst. Other organisms are considered, if at all, merely as rivals for the available resources. We recognize, however, that much of our behavior is determined by our relationships with other people. We do things to get praise and avoid criticism, to win friends and influence people, to gain power and earn prestige. Physiological needs are more basic, since they must be satisfied or the organism will die; but social needs may be more power-ful, as attested by the suicide and the martyr. Murray has defined and cataloged a number of such social needs and initiated much research on them.[75] Let's look at two representative studies of social needs—a study by Milgram on the need for deference and a study by Schachter on the need for affiliation.

19.211   nDeference—Milgram

Murray defines the need for deference (**nDeference**) as the need to "admire and support a superior, to raise, honor, or eulogize. To emulate an exemplar. To conform to custom." Milgram performed a series of experiments on the need for deference that so shocked the academic world that, when I was introduced to those studies in graduate school, he was referred to as Mr. X.[70] Let me describe the experiment before considering the ethical issue it raised. When a subject arrived in the laboratory, he found another subject already in the waiting room. This latter "subject" was a stooge following Milgram's instructions. The two were ushered into the experimental room, where they were told that they were about to participate in an experiment on the effects of punishment on learning. They drew lots to determine who would be the teacher and who the learner. By prearrangement, the stooge was always the learner. After watching the stooge being strapped into an electric-chair-like apparatus with all sorts of electrical gadgets attached, the teacher was seated in front of an impressive panel with a row of levers marked from 15 to 450 volts at 15-volt intervals (Figure 19-1). He was told to give the learner problems and to administer shocks (starting with the lowest and working up) every time he made a mistake. The stooge made prearranged errors and exclamations, as indicated in Figure 19-1. Milgram was interested in how far the subject would go before he refused to obey the instructions. All of the 40 subjects went to at least 300 volts, and 26 went all the way to 450 volts. The average maximum shock varied directly with number of years in military service and inversely with number of years in school. That is, the more years one spends in the army, the more likely he is to obey; the more years one spends in school, the less likely he is to obey.

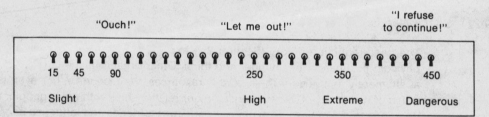

Figure 19-1. Diagram of Panel Used in Studies of Obedience. Prearranged exclamations by the stooge are indicated above the "voltage" at which they were emitted.

Many psychologists were disturbed by this experiment on ethical grounds. They feared that some of the subjects would be upset when they reconsidered what they had done, even though they were told the true nature of the experiment afterward. Milgram countered with the argument that the remote possibility of some minor damage to the self-images of a few individuals is small risk compared with the tremendous advantage of gaining some understanding of this important phenomenon. Its importance is obvious when we recognize that Milgram was studying the **Eichmann effect**—the fact that an individual is willing to commit atrocities he would not normally commit when he sees himself as merely an instrument of some higher authority. The experiment leaves little doubt about the response a military man would make when commanded to press a button leading to the slaughter of thousands of remote victims. Such phenomena must be understood to be controlled. Milgram has contributed a great deal to such an understanding.

Murray defines the need for affiliation (**nAffiliation**) as the need to "draw near and enjoyably cooperate or reciprocate with an allied other (an other who resembles the subject or who likes the subject). To please and win affection of a cathected object. To adhere and remain loyal to a friend." The experience is much more real than any definition can evoke. You have all felt it. You come home alone to your hotel room in a strange city. There is something missing. Is it food? No, you have just eaten. Is it stimulation? No, you flip idly through TV channels and magazines, but there is no interest. You finally find yourself walking the streets or sitting in a bar, looking for someone to be with. You have a need for affiliation. Schachter performed a series of experiments to provide a more intimate understanding of this need.[85] He collected reports of the experiences of prisoners in solitary confinement, of religious ascetics in retreat, of hermits, of castaways, and of other individuals who, by choice or circumstance, found themselves alone for long periods of time. The most consistent finding was that isolation produces anxiety. He reasoned that the need for

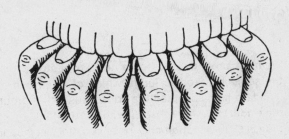

affiliation—the need not to be alone—would increase with anxiety. To test this hypothesis, he randomly divided a group of coeds at the University of Minnesota into two groups. One group (high-anxiety group) was given instructions that led them to believe they were going to be subjected to a severe shock; the other group (low-anxiety group) was given instructions that suggested they were going to receive a very mild shock. As anticipated, the high-anxiety group contained significantly more girls who wanted to be with others than did the low-anxiety group. What others? Two groups in the high-anxiety condition were asked, respectively, if they wanted to be with others in the same situation or with others waiting to see their professors. There was a marked preference to be with others in the same predicament. Misery doesn't love any old company but only miserable company.

Not all members of the high-anxiety group wanted to be with others when they were anxious. Was there any consistent difference between those who did and those who did not? Yes. First-borns have a greater tendency than later-borns to seek out others when they are anxious. Schachter followed up this surprising fact. He found that first-borns are more likely to seek psychiatric help than later-borns, and later-borns are more likely to become alcoholics than first-borns. When they are anxious, first-borns turn to others, but later-borns turn to the bottle. If being alone leads to anxiety and anxiety interferes with performance, later-borns should perform better in lonely tasks. Sure enough, Schachter found that later-borns are better fighter-pilots than first-borns. Schachter explains this peculiar relationship in terms of child-training practices. When the first child is born, the parents are inexperienced and insecure. They try to attend to the child's needs as soon as he begins to cry. Since the pattern of emotional life is set at an early age, the first-born continues to seek others when he is anxious. When the second, third, and fourteenth children are born, the parents are more sophisticated and more secure. They do not have the same tendency (or the time) to rush to the child as soon as he begins to cry for attention. Thus later-borns do not learn to seek out others when they are anxious but turn to other things.

19.22 Conformity

19.221 Studying Conformity

We have already discussed a number of studies of conformity. In Asch's study the subject, asked to judge which of three comparison lines was equal to a standard line, accepted the consensus of the group although it conflicted with the evidence of his senses (Section 16.212). In Sherif's study subjects, asked to indicate the direction and distance a light moved in a dark room, agreed more

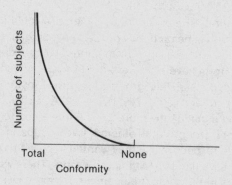

Figure 19-2. The J Curve of Conformity

when tested in a group than when tested individually (Section 16.212). In Milgram's study subjects, when commanded by a man in a white lab coat, "shocked" other "subjects" (Section 19.211). The most significant finding across all these studies is the surprisingly high degree of conformity. Indeed, whereas most psychological phenomena are best described by the normal distribution, conformity best fits the *J curve* (Figure 19-2). That is, most people conform completely to a law, and very few ignore it completely. This curve was generated by a psychologist who stood by a set of traffic lights and observed responses to the stimulus of the red light. Most drivers stopped completely, some slowed down but went through, and very few ignored it completely. This fact brings us to the next point. It is very comforting to be able to go through a green light and be almost certain that you are not going to be annihilated by someone coming through the red light. No one likes to be called a conformist. It has become a derogatory term. Fortunately, we are all conformists. A society is, by definition, a bunch of conformists.

19.222   Producing Conformity

Much of man's dealings with man involves producing conformity. The salesman selling cars, the minister making converts, the policeman eliciting confessions, the parent raising children, the teacher stating opinions, and the politician soliciting votes are all attempting to make others conform. Let's turn from the theoretical study of behavior to the practical business of changing behavior.

Let's focus on the method of changing behavior that has been called brain-washing.

A number of United Nations soldiers, captured by the Chinese Communists during the Korean War, refused repatriation. Their transformation from Capitalists to Communists was attributed to the process of brainwashing. Much concern was expressed over a device powerful enough to make anyone prefer Communism to Capitalism. The Chinese Communists must be as far ahead of the United States in their conquest of inner space as the United States is ahead of them in their conquest of outer space. Many of the servicemen did choose repatriation. A psychologist named Schein interviewed them in transit home and published the following summary of the principles underlying the Chinese technique of brainwashing.[88]

Several general principles underlay the various phases of the Chinese indoctrination, which may be worth summing up at this point. The first of these was *repetition.* One of the chief characteristics of the Chinese was their immense patience in whatever they were doing; whether they were conducting an interrogation, giving a lecture, chiding a prisoner, or trying to obtain a confession, they were always willing to make their demand or assertion over and over again. Many men pointed out that most of the techniques used gained their effectiveness by being used in this repetitive way until the prisoner could no longer sustain his resistance. A second characteristic was the *pacing of demands.* In the various kinds of responses that were demanded of the prisoners, the Chinese always started with trivial, innocuous ones and, as the habit of responding became established, gradually worked up to more important ones. Thus after a prisoner had once been "trained" to speak or write out trivia, statements on more important issues were demanded of him. This was particularly effective in eliciting confessions, self-criticism, and information during interrogation.

Closely connected with the principle of pacing was the principle of constant *participation* from the prisoner. It was never enough for the prisoner to listen and absorb; some kind of verbal or written response was always demanded. Thus if a man would not give original material in question-and-answer sessions, he was asked to copy something. Likewise, group discussions, autobiographical statements, self-criticisms, and public confessions were all demanded as active participation by the prisoner.

No matter which technique the Chinese were using, they always structured the situation in such a way that the correct response was followed by some form of *reward*, while an incorrect response was immediately followed by *threats* or *punishment.* The fact that the Chinese had complete control over material resources and had a monopoly of power made it possible for them to manipulate hunger and some other motives at will, thereby giving rewards and punishments their meaning.

In essence, the prisoner-of-war experience in camp can be viewed as a series of problems which each man had to solve in order to remain alive and well integrated. Foremost was the problem of physical privation, which powerfully motivated each man to improve his living conditions. A second problem was to overcome the fears of nonrepatriation, death, torture, or reprisals. A third problem was to maintain some kind of cognitive integration, a consistent outlook on life, under a set of conditions where basic values and beliefs were strongly undermined and where systematic confusion about each man's role in life was created. A fourth problem was to maintain a valid position in a group, to maintain friendship ties and concern for others under conditions of mutual distrust, lack of leadership, and systematically created social disorganization. The Chinese had created a set of conditions in which collaboration and the acceptance of Communism led to a resolution of conflicts in all these areas.

It is interesting to compare these statements with the following.

If one wishes to produce Conformity for good or evil, the formula is clear. Manage to arouse a need or needs that are important to the individual or the group. Offer a goal which is appropriate to the need or needs. Make sure that Conformity is instrumental to the achievement of the goal and that the goal is as large and as certain as possible. Apply the goal or reward at every opportunity. Try to prevent the object of your efforts from obtaining an uncontrolled education. Choose a setting that is ambiguous. Do everything possible to see that the individual has little or no confidence in his own position. Do everything possible to make the norm which you set appear highly valued and attractive. Set it at a level not too far initially from the starting point of the individual or group, and move it gradually toward the behavior you wish to produce. Be absolutely certain you know what you want and that you are willing to pay an enormous price in human quality, for whether the individual or the group is aware of it or not, the result will be CONFORMITY.

This quote is from a manual for potential dictators, a twentieth-century version of Machiavelli's *The Prince* provided by two American psychologists, Walker and Heyns, as a summary of their *Anatomy for Conformity.*[108] The principles uncovered by both studies are essentially the same. Chinese psychologists do not know any more about changing behavior than American psychologists do. Indeed, Chinese psychologists do not know any more about changing behavior than attentive students of an introductory course in psychology do. You recognize, of course, in the preceding summaries, the now-familiar need-reduction theory, law of effect, and method of successive approximations.

19.3 The Group as a System

19.31 Two-Person Group

19.311 The Communication Unit

You and I, at this moment, form a group—a cozy little group of two but neverthe-less a group. It is a most precarious group, since you may choose at any time to break our communication link by tossing this book away. But as long as you continue reading, we are a group. (Are you still there?) In the language of communication theory, I am the source, you are the destination, and we are communicating over the visual channel. Since I cannot communicate my thoughts to you directly, I encode them by writing and you decode them by reading. If you were to write me a letter explaining why you tossed my book away, we would become a group again while I was reading your letter. This time, however, you would be the source and I would be the destination. If you were to phone me demanding an apology for wasting your time with this book, you would re-establish our group, but you would have switched channels. Speaking and listening are means of encoding and decoding to communicate over the auditory channel. If I had the nerve to argue with you, we would then alternate the roles of source and destination. This possibility of two-way communication is one of the advantages of the auditory over the visual channel. The counterad-vantage of the visual channel is, of course, that cold print is more permanent than hot air. If you were to come here and confront me face-to-face with your complaints, you would add the rich communication of gestures and expressions of the visual channel. Until then, why don't you settle for writing rude remarks in the margin?

19.312 Behavioristic Analysis

No matter how intimate we become, however, your only source of information about me is my behavior. The information may be first-hand, as when we meet and you observe my behavior directly, or it may be second-hand, as when you get an account of my behavior from someone who has met me or when you read this book, which is a product of my behavior. Similarly, all I can ever know of you is what you choose to show me by your behavior and what I hear about your behavior from other people. I cannot see your hypothalamus. (Even if I could, I doubt that I would recognize it as a hypothalamus and certainly not as your hypothalamus.) Your intervening variables and your hypothetical constructs don't show. Thus, in the analysis of groups, only the behavior of the members is relevant.

We tend to think that the behaviorists are right only about simple phenomena and that their argument breaks down for complex phenomena. Strangely, however, it appears that their simple theory applies most aptly to this complex phenomenon of interpersonal communication. This obvious but neglected fact is being rediscovered by encounter groupies who would shudder at being described as behaviorists. Since other people have no source of direct information about you other than your behavior, you must keep everything up front. If someone you love has an annoying habit that bothers you, he or she will never know unless you say so. You cannot assume that that person will know unless you provide evidence of your dissatisfaction through your behavior. We can know people only through the immediate evidence contained in their behavior, not through inferences about their behavior. Isn't it too bad that our interpersonal communication has degenerated so much that such obvious facts need to be rediscovered and heralded as inventions?

19.313   A Web or a Net?

Your relationship with me is only one—and a minor one—of thousands of relationships you have, off and on, with thousands of people. You are an element in a complex system of communication units. Perhaps you view this situation as one of being entangled in a web—a web from which there is no escape. No man is an island or even a peninsula. Even the hermit does not escape. Since he could not have survived his early years without the care of others, he must have introjecting others within himself. The hermit may no longer be in society, but society is still in him.

It would be more fruitful, however, to consider this communication network as a net in which you are supported rather than as a web in which you are entangled. Other people are your major sources of information. Write down ten propositions that you know you know. From the most simple ("I'm Helen Chesterfield") to the most complex ("$E = mc^2$"), you will almost always find that you learned them from someone else. Other people are also your major source of feedback. You may be your own theory, but other people provide you with the evidence for it. You see yourself in the mirrors of other people. This does not necessarily mean that you must become a victim of other-control. By constantly checking your conceptual map against the more immediate perceptual map, you can retain self-control. If you establish sound standards for evaluating, comparing, and organizing the information you receive from other people, you can counter the tendency to other-control, which is an inevitable outcome of the fact that we are each an element in a complex communication network.

19.32   Small Group

In any typical day, you will find yourself constituting an element of a small group: in a row of people waiting for a bus, in a seminar in a classroom, in a bull session in a cafeteria, in a cozy group squashed in an elevator, in a group-therapy session at a hospital, in an audience at a play. The seminar, bull session, and therapy groups seem different somehow from the bus, elevator, and audience groups. In the former the behavior of one member tends to influence the behavior of the others. Such groups, then, possess the basic characteristic of a

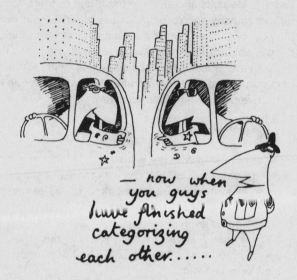

— now when you guys have finished categorizing each other......

system: changes in one element produce predictable changes in the others. Thus they may be studied scientifically. Many techniques have been devised for the scientific study of such small, face-to-face groups. Chapple had an observer for each member of the group press a pen to a moving tape while his member was talking and raise the pen when he was not talking. This simple on-off system provides not only quantitative information about the volume of talking but qualitative information about the tendency for one member to interrupt others or for another member to contribute many short interjections rather than a few long monologues. A famous study by Barker and Wright involved following boys in Midwestern towns throughout the day, recording every detail of their interactions with the social and physical environment. Predictably, then, when they turned to the study of small groups, they produced complete videotapes of every second of each session from many angles.

19.321   How Small Is "Small"?

Those techniques apply only when the elements are interdependent. The people in the line-up waiting for a bus or in the theater audience are simply a set, not a system. A set becomes a system when the independent elements become interdependent. We see this process when the set of people selected for a jury evolves into a system as they discuss the case, as dramatized in the movie *12 Angry Men*. If the system is too large, however, it tends to degenerate into subsystems and can be studied only in terms of the interaction between subsystems. How large is too large? It is probably smaller than we tend to think. As the number of members of a group increases linearly (2, 3, 4, 5, . . .), the number of communication links between them increases factorially (1, 3, 6, 10, 15, . . .). Very soon there are too many communication links to keep open simultaneously. It has been estimated that five is the optimal number of people to have for dinner. Any fewer and interest tends to lag; any more and some people tend not to be personally engaged. Groups larger than five tend to break down into subgroups.

19.322   *Interaction Process Analysis—Bales*

Let's look in detail now at another technique for studying small groups—a technique that walks the tightrope between the contentless form of Chapple and the formless content of Barker and Wright. This technique, called **interaction process analysis**, was developed by Bales.[4]

Let's imagine that you are an observer trained by Bales. A small group is working on a problem in one room, and you are recording their interaction in another room. You are separated by a one-way glass and linked by a one-way microphone so that you can observe them but they cannot observe you. You record each of the acts of each of the members of the group in one of the 12 categories listed in Figure 19–3. At the end of the session you have a large number of statements of the form "Subject *X* (initiator) directed act *Y* to subject *Z* (target) during time period *W*." You can organize this information according to initiators and targets to yield a **matrix**, according to acts to yield a **profile**, or according to time to yield a **phase sequence**, as indicated in Figure 19–4. Organization of the information in these summary forms reveals certain regularities. Matrices reveal a tendency for the members of a group to reach a balance with respect to the relative amount of activity they initiate and receive. Each member receives about half as many acts as he initiates. The more acts a member initiates, the more acts he tends to receive. Profiles reveal a tendency for attempted answers to outnumber their related questions and for positive reactions to outnumber their related negative reactions. This sounds reasonable. Group interaction would not continue unless there were more answers than questions and more positive reactions than negative reactions. Phase sequences reveal that groups presented with a problem tend to shift their emphasis from the problem of orientation (What is it?) to the problem of evaluation

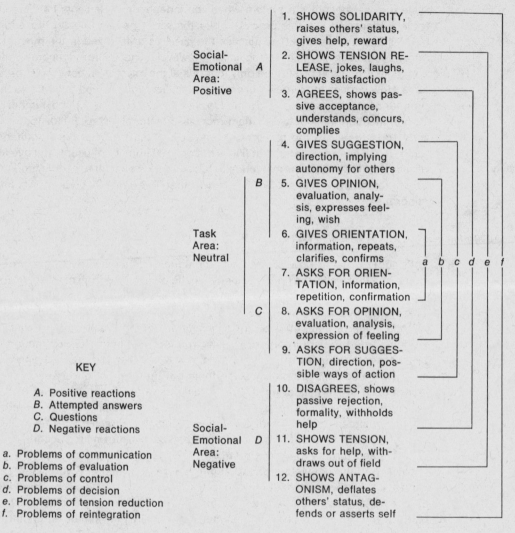

Social-Emotional Area: Positive	A	1. SHOWS SOLIDARITY, raises others' status, gives help, reward
		2. SHOWS TENSION RELEASE, jokes, laughs, shows satisfaction
		3. AGREES, shows passive acceptance, understands, concurs, complies
Task Area: Neutral	B	4. GIVES SUGGESTION, direction, implying autonomy for others
		5. GIVES OPINION, evaluation, analysis, expresses feeling, wish
		6. GIVES ORIENTATION, information, repeats, clarifies, confirms
	C	7. ASKS FOR ORIENTATION, information, repetition, confirmation
		8. ASKS FOR OPINION, evaluation, analysis, expression of feeling
		9. ASKS FOR SUGGESTION, direction, possible ways of action
Social-Emotional Area: Negative	D	10. DISAGREES, shows passive rejection, formality, withholds help
		11. SHOWS TENSION, asks for help, withdraws out of field
		12. SHOWS ANTAGONISM, deflates others' status, defends or asserts self

a b c d e f

KEY

A. Positive reactions
B. Attempted answers
C. Questions
D. Negative reactions

a. Problems of communication
b. Problems of evaluation
c. Problems of control
d. Problems of decision
e. Problems of tension reduction
f. Problems of reintegration

Figure 19-3. The Set of Categories in Interaction Process Analysis

(How do we feel about it?) to the problem of control (What shall we do about it?). As the session progresses, both positive and negative reactions tend to increase. By systematically varying the size, composition, and problems of the group, you can use this objective and organized method of recording to study the effects of changing these variables on the interaction.

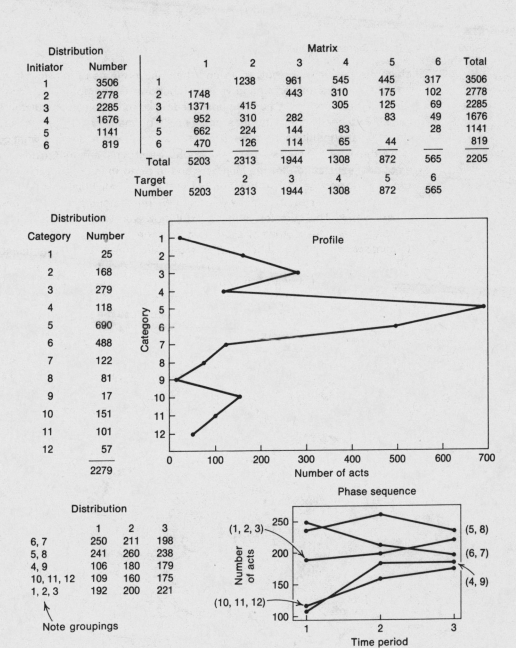

Distribution

Initiator	Number
1	3506
2	2778
3	2285
4	1676
5	1141
6	819

Matrix

	1	2	3	4	5	6	Total
1		1238	961	545	445	317	3506
2	1748		443	310	175	102	2778
3	1371	415		305	125	69	2285
4	952	310	282		83	49	1676
5	662	224	144	83		28	1141
6	470	126	114	65	44		819
Total	5203	2313	1944	1308	872	565	2205
Target	1	2	3	4	5	6	
Number	5203	2313	1944	1308	872	565	

Distribution

Category	Number
1	25
2	168
3	279
4	118
5	690
6	488
7	122
8	81
9	17
10	151
11	101
12	57
	2279

Profile

Category

Number of acts

Phase sequence

Distribution

	1	2	3
6, 7	250	211	198
5, 8	241	260	238
4, 9	106	180	179
10, 11, 12	109	160	175
1, 2, 3	192	200	221

Note groupings

(1, 2, 3)

(5, 8)

(6, 7)

(4, 9)

(10, 11, 12)

Number of acts

Time period

Figure 19-4.   Matrix, Profile, and Phase Sequence

Much discussion has revolved around the relative merits of individuals as opposed to groups for performing various functions. Grandmother has, as usual, two contradictory bits of conventional wisdom so that she can postdict in every case: ''Two heads are better than one,'' but ''Too many cooks spoil the broth.'' Under what conditions does the former statement apply and under what conditions the latter? The two basic functions of groups are to provide social-emotional satisfaction for the members and to perform tasks. By definition, the group performs the former function better than the individual, and the impressive success of Alcoholics Anonymous and Weight Watchers attests to how well it performs it. The question is meaningful, however, with respect to the latter function. Does the output of a group correspond to the lowest common denominator or to the highest common multiple of the output of its members? Advocates of **brainstorming**, in which members of a group toss out spontaneous ideas on some topic with the understanding that the other members will not criticize them, argue that the number of ideas generated is greater than the sum of ideas that each individual could generate, because the suggestions of others

stimulate ideas that the individual would not have thought of on his own. On the other hand, Janis[49] has pointed out the limitations of "groupthink," which has resulted in some poor decisions by various U.S. presidents and their advisers.

Since problem solving involves information processing and decision making, it may be that the group is superior for information processing and the individual for decision making. A group must have at least the sum of the information of its members and thus perhaps inevitably performs the former function better. An individual is a more tightly organized system than is a group and thus perhaps is better able to organize this information and make a decision based on it. However, decision making affects other people more than information processing does. Therefore, in a democracy, information processing tends to be the function of the individual and decision making tends to be the function of the group.

19.33 Large Group

19.331 How Large Is "Large"?

As the social scientist steps farther and farther back from you to view larger and larger groups, you shrink smaller and smaller. If the group is very large, you dwindle to a dot. The sociologist who studies large groups cannot make any predictions about you but only about some limited aspect abstracted from you. From his lofty perspective you are no longer an individual but a member. He can, however, make statistical predictions about the set of which you are a member. Thus he cannot predict that you will kill yourself on the road on Thanksgiving Weekend but only that 500 plus or minus 25 people like you will do so. Similarly, the physicist cannot make absolute statements about the behavior of individual molecules but only statistical statements about the behavior of large numbers of molecules. The larger the number, the greater the accuracy of the prediction. The number of molecules is so large that random variation is essentially removed and statistical statements become absolute statements. Sociologists are not so fortunate. Because the numbers they deal with are not sufficiently large for the law of large numbers to fully apply, sociologists are condemned to using statistical statements. "Large," then, is large enough to make predictions with the desired degree of accuracy.

The sociologist can make you even more anonymous by choosing as his element not you as an individual but a group to which you belong. You become not a person but a motorist. He could study the conflict between the subgroup of motorists who want a highway built through a scenic area and the subgroup of motorists who are more ecology-minded and want the area left alone. You may be a member of both subgroups and thus have the same conflict in microcosm within yourself. But your personal conflict would be within the focus of the psychologist, not of the sociologist.

19.332   The Scientific Community

You as an individual have a store of information and a set of rules for processing that information. You as a member of a group share some of this information and some of those rules with the other members of the group. Let's look, by way of example, at a group in which the shared information and the rules are more explicit than in most groups. Let's focus on the group of scientists.

A useful basic unit of information within this group is the research article. In it a member of the group describes very formally his hypothesis, his method for testing it, his results, and his conclusions. Another member of the group may collate this primary article with related articles in a theoretical summary of the area. A third member may collate those theoretical articles into a textbook. Each individual scientist is expected to assimilate the relevant information before conducting his experiment and adding his research paper to the pile.

The group of scientists, like the individual scientist, needs to be both persistent and flexible to be creative. The traditional process just described shows that the group is persistent. By reviewing the literature, the individuals assimilate the zeitgeist and continue within that tradition. Kuhn[58] has demonstrated the flexibility of the group. He argues that the progress of a science appears cumulative only in retrospect; actually it is made by a series of revolutions in which an old model becomes replaced by a new one. Psychology appears to be in the throes of such a revolution right now, with the reflex-arc model being replaced by the feedback loop (Section 13.221). Those raised within the reflex-arc model will tend to persist within that framework, but the emphasis within psychology will shift to information generated by those working within the new model—until that in turn becomes part of the museum of back journal articles as it is replaced by yet another model.

As an individual scientist you can gain some flexibility by reviewing the literature *after* you have thought about a problem, created hypotheses, and designed experiments to test them. You can thus be saved from the blinkering effect of being told how you are *supposed* to approach the problem. You may also find that reviewing the literature is not the dull task you had anticipated. You may experience warm feelings of familiarity as you encounter hypotheses you have already thought of yourself and cold shudders of "why didn't I think of that?" as you encounter those brilliantly obvious hypotheses that somehow eluded you. You may utter "aha!" as you stumble on evidence for a pet hypothesis and "ah!" as you find evidence against it.

In this age of specialization two scientists may overlap very little in terms of shared information. However, any two scientists, no matter how unrelated their specialties, overlap a great deal in terms of shared rules for processing information. As in all groups, those rules are determined by consensus. Some of the rules are explicit. For example, "your experiment should be described so that any competent person can follow the same procedures and obtain the same results." Some of the rules are implicit, and it is these implicit rules that constitute the dogma of science. "It is better to know than not to know." "The only sources of knowledge are observation and reason." "Everything is potentially knowable." "Everything known can be communicated to and verified by competent others." The dogma is, however, one of rules for processing information rather than one of information itself. That is, it is better to know than not to know, but it is not better to know X than to know Y. Because science is not dogmatic about information, the group of scientists has developed the best strategies to date for deriving an accurate subjective map of the objective world.*

*There is, of course, an unfortunate tendency to stray from time to time from this basic antidogmatic stance. A layman used to be someone who was not a priest but is now someone who is not a scientist. One used to gain authority by wearing a white collar backward, but now one gains authority by wearing a white lab coat.

The ignorant man marvels at the exceptional; the wise man marvels at the common.

C. D. Broadman

20 Idiographic Approach

Most of this book has focused on the nomothetic approach (the study of specific aspects of all individuals), reflecting the current emphasis within psychology. I would like to present here the idiographic approach (the study of all aspects of specific individuals), in which there is increasing interest. The nomothetic approach is embodied in experimental studies and the idiographic approach in clinical studies. Since clinical studies are more meaningful when contrasted with experimental studies, I will discuss experimental studies first (Section 20.1), then clinical studies (Section 20.2), and finally the two in contrast (Section 20.3).

20.1 Experimental Studies

20.11 As Sophistication of Common Sense

You often hear it said (even by some apparently sensible people who fail examinations in psychology) that psychology is nothing but common sense. Like most nothing-buttery arguments, this one is pretty slippery. Common sense is commonly couched in clichés that predict one thing on one occasion and the opposite on another. "Absence makes the heart fonder." Or is it "Absence makes the heart wander"? Apparently, it doesn't matter, for "Familiarity breeds contempt." Or is it "Familiarity breeds content"? This tangle can be cleared only by systematic variation of the psychological distance between two people and measurement of their liking for each other at different distances. It may be that such a study would reveal both clichés to have some truth. Perhaps absence makes fond hearts grow fonder and not-so-fond hearts wander—just as wind fans a strong flame but extinguishes a weak flame.

Common sense is not only relative to the occasion but relative to the times. What was common sense yesterday is nonsense today. It was once common sense to believe that the world was flat. You can imagine the ridicule heaped on the first crank who suggested that it was a ball with people and buildings clinging upside down to its underside. Today it is common sense to believe that the world is round.* What was nonsense yesterday is common sense today. Physicists have converted us to the noncommonsensical notion that the chair on which you are sitting is not solid but composed of myriads of microscopic elements in constant motion through spaces infinitely more vast than themselves. Microbiologists have convinced us that we can be killed by animals so small that we cannot even see them. The stigma of being nothing but common sense has been removed from physics and biology but not yet from psychology. Perhaps this is true because we are not all physicists and biologists but are all, in a sense, psychologists. That is, we all observe, generalize about, try to explain, predict, and control the behavior and experience of ourselves and of others. If you are already a psychologist, you may reasonably question the value of a book that introduces you to psychology. The psychologist, however, thinks about behavior and experience in a more systematic manner than the layman.

We all observe things happening around us. The professional psychologist differs from the amateur in that he does not wait for things to happen but arranges for things to happen. When he does so, he is said to be conducting an experiment. Consider some of the happenings organized by psychologists that were described in the previous chapters. Do you remember Blodgett's experiment on latent learning (Section 5.312)? What did he arrange to happen? He arranged for food to be placed in the goal box on a certain trial. What did he observe? He observed a sudden improvement in performance. Do you remember Tinklepaugh's experiment on the depression effect (Section 5.313)? What did he arrange to happen? He arranged for lettuce to be substituted for grapes under the flowerpot. What did he observe? He observed that the monkey threw temper tantrums and flowerpots. Do you remember the experiment on subliminal perception (Section 8.251)? What did the experimenter arrange to happen? He arranged for the words "Drink Coke" to be flashed on the screen. What did he observe? He observed that the sale of Coke increased.

We all ask questions and seek answers. The professional psychologist differs from the amateur in the precision with which he couches the question and the care with which he seeks the answer. He couches the question in the form of a

---

*There are, of course, still some people who are not convinced. However, membership in the Flat World Society has dwindled somewhat as a result of the recent photographs taken by astronauts.

hypothesis and seeks the answer by conducting an experiment to test this hypothesis. He realizes that nature must be asked clear questions before she will yield clear answers. The hypothesis is an intelligent guess that there is an interesting relationship between two variables. It is the hypothesis that guides the psychologist to which variables, of the myriad possible variables, to manipulate and observe.

20.12   Independent, Dependent, and Extraneous Variables

The most powerful and pervasive way to test a hypothesis is to conduct an experiment. We have already seen that an experiment involves arranging for something to happen and observing the effect on something else. More precisely, the thing the psychologist arranges to happen is called the **independent variable,** and the thing he observes is called the **dependent variable.** It is of interest to note that, almost invariably in psychological research, the independent variable is a stimulus and the dependent variable is a response. In designing an experiment to test his hypothesis, the psychologist must decide exactly how he will present the stimulus and how he will measure the response. He aspires to the conclusion that the stimulus is the cause of the response as effect. Such cause-effect relationships are, of course, the basic building blocks of a science. To make this conclusion, however, he must eliminate all other variables that could possibly have been the cause. He must control the **extraneous variables.** Let's consider, in turn, each aspect in the design of the experiment.

20.121   Manipulating the Independent Variable

It is not always easy to arrange for certain things to happen. A subliminal-perception experiment requires the presentation of a stimulus to be long enough to have an effect but short enough not to be consciously observed. The consistent presentation of stimuli for exactly the correct time interval had to await the invention of the tachistoscope. Great breakthroughs in psychology often result from the development of an instrument to present stimuli or measure responses that could not be presented or measured before.* The independent variable is sometimes impossible to manipulate. In Bruner's study of the effect of socioeconomic status on the perception of coins (Section 16.212), he could not make some kids poor and some kids rich. (He could—but he was

*Some sciences are entirely dependent on the development of instruments, without which they could not even observe the phenomena with which they deal. Microbiology began with the invention of the microscope to make the too-small large enough to see; astronomy progresses with the improvement of the telescope to bring the too-far near enough to see.

interested in the persistent state of the mind rather than the transitory state of the pocket.) He had to select a group that was already rich and a group that was already poor. Here the independent variable is a characteristic of the subject rather than of the environment.

20.122 Measuring the Dependent Variable

Having arranged for something to happen, the experimenter must measure the effect of his happening. It is not enough simply to describe the effect. Tinklepaugh's experiment was very amusing, but it was not very scientific. He could only make the vague statement that he changed grapes for lettuce and the monkey threw temper tantrums. Crespi's experiment (Section 5.313) to test the same hypothesis was less amusing but more scientific. He stated precisely that he substituted two pellets for eight pellets in the goal box and observed an average increase of 11.2 seconds in the time to run the maze.

20.123 Controlling Extraneous Variables

The conclusion of the subliminal-perception experiment was that the flashing of "Drink Coke" (independent variable) was the cause of the increase in Coke sales (dependent variable). This conclusion was not valid, since the effect could have been caused by a number of extraneous variables (heat, suggestion, salt in the popcorn, and so on). The experimenter could have controlled those variables by presenting the same movie in the same theater at the same temperature to audiences on two successive evenings. On one night the subliminal stimuli are not presented; on the other night the subliminal stimuli are presented. This technique of control, involving one group submitted to the independent variable and the other not submitted to it, is the basic experimental design in psychological research. The first group is the **experimental group,** and the second group is the **control group.** An interesting control is involved in cases in which the experimental group is given a pill. Any effect on the dependent variable may be caused by the pill or by the suggestion that the pill will help. The second possibility may be eliminated by giving the control group a pill also—but one with no physical effect. Such a pill is called a **placebo.*** A further control is necessary when the vested interests of the experimenter who administers the pill may

*Some doctors use placebos to cure hypochondriacs. People who just think they are sick can be cured by pills that they just think will cure them. This situation poses an ethical question: is a doctor justified in charging high prices for useless pills on the ground that, the higher the price, the greater the faith in their efficiency and the more effective the cure?

cause him to unconsciously favor the experimental group. This variable may be eliminated by the **double-blind technique,** in which neither the subject nor the experimenter knows which pill is the placebo.

20.2   Clinical Studies

20.21   As Sophistication of Common Sense

The vast majority of investigations considered in this book are experiments. That is, they deal with limited aspects of a number of subjects. In contrast, the **case study** focuses on all aspects of a single subject. Whereas the experiment keeps the environment constant and varies the subject, the case study keeps the subject constant and varies the environment.

This strategy for studying man is more familiar to the layman than the experiment is. It is used by directors in movies that focus on a single personality. We have come to know *Hud, Jeremiah Johnson, Dirty Harry, Joe, Alfie,* and many others in this way. It is used by biographers and autobiographers. Information is gleaned from various sources and organized to paint a picture of a personality. It is used by the press. When an individual becomes of interest to the public, the mass media build a picture of his personality from various sources. In the turbulent wake of some recent assassinations, we have seen the personalities of some obscure individuals constructed by the mass media in this way, with the result that an unknown becomes known to all. It is used by psychoanalysts and psychiatrists. Some recently published collections of case histories give a flavor of this approach. Such accounts tend to be somewhat sensationalistic—*The Case of the Jet-Propelled Couch* or *The Case of the Castration Complex*—but they do provide some insight into the profession and prove to be as exciting as anything out of Perry Mason or Sherlock Holmes.

The case-study method is used by everyone. The various techniques employed by psychologists in collecting information about an individual for a case study are simply refinements of everyday techniques used by the layman. Consider the familiar situation in which a young man ostensibly studying in the library notices a young lady who looks like someone he would like to know. He saunters past her seat on some pretended errand and glances casually over her shoulder to read her name on her exercise book. From the student directory, he can now find her address, telephone number, major, and year. The psychologist likewise uses documents and records as a source of information. Records from schools and jobs, birth certificates and marriage licenses, police blotters and government records, diaries and biographies—all are of value.

The young man now dials the phone number and breaks the good news that he would like to meet her for coffee. Over the coffee, he gets to know more about her by talking to her. This technique, in the hands of the psychologist, is known as an **interview.** The interview may be totally unstructured at one extreme (like the psychoanalytical interview, in which the patient lies on a couch and rambles on about whatever he wishes) or highly structured at the other extreme (like some job interviews, in which the applicant is asked a precise series of predetermined questions). In fact, some interviews are so highly structured that the interviewer merely reads the questions and writes the answers. An improvement over this type (since it reduces errors of interpretation and frees the interviewer to do something useful) is to have the subject read the questions and write the answers himself. The form used is called a **questionnaire.**

After the meeting over coffee, the young man begins to take his lady out on dates. Whether consciously or unconsciously, he submits her to a variety of tests. He expresses a way-out opinion and observes her reaction; he introduces her to his friends and notices how they get along. Psychologists use this technique more consciously and systematically. When selecting and training spies, they put the applicants in various situations in which spies would be likely to find themselves and observe how they behave. This **situational-test** technique is very expensive, time-consuming, and difficult to standardize. These shortcomings can be avoided somewhat by describing the situations and having the applicants write what they would do. A **paper-and-pencil test** on "what I would do were I James Bond in the following situation" seems remote from the corresponding real-life situation, but symbolic responses to the symbolic situations should provide some indication of real responses to the real situations. Most psychological tests are not direct symbolic representations of the relevant real situations but are designed so that performance on them is correlated with performance in the real situation.

In summary, the psychologist collects information about an individual by (1) asking about him (records and documents), (2) asking him (interviews and questionnaires), and (3) observing him (situational and paper-and-pencil tests).

20.22   A Case of Multiple Personality

20.221   The Three Faces of Eve

The Three Faces of Eve is a classic case study that will illustrate this method of investigation.[100] A 25-year-old married woman came to the office of a psychiatrist complaining of severe headaches followed sometimes by blackouts. Eve White seemed to suffer from the routine suburban syndrome of personal frustration and marital unhappiness. One day, however, the case took a peculiar turn. A letter arrived at the psychiatrist's office from Eve White. At the bottom of the letter, in a childish scrawl, there was a message apparently from someone else. On her next visit, Eve White appeared agitated and finally asked if hearing imaginary voices meant that one was insane. While the psychiatrist was trying to think of a tactful reply, a strange expression crossed Eve's face, and she buried her head in her hands as if seized by a sudden pain. After a tense moment of silence, she looked up and, with a quick, restless smile, said "Hi there, Doc!" The shy and conventional manner of Eve White had been replaced by the childishly daredevil air and erotically mischievous glance of—let us call her—Eve Black. She spoke casually of Eve White and her problems, always using the third person. She denied being the wife of Eve White's husband and showed no affection for Eve White's child. She laughed as she described the times she had disobeyed her parents and then "went in" to leave Eve White to receive the resultant beating or the times when she had gotten drunk and left Eve White to wake up with the resultant hangover. She was perfectly aware of the existence of Eve White, but Eve White did not know of her. Indeed, she had been married once without Eve White's knowing anything about it.

Eve White-Black seemed to be making some progress under therapy, but then the headaches and blackouts reappeared. This time Eve Black shared the blackouts. As she put it, "I don't know where we go, but go we do." During one session Eve White fell asleep and, on awakening, looked at the psychiatrist and said "Who are you?" Another personality—calling herself Jane—had emerged. The psychiatrist was able eventually (with the aid of another psychiatrist—not a group therapist, as was the rumor) to trace the source of the split in personality to a traumatic childhood episode in which Eve White had been forced to kiss a dead grandmother good-bye, as was the tradition in her subculture. He also achieved some integration of personality around Jane by calling out Eve White and Eve Black less and less in each session. In time Jane embarked on a reasonably well-adjusted life, although not with Eve White's husband. Apparently a fourth personality subsequently emerged, and her account of the case can be read in *The Final Face of Eve*.[59]

20.222 Ethical and Theoretical Issues

This case poses some ethical and theoretical problems. Since that integrated function that we call personality is more the essential self than the physical structure in which it is housed, the psychiatrist, in phasing out two of the personalities, was in a sense committing murder. This fact becomes clearer when we recognize that Eve White was the only one of the three personalities who was, in any real sense, the mother of the child. Whereas few people would prosecute, most would caution about the tremendous responsibility involved in deciding which personality to preserve.

Such cases of **multiple personality** (involving a split within the individual) are extremely rare as compared with cases of split personality, or **schizophrenia** (involving a split between the individual and his environment), which are extremely common. Even though they are rare, however, they need to be explained. Bizarre cases like this probably represent extremes of normal deviations. We all have many personalities within us. Perhaps we have as many personalities as there are people who know us. Think of the different faces you present to your mother, your mate, your brother, and your dentist. In your case those various yous know of one another. However, if there was one of those yous of which the others did not approve, it could be repressed. Perhaps this is what happened in the case of Eve White. Her good self (Eve White) repressed her bad self (Eve Black), and thus two distinct personalities coexisted in the same body.

20.3 Experimental and Clinical Studies

20.31 Analysis and Synthesis

The experiment exemplifies the essentially analytic nature of scientific thinking. That is, it analyzes a system into its elements and studies those elements. It divides and conquers. The strategy has been tremendously effective and has dramatically increased our knowledge of the world and of ourselves over the last few centuries.

However, sounds of revolution are in the air. First came a whisper from Whitehead in the 1930s, when he accused the scientific establishment of the twentieth century of living on the intellectual capital of the seventeenth century by persisting in the analytic tradition. The whisper is now swelling into a dull roar, which can be picked up by those with antennae tuned to the future. It is heard in architecture and anthropology, in ecology and ethology, in psychology and psychiatry. It is seeping through the seams between the disciplines into the various hyphenated hybrids. If you tune into those rumblings, you may pick out a common theme: analysis is fine, but then synthesis is necessary. We must start to put Humpty Dumpty together again. If you listen very carefully, you may discern an even more subtle theme: the synthesis may reveal the limitations of the analysis. Some systems are not the simple sum of their elements. All the specialist scientists and all the specialist technologists cannot put Humpty Dumpty together again. Analysis is appropriate only for certain systems. One penny plus one penny equals two pennies. But one acid plus one alkali does not equal two acid alkalis, and one rabbit plus one rabbit does not necessarily equal two rabbits. A system must therefore be studied as a whole rather than as the sum of its elements. We must leave the Age of Analysis and enter the Age of Synthesis. One symptom of the dawning of the Age of Synthesis is increased criticism of the experiment, which analyzes the person into elements, and increased emphasis on the case study, which considers the person as a whole.

20.32 *Explanation and Understanding*

The experiment is aimed at the explanation of a specific aspect of the behavior of all individuals; the case study is aimed at the understanding of all aspects of the behavior of a specific individual. The experiment is designed to derive laws that apply to all individuals **(nomothetic laws)**; the case study is designed to derive laws that apply to a specific individual **(idiographic laws)**. The experiment is the major tool of experimental psychologists; the case study is the major tool of clinical psychologists. A perennial debate rages between experimental and clinical psychologists on the relative merits of the two approaches and the two types of laws derived by them. The experimental psychologist argues that there is no such thing as a law that applies to only one individual. Just as there are no laws that apply to a specific snowflake but only general laws that apply to all snowflakes, with each of the tremendous variety of snowflakes representing a specific instance of those laws, so there are no specific laws that apply to an individual organism but only general laws applying to all individuals, of which each individual represents a specific instance. The clinical psychologist retorts that the personality cannot be reconstructed from the little bits and pieces into which it is analyzed for experimental purposes, that the whole personality is more than the sum of its parts, and that personality is an organization rather than simply a profile of traits. Gordon Allport, who was an experimental psychologist but a gadfly in the nomothetic ointment, illustrated this idea with a quotation by Chesterton about one of Thackeray's characters: "She drank but Thackeray did not know it."[2]

This cleavage between experimental and clinical psychologists may perhaps be an aspect of the broader split between scientists and artists. Gleitman concluded a lecture on Freud by asking the audience the following questions: "If you were to have your appendix removed, would you choose for your surgeon the great Greek doctor Hippocrates or a mediocre graduate student of an average medical school today?" (They chose the latter.) "If you were to have a portrait painted, would you choose for your artist Leonardo da Vinci or a mediocre graduate of an average art school today?" (They chose the former.) "If you were to be psychoanalyzed, would you choose for your analyst Sigmund Freud or a mediocre graduate of an average psychoanalytic school today?" (They chose the former.) Thus they aligned Freud with da Vinci rather than with

Hippocrates—with the artist rather than with the scientist. They recognized psychoanalysis as an art, in which the intuitive insight of the artist is most important, rather than as a science, in which the cumulative information of the science is most important. They realized that the mediocre graduate student in psychoanalysis does not stand on the shoulders of Freud, as the mediocre graduate student in medicine stands on the shoulders of Hippocrates. Clinical psychology is an art that seeks the understanding of an individual; experimental psychology is a science that seeks the explanation of specific behaviors of all individuals.

We are as gods and might as well get good at it. So far remotely done power and glory—as via government, big business, formal education, church—has succeeded to a point where gross defects obscure actual gains. In response to this dilemma and to these gains a realm of intimate, personal power is developing—power of the individual to conduct his own education, find his own inspiration, shape his own environment, and share his adventure with whoever is interested.

The Last Whole Earth Catalogue

21 Applied Approach

21.1 Pure and Applied Psychology

21.11 Understanding and Control

The aim of pure science is understanding; the aim of applied science is control. The aim of pure psychology is self-understanding; the aim of applied psychology is self-control. Since I am pure, the emphasis in this book has been on self-understanding, but in this chapter I'll focus on self-control.

Understanding is not necessary for control—you can drive your car without understanding the internal-combustion engine—but it helps. An understanding of what is happening when you depress the clutch and the accelerator helps you prevent stalling during that initial learning period before the synchronization of the two pedals becomes automatic. The more evolved the pure science, the more effective the applied science. The validity of the theory determines the utility of the practice. As you gain self-understanding, you increase self-control.

Understanding is not sufficient for control either. Understanding is to control as thought is to action. Any self-understanding you may gain from this book is useless unless it is translated into an increase in self-control.

There should be an intimate interaction between self-understanding and self-control. The motivation to gain more self-control should lead to greater self-understanding, and each gain in understanding should result in greater self-control. Our failure as laymen to thus orchestrate thought and action is reflected in our failure as psychologists to orchestrate the work of the **pure psychologist** and the work of the **applied psychologist**. The pure psychologist tends to criticize the applied psychologist for applying principles that have not yet been adequately tested, and the applied psychologist tends to criticize the pure psychologist for cloistering himself in an ivory tower far from the "real" problems of a troubled world. Both criticisms are unreasonable. The applied psychologist must do what he can with what he has, and the pure psychologist must do what he can with what he has so that the applied psychologist can have more later. The pure psychologist derives theoretical principles, and the applied psychologist translates them into practical solutions. Perhaps the intimate interaction between self-understanding and self-control can best be achieved by making the pure psychologist and the applied psychologist one and the same person. Action leads to thought, but thought also leads to action. Necessity is the brother of invention. Each of us should aspire, then, to be both a pure and an applied psychologist.

21.12   From Other-Control to Self-Control

The emphasis within applied psychology has always been on other-control: the vocational counselor tries to find an appropriate job for you; the personnel officer tries to find if you are appropriate for a particular job; the probation officer regulates your present because of your wicked past; the psychoanalyst probes your wicked past for clues to your neurotic present. Perhaps this is why, however benevolent we psychologists are, you picture us as scheming to control you. Perhaps this is also why you titter when you see the bibliographical abbreviation for the *Psychological Bulletin* (*Psychol. Bull.*) and why you refer to behavioral science by its initials. Psychologists will develop a better public image only when they shift their emphasis from other-control to self-control. This does not mean that they must start all over again from scratch. Each technique for other-control is also a technique for self-control. (Since, conversely, each technique for self-control is also a technique for other-control, I hesitate to teach such methods. But if they're available to some, then they should be available to all.) The only effective antidote to other-control is self-control. You are controlled either by yourself or by others, or you are out of control. Take your pick.

Many psychologists will resist a shift to self-control because it implies free will and thus violates the basic deterministic axiom of science. However, in the special case of the nervous system of our species, the deterministic dogma does not apply. It is a self-controlled system. This fact is made increasingly evident by the current movement in psychology away from an S-R and toward an R-S model. In the former model your responses are reactions to stimuli; you are controlled from the outside. In the latter model your responses are actions that elicit stimuli; you control yourself from the inside. As we switch from the S-R reflex arc to the R-S feedback loop, we shift from an emphasis on other-control to an emphasis on self-control, a once-taboo term that is beginning to appear more and more in the professional literature.

In exerting self-control and trying to write your own script, you may be accused of magical thinking. Surely, however, it is more magical to assume that your script was prewritten by some great ghost-writer in the sky or by other people who are mysteriously capable of other-control but not self-control. At any rate, assume self-control as a hypothesis, and collect evidence for or against it. You can't be any more scientific than that. Perhaps, by assuming self-control, you will gain it. The hypothesis is self-fulfilling. Perhaps, if you are determined to be determined (and are undisturbed by this apparent contradiction), you will be determined. Be a determinist about the past and the present and a free-willist about the future. Whatever was was, whatever is is, but whatever will be may be.

21.2 An Operating Manual for Species Homo sapiens

21.21 Need for an Operating Manual

When I got my typewriter, I got an operating manual. When I got my car, I also got an operating manual. When I got my nervous system—the most complex and mysterious system in the universe—no operating manual. After bumbling along without a manual for 35 years, I decided to write my own.* I have offered my manual to many people. "Hello. Are you a member of species Homo sapiens? Yes? I have just the thing you've been waiting for all your life—an operating manual for species Homo sapiens." Needless to say, I have encountered much resistance. The most common reaction is one of amazement that anyone would be so presumptuous as to assume that he is the operator. Initially I was amazed that they were amazed. Yet perhaps it is not so surprising. The prevailing models of man in our culture involve other-control. Christian man is a puppet dangling at the fingertips of God. Scientific man is an automaton reacting mechanically to the environment. Even some of those who share my belief that we are self-controlled questioned the value of an operating manual. We can operate our nervous systems, but we shouldn't. We should let them operate naturally. It is true that many of our social and personal problems stem from operating our nervous systems—but only from operating them badly. We must therefore learn how to operate them well.

*I haven't found a publisher for it yet. Textbook publishers tell me it is a trade book, and trade publishers tell me it is a textbook. Someday soon a publisher who is not suffering from hardening of the categories will realize what a big market species Homo sapiens is and will publish the book. Until then you'll just have to struggle along as well as you can without an operating manual.

Some individuals accepted the value of an operating manual but questioned the value of *my* operating manual. "That's how you operate your head but not how I operate mine." We are, however, all members of the same species on the same planet in essentially the same predicament and with essentially the same

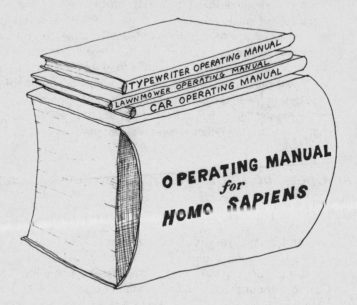

equipment. Although the contents of our nervous systems vary tremendously, the functions and structures are pretty much the same. Thus principles that are valid for operating my nervous system are valid for operating your nervous system. One implication of this argument is that you and I have essentially the same equipment as Albert Einstein and Pablo Picasso. Well, we do. They have simply developed better strategies for using their equipment.

Some individuals were apprehensive about self-control because it conjured up visions of grim, puritanical, teeth-gritting self-discipline. But self-discipline implies doing what you don't want to do. Self-control involves doing well whatever you want to do, living with grace, making of your life a beautiful movie.

21.22 *Description of an Operating Manual*

Let me introduce you to my operating manual and to other recent works that could be considered part of an operating manual.

Species *Homo sapiens* is a set of interacting systems: a circulatory system to process blood, a digestive system to process food, a nervous system to process information, and so on and so on. The nervous system is the only one of those subsystems that is under voluntary control. That is, whereas it is reasonable to say "stop talking," because talking is a subfunction of the nervous system, it is not so reasonable to say "stop digesting," because digesting is a subfunction of the digestive system. There is, of course, evidence that other subsystems can be controlled, but only through the mediation of the nervous system. Therefore, since the nervous system is the only system under direct control, it is the only system that can be "operated." Look at *Man's Presumptuous Brain*, by Simeons,[91] for the section of our manual that deals with operating your other subsystems through your nervous system.

A closer look at the nervous system reveals that it consists of an autonomic nervous system to deal with the internal environment and a central nervous system to deal with the external environment. Until recently it had been assumed that the autonomic nervous system could not be "operated." However, it has been demonstrated that we are simply not *aware* of the functioning of the autonomic nervous system because it is obscured by the functioning of the central nervous system—just as we are not aware of the light from the stars during the day because it is obliterated by the light from the sun. We have learned techniques for brightening the light from the stars **(biofeedback)** and for dimming the light from the sun **(meditation).** As a result, we have become aware of the operation of the autonomic nervous system and have learned to control it. Look at *Biofeedback and Self-Control,* edited by Barber,[5] and at *Altered States of Consciousness,* edited by Tart,[98] for the section of our manual that deals with operating your autonomic nervous system.

A closer look at the central nervous system reveals that it consists of an old brain for biological responses to the external environment and a new brain for cultural responses to the external environment. This dichotomy could be roughly identified with the traditional distinction between emotion and reason. Since the biological responses are built-in, it would appear that you could not operate your old brain. Moreover, since the biological responses are built in to aid in your survival, it would seem that you *should* not operate your old brain. Lorenz has argued that cultural innovations have created a situation in which the biological response of aggression, although designed for the survival of our species, could instead result in the extinction of our species. We must therefore learn cultural means of controlling our biological responses. Therapists also have argued that we often learn inappropriate emotional responses, and they provide a variety of therapies for unlearning such responses. Thus you can learn to operate your old brain (or, rather, unlearn in order to permit it to operate as it should) by undergoing therapy. Look at *On Aggression,* by Lorenz,[63] and *Guide to Rational Living*, by Ellis and Harper,[22] for the section of our manual that deals with operating your old brain.

A closer look at the new brain reveals that it consists of a right hemisphere for the processing of visual information and a left hemisphere for the processing of verbal information. The right and the left hemispheres could be roughly identified with the artist and the scientist, respectively, in each of us. Shake your left hand with your right hand and say "hello" to your other half. Bridge the gap between the two cultures. Look at *Experiences in Visual Thinking*, by McKim,[69] and *Five-Day Course in Thinking*, by de Bono,[17] for the section of our manual that deals with operating your right and left hemispheres, respectively.

As missing parts of our operating manual emerge, we will get our right hemisphere connected to our left hemisphere, our new brain connected to our old brain, our central nervous system connected to our autonomic nervous system, and our nervous system connected to our other systems. Eventually, in the vague language of a previous generation, we will "educate the whole person"—or, in the equally vague language of the current generation, we will "get it all together."

Man is a biped without feathers.

Plato
Politics

God created man in his own image, in the image of God created he him; male and female created he them.

Genesis 1:27

What a piece of work is a man! How noble in reason! How infinite in faculty! in form, in moving, how express and admirable! in action how like an angel! in apprehension how like a god!

William Shakespeare
Hamlet, Act II, Scene 2

Man is a rational animal who always loses his temper when he is called upon to act in accordance with the dictates of reason.

Oscar Wilde
The Critic as Artist

22

Epilogue

The search continues, but the story must end; it is necessarily a to-be-continued story. The story is not only unfinished but unsophisticated; it is necessarily a superficial story. Further courses in psychology will enable you to delve deeper into the various topics touched on here. The courses typically offered in an undergraduate psychology program are listed in Figure 22-1, alongside the chapters of this book on which they expand. Thus, for example, if you wish a more intensive study of the material covered in Chapter 12, you will take the course labeled Abnormal Psychology.

Man's search for self-understanding involves many people in many places doing many different things. We have peered over the shoulder of Hebb in Montreal as he probed theoretically into the nervous systems of his subjects and sat behind Freud in Vienna as he probed into the pasts of his patients. We have observed McConnell mincing worms and Minami and Dallenbach freezing cockroaches. We have memorized nonsense syllables with Ebbinghaus at breakfast and analyzed factors with Thurstone at supper. One could leave with the impression that the story of the search has, like a telephone directory, many characters but no plot. One could conclude that psychology is an account of thousands of psychologists scurrying in thousands of different directions.

I might have avoided giving this impression if I had organized the story around problems rather than approaches. Thus a chapter on the problem of memory could have described the diverse activities just noted and demonstrated their common focus. Penfield and McConnell were both seeking the physical basis of memory, Minami and Dallenbach and Freud and Ebbinghaus were seeking factors influencing the efficiency of memory, and Thurstone was measuring individual differences in efficiency. The tremendous diversity of activities that constitutes "doing psychology" reflects, then, not unhealthy schisms within psychology but a healthy variety of approaches focusing on a common problem.

A chapter on the problem of memory could have continued from the theoretical to the practical aspect of the problem. It is no secret that efficient techniques for remembering can enable you to learn twice as much in the time you now spend studying (or, for those who are more interested in time than in learning, the same amount in half the time), and it is no surprise that the theoretical findings of psychologists can be applied to increase your efficiency. Let's consider, by way of illustration, one theoretical finding and its practical application in helping you learn the content of this book more efficiently. It is easier to remember a set of propositions when they are organized in a meaningful way. The organization is to the propositions as the basket is to the eggs. Many of the propositions in this book are definitions of technical terms. You must first learn to speak the language of a discipline before you can talk about the system with

CHAPTERS	COURSES
2 Functional Approach	Emotion and Motivation
3 Genetic Approach	Behavioral Genetics
4 Behavioristic Approach	Learning
5 Mediational Approach	Cognition
6 Approach through Verbal Response	Language
7 Approach through Novel Response	Creativity
8 Psychophysical Approach	Psychophysics
9 Psychophysiological Approach	Sensory Processes
10 Phenomenological Approach	Perception
11 Psychometric Approach	Tests and Measurements
12 Pathological Approach	Abnormal Psychology
13 Ontogenetic Approach	Child Development
14 Phylogenetic Approach	Comparative Psychology
15 Approach through Altered States	
16 Normative Approach	
17 Analogical Approach	
18 Physiological Approach	Physiological Psychology
19 Sociological Approach	Social Psychology
20 Idiographic Approach	Personality
21 Applied Approach	Applied Psychology

Figure 22–1. Correlation Chart of Chapters in This Book and Typical Undergraduate Courses in Psychology. The chapters with no corresponding courses cover approaches so recently emphasized that, in most universities, equivalent courses have not yet evolved.

which that discipline deals. This grim fact has been disguised in this text, but many bitter pills have been smuggled in under the sugar coating. These technical terms appear in boldface in the text and are organized into categories preceding the back cover. Those particular sets of categories are retrospectively inevitable when we consider the nature of psychological research. It involves a confrontation between *experimenter* and *subject* in which the experimenter presents *stimuli* to which the subject emits *responses*. The presentation of the stimulus and the measurement of the response may require the use of *tools* and *techniques*. The response is subjected to statistical analysis to transform the data into *facts*, which in turn are organized into *theories*. The facts may be expressed in terms of *numbers* or *pictures*. The theories may be expressed purely in terms of stimuli and responses or in terms of "something" between the stimulus and the response. This "something" may refer to a *function* of the nervous system or to a *structure* within it.

We should not lose sight of the fact that we are ultimately seeking an understanding not just of subfunctions like memory but of man. In Section 17.222 I suggested that one reason why we fail to solve problems is that we are not able to recognize solutions. As a service to the aspiring Darwins and Newtons of psychology, here is a sketchy summary of what the ultimate psychological theory may look like, so that you will recognize it should you happen to stumble over it. In this State of the Science message I will attempt a broad summary of the product of the various approaches presented in this book.

As a child I was addicted to jigsaw puzzles. I would compulsively do first the outside border, then the next border, and so on, working in toward the center. In the process, however, I would get little clumps of pieces together that fit one another but did not yet fit into the general framework. As an adult I am still addicted to puzzles, and I am still working compulsively from the outside border toward the center. My major current puzzle is to construct a description of the nervous system such that the manifestations of its functioning from the outside (behavior) and from the inside (experience) can be explained. Writing this book is one means toward the end of solving that puzzle. It appears that the first three outer borders are almost complete. Darwin's theory of evolution is the outermost border (Section 2.1). The basic function of the nervous system is to help the organism to survive. Freud's theory is the second border (Section 12.21). It focuses the theory of evolution on the nervous system of our species. It describes the development of sex and love, which are so important for the survival of our species, and shows how things may go wrong during that long period of development. It also describes the struggle of our psychological aspect (ego) to build an accurate subjective map of the objective world so that we can cope with it, despite the pressures of our biological and sociological aspects (id and superego). Piaget's theory is the third border (Section 13.33). It describes how the nervous system assimilates and accommodates to the objective world so that the ego may build up an accurate subjective map of it. Within these broad borders there are a number of clumps that fit together but do not yet fit neatly within the general framework. Let me simply list them as propositions about the nervous system of our species.

1. The function of the nervous system is to process information. The nervous system deals not only with input information, as assumed in the behavioristic approach (Chapter 4), or with input and stored information, as assumed in the mediational approach (Chapter 5), but with input, stored, and fedback information, as assumed in the phenomenological approach (Chapter 10).

2. The nervous system processes information in order to build a subjective map of the objective world so that the organism can cope with that world. This subjective map consists of a perceptual map based on percepts and a conceptual map based on concepts.

3. The nervous system has one mechanism for preserving gains and another mechanism for taking advantage of the possibility of further gains. This theme runs throughout this book (for example, the discussion of perseverance and flexibility in creativity in Section 7.33, of accommodation and assimilation in adaptation in Section 13.331, and of continuous discontinuity in both ontogenetic and phylogenetic development in Section 14.1). There are equivalent mechanisms in the social system (for example, see the discussion of evolution

and revolution in Section 5.212 and the discussion of the scientific community in Section 19.332).

4. The nervous system is a self-controlling system. Through fedback information it can maintain a balanced state and attain a desired state. Further, since each nervous system creates its own desired state, it is a self-inventing system. Each of us, then, is our own invention and can possibly be fully understood only by the inventor.

5. The nervous system is a conscious system. Therefore we need to explain experience (the view from inside) as well as behavior (the view from outside). Further, since the self is an important aspect of experience, the nervous system is a self-conscious system. Even further, since each nervous system may set self-understanding as its desired state, the nervous system is potentially a self-understanding system. This is the ultimate search in which we are engaged in this book.

The search has been described as a story rather than as a history. The organization has been logical rather than chronological. We have met Skinner before Fechner, even though Fechner was dead before Skinner was born. This story could be called history only in the sense that psychology has many histories, each characterized by a particular logical approach to the understanding of man. Thus Chapter 11, which traces the evolution from Binet's one intelligence through Thurstone's seven abilities to Guilford's 120 factors, could be considered as a historical sketch of the psychometric tradition. A minihistory of the broader evolution of man's study of himself could be traced by reading the account of the introspective approach in which the stimulus was controlled (Section 10.211) and the behavioristic approach in which the stimulus was controlled and the response was measured (Section 10.212), the Gestalt reaction to the reductionism of behaviorism (Section 16.211), and the cognitive reaction to the peripheralism of behaviorism (Section 5.1).

A historical organization might have provided a longer barrel from which to project more accurately the direction in which psychology will move in the future. It is impossible, of course, to predict the content of the psychology texts of the future, but there is little doubt about the increasing importance of that content. As the search continues, the findings will accumulate and be applied to the understanding and control of ourselves and of others. Whereas this improved understanding of ourselves can be applied to good or bad ends, understanding is valuable in itself. We laugh when the social worker in *A Thousand Clowns* says "I didn't like the kid, so I tried to understand him. Now I understand him. I hate him" or when the boozer in the bar says "My wife and I don't get along. She understands me." We laugh because we intuitively recognize that understanding leads to affection for others or, at the very least, acceptance of others. If that is all the search produces, it will have been worthwhile.

References

1 Adler, M. J. *The difference in man and the difference it makes.* New York: World, 1967.

2 Allport, G. W. *Pattern and growth in personality.* New York: Holt, Rinehart & Winston, 1961.

3 Asch, S. E. Effects of group pressure upon the modification and distortion of judgments. In E. E. Maccoby, T. M. Newcomb, & E. L. Hartley (Eds.), *Readings in social psychology.* (3rd ed.) New York: Holt, Rinehart & Winston, 1958.

4 Bales, R. F. *Interaction process analysis: A method for the study of small groups.* Reading, Mass.: Addison-Wesley, 1950.

5 Barber, T. X. (Ed.) *Biofeedback and self-control: An Aldine reader on the regulation of bodily processes and consciousness.* Chicago: Aldine, 1971.

6 Bayley, N. The development of motor abilities during the first three years. *Monographs of the Society for Research in Child Development*, 1936, No. 1.

7 Berelson, B., & Steiner, G. A. *Human behavior: An inventory of scientific findings.* New York: Harcourt Brace Jovanovich, 1964

8 Birch, H. G. The role of motivational factors in insightful problem solving. *Journal of Comparative Psychology*, 1945, **38**, 295–317.

9 Birch, H. G. The relation of previous experience to insightful problem solving. *Journal of Comparative Psychology*, 1945, **38**, 367–383.

10 Blodgett, H. C. The effect of the introduction of reward upon the maze performance of rats. *University of California Publications in Psychology*, 1929, **4**, 113–134.

11 Boole, G. *Collected logical works. Vol. 11: Laws of thought.* LaSalle, Ill.: Open Court, 1952.

12 Brady, J. V. Ulcers in "executive monkeys." *Scientific American*, 1958, **199**(4), 95–103.

13 Bruner, J. S., & Goodman, C. C. Value and need as organizing factors in perception. *Journal of Abnormal and Social Psychology*, 1947, **42**, 33–44.

14 Cannon, W. B. Hunger and thirst. In C. Murchison (Ed.), *Handbook of general experimental psychology.* Worcester, Mass.: Clark University Press, 1934.

15 Carnap, R. *The logical syntax of language.* London: Routledge & Kegan, 1937.

16 Crespi, L. P. Quantitative variations of incentive and performance in the white rat. *American Journal of Psychology*, 1942, **55**, 467–517.

17 de Bono, E. *Five-day course in thinking.* New York: Basic Books, 1967.

18   de Bono, E. *New think: The use of lateral thinking in the generation of new ideas.* New York: Basic Books, 1968.

19   de Bono, E. *Dog exercising machine.* New York: Simon & Schuster, 1971.

20   Dennis, W., & Dennis, M. G. The effect of cradling practices upon the onset of walking in Hopi children. *Journal of Genetic Psychology,* 1940, **56**, 77–86.

21   de Ropp, R. S. *Master Game.* New York: Delacorte, 1968.

22   Ellis, A., & Harper, R. A. *Guide to rational living.* Englewood Cliffs, N.J.: Prentice-Hall, 1961.

23   Festinger, L., Reicken, H. W., & Schachter, S. *When prophecy fails.* Minneapolis: University of Minnesota Press, 1956.

24   Flavell, J. H. *Developmental psychology of Jean Piaget.* New York: Van Nostrand Reinhold, 1963.

25   Funkenstein, D. H. The physiology of fear and anger. *Scientific American,* 1955, **192**(5), 74–81.

26   Gardiner, W. L. An investigation of the understanding of the meaning of the logical operators in propositional reasoning. (Doctoral dissertation, Cornell University.) Ithaca, N.Y.: University Microfilms, 1966, No. 66–4109.

27   Gelb, A. Die "Farbenkonstanz" der Sehdinge. In W. A. von Bethe (Ed.), *Handbuch Normaler und Patholigscher Physiologie* (Vol. 10, No. 1). Berlin: Springer, 1929.

28   Gesell, A., & Thompson, H. Learning and growth in identical infant twins. In R. G. Barker, J. S. Kounin, & H. F. Wright (Eds.), *Child behavior and development.* New York: McGraw-Hill, 1943.

29   Gibson, E. J., & Walk, R. D. The "visual cliff." *Scientific American,* 1960, **202**(4), 64–71.

30   Gibson, J. J. *The perception of the visual world.* Boston: Houghton Mifflin, 1950.

31   Gibson, J. J. *The senses considered as perceptual systems.* Boston: Houghton Mifflin, 1966.

32   Goldstein, K., & Scheerer, M. Abstract and concrete behavior: An experimental study with special tests. *Psychological Monographs,* 1941, **53** (2, Whole No. 239).

33   Gorer, G. Man has no "killer" instinct. In M. F. A. Montagu (Ed.), *Man and aggression.* New York: Oxford University Press, 1968. Pp. 27–36.

34   Gray, G. W. The great raveled knot. *Scientific American,* 1948, **178**, 27–38.

35   Greenspoon, J. The reinforcing effect of two spoken sounds on the frequency of two responses. *American Journal of Psychology,* 1955, **68**, 409–416.

36 Guilford, J. P. *The nature of human intelligence.* New York: McGraw-Hill, 1967.

37 Hall, C. S. What people dream about. *Scientific American,* 1951, **185**(5), 60–63.

38 Harlow, H. F. The formation of learning sets. *Psychological Review,* 1949, **56**, 51–65.

39 Harlow, H. F. The nature of love. *American Psychologist,* 1958, **13**, 673–685.

40 Hartline, H. K. The response of single optic nerve fibers of the vertebrate eye to illumination of the retina. *American Journal of Physiology,* 1938, **121**, 400–415.

41 Hebb, D. O. *The organization of behavior: A neuropsychological theory.* New York: Wiley, 1949.

42 Hebb, D. O. The mind's eye. *Psychology Today,* November 1971, pp. 43–46, 74–76.

43 Hebb, D. O. *A textbook of psychology.* (3rd ed.) Philadelphia: Saunders, 1972.

44 Heron, W. The pathology of boredom. *Scientific American,* 1957, **196**(1), 52–56.

45 Hochberg, J. E., Triebel, W., & Seaman, G. Color adaptation under conditions of homogeneous visual stimulation (Ganzfeld). *Journal of Experimental Psychology,* 1951, **41**, 153–159.

46 Hockett, C. F. Animal "languages" and human language. *Human Biology,* 1959, **31**, 32–39.

47 Hubel, D. H., & Wiesel, T.N. The visual cortex of the brain. *Scientific American,* 1963, **209**(5), 54–62.

48 Hull, C. L. *Principles of behavior: An introduction to behavior theory.* New York: Appleton-Century-Crofts, 1943.

49 Janis, I. L. Groupthink. *Psychology Today,* November 1971, pp. 43–46, 74–76.

50 Jenkins, J. G., & Dallenbach, K. M. Oblivescence during sleep and waking. *American Journal of Psychology,* 1924, **35**, 605–612.

51 Jensen, A. R. How much can we boost IQ and scholastic achievement? *Harvard Educational Review,* 1969, **39**(1).

52 Kellogg, W. N., & Kellogg, L. A. *The ape and the child.* New York: McGraw-Hill, 1933.

53 Kelly, G. A. *Theory of personality: The psychology of personal constructs.* (2 vols.) New York: Norton, 1955.

54 Kinkade, K. *A Walden Two experiment.* New York: Morrow, 1973.

55 Kleitman, N. Patterns of dreaming. *Scientific American*, 1960, **203**(5), 82–88.

56 Kohler, I. Experiments with goggles. *Scientific American*, 1962, **206**(5), 62–72.

57 Köhler, W. *The mentality of apes.* (Trans. by E. Winter.) New York: Harcourt, 1925.

58 Kuhn, T. S. *Structure of scientific revolutions.* Chicago: University of Chicago Press, 1962.

59 Lancaster, E., & Poling, J. *The final face of Eve.* New York: McGraw-Hill, 1958.

60 Lashley, K. S. Mass action in cerebral function. *Science*, 1931, **73**, 245–254.

61 Leonard, W. E. *The locomotive god.* New York: Appleton-Century-Crofts, 1927.

62 Lorenz, K. *King Solomon's ring.* (Trans. by M. K. Wilson.) London: Methuen, 1952.

63 Lorenz, K. *On aggression.* (Trans. by M. K. Wilson.) London: Methuen, 1966.

64 MacLeod, R. B. The place of phenomenological analysis in social psychological theory. In J. H. Rohrer & M. Sherif (Eds.), *Social psychology at the crossroads: The University of Oklahoma lectures in social psychology.* New York: Harper & Row, 1951. Pp. 215–241.

65 MacNichol, E. F., Jr. Three-pigment color vision. *Scientific American*, 1950, **182**(3), 38–43.

66 Maslow, A. H. *Toward a psychology of being.* (2nd ed.) Princeton, N. J.: Van Nostrand, 1968.

67 Masserman, J. H. Experimental neuroses. *Scientific American*, 1950, **182**(3), 38–43.

68 McConnell, J. V. Memory transfer through cannibalism in planarians. *Journal of Neuropsychiatry*, 1962, **3**, Supp. 1, 42–48.

69 McKim, R. *Experiences in visual thinking.* Monterey, Calif.: Brooks/Cole, 1972.

70 Milgram, S. Behavioral study of obedience. *Journal of Abnormal and Social Psychology*, 1963, **67**(4), 371–378.

71 Miller, G. A., Galanter, E., & Pribram, K. H. *Plans and the structure of behavior.* New York: Holt, Rinehart & Winston, 1960.

72 Miller, N. E. Studies of fear as an acquired drive: 1. Fear as motivation and fear reduction as reinforcement in the learning of new responses. *Journal of Experimental Psychology*, 1948, **38**, 89–101.

73 Minami, H., & Dallenbach, K. M. The effect of activity upon learning and retention in the cockroach. *American Journal of Psychology*, 1946, **59**, 1–58.

74 Mueller, G. E., & Pilzecker, A. Experimentelle Beiträge zur Lehre vom Gedächtniss. *Zeitschrift für Psychologie*, Ergänzungsband, 1900, **1**, 1–288.

75 Murray, H. A., et al. *Explorations in personality.* New York: Oxford, 1938.

76 Olds, J. Pleasure centers in the brain. *Scientific American*, 1956, **195**(4), 105–116.

77 Osgood, C. E., Suci, G. J., & Tannenbaum, P. H. *The measurement of meaning.* Urbana: University of Illinois Press, 1957.

78 Pavlov, I. P. *Conditioned reflexes: An investigation of the physiological activity of the cerebral cortex.* (Trans. and Ed. by G. V. Anrep.) London: Oxford University Press, 1927.

79 Piaget, J. *Logic and psychology.* New York: Basic Books, 1957.

80 Pritchard, R. M. Stabilized images on the retina. *Scientific American*, 1961, **204**(6), 72–78.

81 Rock, I. The role of repetition in associative learning. *American Journal of Psychology*, 1957, **70**, 186–193.

82 Romanes, G. J. *Animal intelligence.* New York: Appleton-Century-Crofts, 1912. Originally published 1882.

83 Rosenblatt, F. The perceptron: A probabilistic model for information storage and organization in the brain. *Psychological Review*, 1958, **65**, 386–408.

84 Rosenthal, R., & Jacobson, L. *Pygmalion in the classroom: Teacher expectation and pupils' intellectual development.* New York: Holt, Rinehart & Winston, 1968.

85 Schachter, S. *The psychology of affiliation: Experimental studies of the sources of gregariousness.* Stanford, Calif.: Stanford University Press, 1959.

86 Schachter, S. Some extraordinary facts about obese humans and rats. *American Psychologist*, 1971, **26**, 129–144.

87 Schachter, S., & Singer, J. Cognitive, social, and physiological determinants of emotional states. *Psychological Review*, 1962, **69**, 379–399.

88 Schein, E. H. The Chinese indoctrination program for prisoners of war: A study of attempted "brainwashing." In E. E. Maccoby, T. M. Newcomb, & E. L. Hartley (Eds.), *Readings in social psychology.* (3rd ed.) New York: Holt, Rinehart & Winston, 1958.

89 Schlosberg, H. The description of facial expressions in terms of two dimensions. *Journal of Experimental Psychology*, 1952, **44**, 229–237.

90 Sherif, M. *The psychology of social norms.* New York: Harper, 1936.

91 Simeons, A. T. *Man's presumptuous brain: An evolutionary interpretation of psychosomatic diseases.* New York: Dutton, 1961.

92 Skinner, B. F. "Superstition" in the pigeon. *Journal of Experimental Psychology*, 1948, **38**, 168–172.

93 Skinner, B. F. *Verbal behavior.* New York: Appleton-Century-Crofts, 1957.

94 Skinner, B. F. *Walden two.* New York: Macmillan, 1960.

95 Skinner, B. F. *Beyond freedom and dignity.* New York: Knopf, 1972.

96 Spalding, D. A. Instinct, with original observations on young animals. *British Journal of Animal Behavior*, 1954, **2**, 2–11.

97 Spitz, R. A. Hospitalism: An inquiry into the genesis of psychiatric conditions in early childhood. In O. Fenichel et al. (Eds.), *The psychoanalytic study of the child*, Vol. 1. New York: International Universities Press, 1945.

98 Tart, C. T. (Ed.) *Altered states of consciousness: A book of readings.* New York: Wiley, 1969.

99 Teitelbaum, P. Disturbances in feeding and drinking behavior after hypothalamic lesions. In M. R. Jones (Ed.), *Nebraska symposium on motivation.* Lincoln: University of Nebraska Press, 1961.

100 Thigpen, C. H., & Cleckley, H. M. *The three faces of Eve.* New York: McGraw-Hill, 1957.

101 Thorndike, E. L. *Animal intelligence.* New York: Macmillan, 1911.

102 Thurstone, L. L. Primary mental abilities. *Psychometric Monographs*, 1938, **1**.

103 Tinklepaugh, O. An experimental study of representative factors in monkeys. *Journal of Comparative Psychology*, 1928, **8**, 197–236.

104 Tolman, E. C., Ritchie, B. F., & Kalish, D. Studies in spatial learning: II. Place learning versus response learning. *Journal of Experimental Psychology*, 1946, **36**, 221–229.

105 Underwood, B. J. Interference and forgetting. *Psychological Review*, 1957, **64**, 49–60.

106 von Frisch, W. *Bees: Their vision, chemical senses, and language.* Ithaca, N.Y.: Cornell University Press, 1950.

107 von Senden, M. *Space and sight.* (Trans. by P. Heath.) London: Methuen, 1960.

108 Walker, E. L, & Heyns, R. W. *An anatomy for conformity.* Monterey, Calif.: Brooks/Cole, 1967.

109 Wallach, H. Brightness constancy and the nature of achromatic colors. *Journal of Experimental Psychology*, 1948, **38**, 310–324.

110 Watson, J. B. *Behaviorism.* Chicago: University of Chicago Press, 1924.

111 Watson, J. B., & Rayner, R. Conditioned emotional reactions. *Journal of Experimental Psychology*, 1920, **3**, 1–14.

112 Woodworth, R. S. *Experimental psychology.* New York: Holt, 1938.

113 Young, J. Z. Visual responses by octopus to crabs and other figures before and after training. *Journal of Experimental Biology*, 1956, **33**, 709–729.

Index

Lewin, K., 150
Light energy, 122
Limen, 110
Linguistics, 86–87
Localization, 270, 272
Locke, John, 37
Locomotive God, case of the, 170
Logarithmic law, 111
Logic, 87, 234, 241
Logical operators, 243, 244
Logical Syntax of Language, The (Carnap), 241
Logic and Psychology (Piaget), 242
Longitudinal method, 191
Lorenz, Konrad:
  aggression, 212–216, 317
  critical period, 192
  and Freud, 176
  imprinting, 40
Loudness, 110–111
Love, 21–22
LSD, 279–280
Lysenko, 12

MacLeod, R. B., 144
Malfunction, 169
Mand, 59, 60
Manipulation, 21
Marbe's law, 81
Maslow, A. H., 95, 184
Mass action, 74–75, 270–272
Masserman, J. H., 182
Master Game (de Ropp), 234
Matrix, 291, 293
Maturation, 191
McConnell, J. V., 34, 274
McKim, R., 318
McLuhan, Marshall, 6
Meaning, 63–66
Mechanisms, 249, 257–258
Meditation, 317
Memory, 75, 274–275, 321
Memory trace, 274–275
Mendel, G. J., 97–98

Mental age (MA), 155
Messing around in the matrix, 102–103
Method of successive approximations, 55, 59, 287
Milgram, S., 281–282, 285
Miller, G. A., 89, 250, 251, 274
Miller, N. E., 180
Mises, Dr., 108–109
Misperception, 118, 234–240
Mnemonics, 85–86
Molyneux, Mr., 37
Moon illusion, 238
Morpheme, 87
Morphology, 87
Morris, D., 212
Motivation, 13–23
Motor development, 189–192
Motor neurons, 266
Motor projection areas, 269–270
Mueller, G. E., 84
Muller-Lyer illusion, 236, 237
Multiple personality, 308
Murray, H. A., 281, 283

nAffiliation, 283–284
Nature-nurture controversy, 35–40, 118, 191
nDeference, 281–282
Need, 15, 20–23, 281–284
Need-reduction theory, 13, 14–18, 20, 281, 287
Nerve gas, 266–267
Nervous system:
  analogical approach, 249
  behavior and experience, 39, 107–108, 143
  as complex system, 4
  and computer, 249–251
  D-state and W-state, 228–229
  evolution of function, 208–211
  evolution of structure, 204–208
  functional disorders of, 170–171, 177–178
  function of, 269
  in hierarchy of systems, 279–280
  and memory, 274
  needs of, 20–23

CLASSIFICATION OF TECHNICAL TERMS IN THE TEXT

EXPERIMENTER

Applied psychologist
Pure psychologist

Behaviorist
Gestalt psychologist
Introspectionist

Environmentalist
Hereditarian

SUBJECT

Agnostic
Aphasic
Apraxic

Color-blind

Control group
Experimental group

Neurotic
    Hysterical
    Obsessive-compulsive
    Phobic
Psychotic
    Multiple personality
    Schizophrenic

STIMULUS

Complementaries

Conditioned stimulus
Unconditioned stimulus

Contact comfort

Cue function
Arousal function

Distal stimulus
Proximal stimulus

Figure
Ground

Ganzfeld

Goal

Higher-order variable
    Texture gradient

Kernel sentence
Morpheme
Phoneme

Limen
    Absolute
    Difference
    Terminal
Serendipity
Zeitgeist

RESPONSE

Echoic response
Mand

Tact
Paradigmatic response
Syntagmatic response

Superstitious behavior

Reflex
    Chain
    Conditioned
    Unconditioned
    Flexor
    Extensor

Tropism

TOOL

Definition
    Analytical
    Operational
    Practical

Distorted room
Trapezoid window

Hypothesis

Hypothetical construct
    Cell assembly
    Phase sequence

Idiographic law
Nomothetic law

Kent-Rosanoff list

Nonsense syllables
Placebo

Puzzle box
Skinner box

Reduction screen

Reversible figure

Tachistoscope

Teaching machine

Test
    California Infant Scale
        of Motor Development
    Ishihari
    Stanford-Binet
    Primary Mental Abilities
    Word-association
    Paper-and-pencil
    Situational

Variable
    Dependent
    Independent
    Extraneous
    Intervening

Visual cliff

TECHNIQUE

Ablation
Stimulation

Biofeedback
Meditation

Brainstorming

Case study

Clinical method

Conditioning
    Backward
    Forward
    Simultaneous
    Classical
    Instrumental

Cross-sectional method
Longitudinal method

Double-blind technique

Factor analysis

Interaction process analysis

Interview
Questionnaire

Introspection

Method of successive
    approximations

Psychophysical methods

Pupillometrics

Total reinforcement
Partial reinforcement
    Fixed schedule
    Variable schedule
    Interval schedule
    Ratio schedule

Repertory Grid Technique
Self-characterization

Sensory deprivation

Shaping

FACT

Aha phenomenon
Eureka effect

Centralization
Differentiation
Encephalization

Conflict
    Approach-approach
    Approach-avoidance
    Avoidance-avoidance

Constancy
    Brightness
    Size
    Shape
    Object

Contrast
    Simultaneous
    Successive

Critical period
Readiness

Dark adaptation

Depression effect
Elation effect

Displacement

Duality of patterning
Displacement
Productivity

Eichmann effect

Facilitation
Occlusion

Functional autonomy

Gradient of reinforcement

Homeostasis

Illusion
   Geometric illusion
   Moon illusion
   Muller-Lyer
   Illusion of movement
   Autokinetic effect
   Phi phenomenon

Inhibition
   Proactive
   Retroactive

Law of effect

Marbe's law

Partial paradox

Perceptual defense
Perceptual vigilance

Physiological nystagmus

Refractory period
   Absolute
   Relative

Serial position effect

Set

Yerkes-Dodson law

THEORY

Activation theory
James-Lange theory

Cognitive dissonance

Confusion theory
Eye-movement theory
Good-figure theory
Perspective theory

Contemporaneity principle

Duplicity theory

Equipotentiality
Mass action
Localization

Hering theory
Young-Helmholtz theory

Logarithmic law
Power law

Need-reduction theory

Oedipus complex

Subception

Theory of evolution

Theory of recapitulation

Weber's law

NUMBER

Deviation score

Percentile score

Mental Age (MA)
Intelligence quotient (IQ)

Raw score

Reliability
Validity

PICTURE

Color cone

Cumulative record

J curve

Profile
Matrix
Phase sequence

STRUCTURE

Acetylcholine

Adrenalin
Noradrenalin

Association areas of cortex
Projection areas of cortex
   Motor
   Sensory

Cognitive map

Cone
Rod

Deoxyribonucleic acid
   (DNA)
Ribonucleic acid (RNA)

Conceptual map
Perceptual map

Erogenous zone

Hypothalamus

Iodopsin
Rhodopsin

Neuron
   Association
   Motor
   Sensory

On-cells
Off-cells
On/off-cells

On-center cells
Off-center cells

Personal construct

Reflex arc

Pain center
Pleasure center

Receptive field

Reticular activating system (RAS)

Retina

Synapse

FUNCTION

Assimilation
Accommodation

Defense mechanism
   Projection
   Rationalization
   Reaction formation
   Repression

Drive
Need
   nAffiliation
   nDeference

Extinction
Generalization
Discrimination

Fixation
Regression

Imprinting

Image
Plan

Learning
   Insight
   Latent
   One-trial
   Place
   Response
   Rote
      Paired-associates
      Serial
   Trial-and-error

Memory
   Short-term
   Long-term

Rationality
Veridicality